Approaches to Teaching
Stoker's *Dracula*

Approaches to Teaching Stoker's *Dracula*

Edited by

William Thomas McBride

The Modern Language Association of America
New York   2025

© 2025 by The Modern Language Association of America
85 Broad Street, New York, New York 10004
www.mla.org

All rights reserved. MLA and the MODERN LANGUAGE ASSOCIATION are trademarks owned by the Modern Language Association of America. To request permission to reprint material from MLA book publications, please inquire at permissions@mla.org.

To order MLA publications, visit www.mla.org/books. For wholesale and international orders, see www.mla.org/bookstore-orders.

The MLA office is located on the island known as Mannahatta (Manhattan) in Lenapehoking, the homeland of the Lenape people. The MLA pays respect to the original stewards of this land and to the diverse and vibrant Native communities that continue to thrive in New York City.

Approaches to Teaching World Literature 178
ISSN 1059-1133

Library of Congress Cataloging-in-Publication Data

Names: McBride, William (William Thomas), editor.
Title: Approaches to teaching Stoker's Dracula / edited by William Thomas McBride.
Description: New York : The Modern Language Association of America, 2025. | Series: Approaches to teaching world literature, 1059-1133 ; 178 | Includes bibliographical references.
Identifiers: LCCN 2024032984 (print) | LCCN 2024032985 (ebook) | ISBN 9781603296779 (hardcover) | ISBN 9781603296786 (paperback) | ISBN 9781603296793 (EPUB)
Subjects: LCSH: Stoker, Bram, 1847–1912. Dracula. | Stoker, Bram, 1847–1912—Study and teaching. | Dracula, Count (Fictitious character)—Study and teaching. | English literature—19th century—Study and teaching.
Classification: LCC PR6037.T617 Z54 2025 (print) | LCC PR6037.T617 (ebook) | DDC 823/.8—dc23/eng/20241120
LC record available at https://lccn.loc.gov/2024032984
LC ebook record available at https://lccn.loc.gov/2024032985

CONTENTS

Acknowledgments	vii
Preface	ix

PART ONE: MATERIALS

Editions and Translations	3
Critical Sources	6
Other Works by Stoker	16
Biographies	17
Classroom Guides	18
Additional Online Resources	18

PART TWO: APPROACHES

Introduction *William Thomas McBride*	21

Critical Reading

Teaching Critical Theory with *Dracula* *Ana Raquel Rojas*	26
Navigating *Dracula* Criticism in the Classroom *Agnes Andeweg*	33
Teaching *Dracula* and the Professions: Work, Money, and Desire *Joshua Gooch*	39

The Gothic

Gothic Abjection in the Original *Dracula* *Jerrold E. Hogle*	44
Dracula and Irish Gothic Fiction *Richard Haslam*	52

Ethnic Studies

Dracula in a Latinx Context *Lisa Nevárez*	61
The Absence and Fear of Black People: *Dracula* in a Course on African American Vampire Fiction *Jerry Rafiki Jenkins*	68
Why Fear Endures: *Dracula* in a Postmillennial Indian Classroom *Srirupa Chatterjee*	75

vi   CONTENTS

Medicine

Nervous Systems: *Dracula* and Fin-de-Siècle Gender Trouble   83
  Elizabeth Way

Contagion and Otherness: *Dracula* in the Age of COVID-19   90
  Ess Pokornowski

Dracula and the Medical Humanities   98
  William Hughes

Sexuality and Gender

Dracula's Fluidity: Beyond Queering the Vampire   105
  Jolene Zigarovich

Dracula and Masculinity   113
  Andrew Smith

"She Interest Me Too": Centering Women in *Dracula*   120
  Patrick R. O'Malley

Film and Television

The Dracula Megatext   127
  Jeffrey Andrew Weinstock

Vampires in a Virtually Flipped Classroom   135
  Peter Gölz

New Media and Digital Humanities

Dracula in the Undergraduate Digital Classroom   143
  Christopher G. Diller

Dracula and New Media   152
  Zan Cammack

Exploring the Transmedia *Dracula*   159
  Shari Hodges Holt

Board Games and Study Abroad

Fury of Dracula: Board Games as Participatory Pedagogy   167
  David Smith

vEmpire 2.0: How to Teach *Dracula*: Where, When, and Why   175
  Dragan Kujundžić

Notes on Contributors   185
Survey Respondents   189
Works Cited   191

ACKNOWLEDGMENTS

I want to express my thanks to Patrick O'Malley, Jerry Hogle, Jeffrey Weinstock, and John Paul Riquelme for sharing their insights with my senior seminar students during the pandemic. My gratitude goes out to James Hatch for his guidance throughout the early stages of this book and to Zahra Brown and Erika Suffern, whose resourcefulness strengthened it. To Cherlyn, Madison, and Brooklyn—thank you for the love and quiet you gave me throughout my working on this book.

I dedicate this book in memoriam to John Paul Riquelme, a stellar scholar and generous man.

PREFACE

Written by an Irish civil servant, theater critic, Oscar Wilde frenemy, Walt Whitman devotee, and manager of the renowned actor Henry Irving, *Dracula* is perhaps the most instantly recognizable and culturally influential novel of the past one hundred years. Published by Archibald Constable (also Sir Walter Scott's publisher) in 1897, Bram Stoker's novel has never gone out of print. Since entering the public domain in 1962, it has appeared in over thirty pulp and scholarly editions, has been translated into more than forty languages, and has generated legions of journal articles and books of criticism. Wall-to-wall remediations of the novel have delivered us into a world where there is no escape from lurking Dracula memes. An apt metaphor for the novel's effect is contagion. The work itself offers a prime model for teaching theories of metaphor, inviting into the classroom thinkers ranging from Aristotle to the likes of Paul Ricœur, George Lakoff, and Susan Sontag. *Dracula* lives up to the often-quoted description of novels wherein Henry James asks, "What do such large, loose, baggy monsters, with their queer elements of the accidental and the arbitrary, artistically *mean*?" (84), and Stoker's baggy monster of a novel welcomes in all of us attracted to the question.

The ever-malleable vampire myth at the heart of Stoker's novel has served as an imaginative figure for artists and philosophers throughout the ages. As Nina Auerbach has put it, "[E]very generation creates and embraces its own vampire" (145). Stoker's novel and vampire narratives more broadly are a pedagogical and hermeneutical gold mine rich with examples of, to use Freudian language, displacement, that process of "dream-censorship" that conceals an untraceable "genuine thing" and exchanges it with strange, "most unusual, external associations" (Freud, *Introductory Lectures* 233). Karl Marx famously wrote that "[c]apital is dead labour, which, vampire-like" sucks only "living labour, and . . . the more labor it sucks," the more it thrives (Marx, *Critique* 342). In a 1990 political speech in support of his Slovenian presidential bid, the post-Marxist gadfly and philosopher Slavoj Žižek proclaimed, "We have had enough of the vampires that live off of us, making us guilty, that are making us pay someone else's dues, and today we need . . . a wooden stake, together with garlic to kill and destroy all sorts of vampires" ("Žižek!"). Žižek also turns to Stoker's novel in his philosophical musings to discuss Lucy's postpenetration struggle with *jouissance* (*For They Know Not* 220). In the "Not All Vampires Suck Blood" chapter of his *Satanic Bible*, Anton LaVey coined the term "psychic vampire" (75) to describe those people who suck the spiritual life force out of other living creatures, a propensity that biographers tell us Stoker experienced in his relationship to Irving. Roughly coinciding with the 1895 conviction of Oscar Wilde for "gross indecency with certain male persons" (Bristow 148), Stoker's Count registers as a threatening, yet exciting, polymorphous sexual other. While *Dracula* exhibits stable gender positionalities on the surface—a bourgeois

X   PREFACE

heterosexual couple, two respectable male members of the medical profession, and an American cowboy wannabe—unconventional erotic situations arise when, for example, three ravishing female vampires bring to Jonathan a "languorous ecstasy" (Stoker, *Dracula* [Browning and Skal] 47) that is jealously interrupted by the Count, who later in the novel forces Mina to drink blood from his breast with her husband looking on. Such sexual "inversions" are struck in relief when the chaplain of the English mission church consecrates the albeit rushed marriage of Mina and Jonathan, whose monogamous union ultimately produces a son.

Historians of the novel agree that the literary origin of Stoker's Count was likely Lord Ruthven of *The Vampyre*, a novella written by Lord Byron's traveling doctor and amanuensis John Polidori and conceived during the famous summer at Lake Geneva when Mary Shelley, in response to a writing challenge devised by Byron, gave birth to her *Frankenstein*. There can be little doubt that prior to writing his novel, Stoker attended any number of stage plays based on *The Vampyre* being performed in London. There's a certain symmetry here, too, in the compositional dynamic engaged by both Stoker and Polidori, for just as it is contended that Polidori based his vampire on his employer Byron, it has been surmised in some circles that Stoker used his boss Irving as the model for his vampire (Skal, Preface x; Ellmann xii; Arata 634). The serialized penny dreadful *Varney the Vampire; or, The Feast of Blood*, by James Malcolm Rymer (some editions credit Thomas Preskett Prest, creator of the demon barber Sweeney Todd, as a contributor [Rymer, *Illustrated* Varney]) added to the *Dracula* recipe by featuring many genre-linked ingredients that Stoker would incorporate, particularly a rape fantasy. In the first pages of *Varney* we read of the trembling, smooth limbs and heaving bosom of a "fair creature, just budding into womanhood" (Rymer, *Varney* 34) who is being dragged by the head to her bed. "With a plunge [Varney] seizes her neck in his fang-like teeth—a gush of blood, and a hideous sucking sound follows" (36). Another source often pointed to, and one Stoker acknowledged having read, comes from his countryman, that "professor of the flesh-creeping school" Joseph Sheridan Le Fanu, whose steamy lesbian ghost story *Carmilla* was published as a serial in 1872.

Within English studies *Dracula* is often dismissed as a cheapjack exercise in the gothic whose prose never quite saves the novel from potboiler status. Contemporary reviews were mixed. One of its very first reviewers, writing in the London literary magazine *The Athenaeum*, declared, "'Dracula' is highly sensational, but it is wanting in the constructive art as well as in the literary. It reads at times like a mere series of grotesquely incredible events" (Review). Stoker's obituary in *The Times* of London deemed *Dracula* a "particularly lurid and creepy kind of fiction" ("Obituary"), and the editor of the 1983 Oxford edition, A. N. Wilson, writes in his introduction that the novel is a "second-rate classic" and "not a great work of literature" (Wilson xi). Christopher Craft remarks that Stoker's readers have to suffer through "a hundred rather tedious pages" ("Kiss Me" 126), and Clive Leatherdale characterizes Stoker as a "hack" (75). That these and several other *Dracula* scholars can dismiss and simultaneously champion Stoker's work (note the second half of Leatherdale's title, *A Study of Bram Stoker's Gothic Masterpiece*) speaks to

PREFACE   xi

the attraction/repulsion most of Stoker's characters and readers feel toward the Count. The novel is acknowledged as a cultural phenomenon by esteemed writers such as T. S. Eliot and James Joyce. In *The Waste Land* we read of "bats with baby faces" who, like Stoker's Count, "crawled head downward down a blackened wall" (380). In *Finnegans Wake*, Stoker's fellow Irishman poeticizes the author and his novel this way: "Let's root out Brimstoker and give him the thrall of our lives" (Joyce 145).

The universal appeal of Stoker's work, for better or worse, has spawned a slew of adaptations that begins with John L. Balderston's revision of Hamilton Deane's 1924 authorized stage play, *Dracula* (Deane and Balderston). A cultural studies seminar could examine the novel's shape-shift in response to an obsessional fan base comprising various vampire subcultures and Goth enthusiasts, as evidenced by Dracula's haunting of graphic novels, blogs, and online role-playing. The Count will continue to star in the latest series from streaming services and to provide fodder for comedians and late-night talk show writers who want to send up political figures and celebrities. He's a benign mathtutoring puppet on public television and is merchandized as the namesake of a General Mills breakfast cereal still in production fifty years after its debut. Finally, teachers and students of film and film history are met with an overabundance of film adaptations, more than two hundred of them and still counting. It is the singular distinguishing feature of Stoker's novel that, like the Count feeding Mina, *Dracula* continues to feed itself to cinema, beginning in 1920 with the rumored Soviet film *Дракула* (*Dracula*), followed by the Hungarian director Károly Lajtha's now lost 1921 *Drakula halála* (*Dracula's Death*) and, the following year, that spectacularly unsettling performance by Max Schreck in F. W. Murnau's classic *Nosferatu: A Symphony of Horror*. Ten years later, Universal provided the model for nearly all Draculas to come, Bela Lugosi's iconic Count, in Tod Browning's *Dracula*. Nine *Dracula* films from Hammer Film Productions followed between 1958 and 1974. Each new film adaptation adds elements and customs not found in the novel. Henrik Galeen's script for Murnau's *Nosferatu*, written twenty-five years after the novel's publication, has the Count being destroyed by sunlight. Garrett Fort's dialogue adds Bela Lugosi's line about never drinking . . . wine. Stoker's story has been taken up by directors as various as Roman Polanski, Werner Herzog, and Francis Ford Coppola; more recently, Universal released the dreadfully unfunny feature film *Renfield*, starring Nicholas Cage as Dracula. Having failed more than once in his attempt to bring Stoker's novel to the screen, Orson Welles told Peter Bogdanovich:

> *Dracula* would make a marvelous movie. In fact, nobody has ever made it; they've never paid any attention to the book, which is the most hairraising, marvelous book in the world. It's told by four people, and must be done with four narrations, as we did on the radio. There's one scene in London where he throws a heavy bag into the corner of a cellar and it's full of screaming babies! They can go that far out now.
>
> (Welles and Bogdanovich 13)

xii   PREFACE

In the film *Ghost Dance*, directed by Ken McMullen, Jacques Derrida classifies the art of cinema as a "contest of phantoms" that allows "ghosts to come back" (00:17:44). *Dracula* was published a year after the first public screening of the Lumière brothers' *Arrivée d'un train à la Ciotat* (*Arrival of a Train at La Ciotat*), where reportedly audience members ducked from the image of the oncoming locomotive or ran screaming out of the theater. As long as preservation and digital duplication allows, like the undead vampire, the medium of film, its actors and narrative conceits, will live on in perpetuity.

As a classic of late Victorian horror fiction, *Dracula* is read and taught across the world. It is equally "at home" in the high school English class and in the PhD seminar. Teachers report that some students struggle with the book's length and its unfamiliar epistolary form, while others balk at its semipornographic content and its uncritical treatment of the violent possession of women. These perceptions are engaged by critics and by the contributors to this volume. Stoker's novel can spark discussions of science and medicine, money and postcolonial theory, monster theory, the gothic, gender and queer theory, fin-de-siècle anti-Semitism, cinema studies, new technologies, and popular culture. The original title of the book, *The Un-Dead*, was changed to *Dracula* by the publisher only at the last minute before going to press (Kelly). In a heartfelt talk with Lord Godalming, Van Helsing refers to Lucy as "the dead Un-Dead" (Stoker, *Dracula* [Browning and Skal] 196), and *The Oxford English Dictionary* cites *Dracula* as containing an example of the double-truth term the "undead" ("Undead"). Teachers of global and dramatic literature might present Dracula's dilemma as that of a sympathetic antihero cursed with a soulless immortality à la Faust. Stoker's novel can serve literature classes by considering the Count's work as the devil's work, and students of the Bible as literature can contemplate the self-contradictory dead/undead notion applicable to two of Pauline Christianity's main tenets, namely the fully human / fully divine Jesus and his resurrection. The 1897 novel's release coincided with the emergence of the protofeminist, sexually liberated New Woman and the publication of *Sexual Inversion*, by Havelock Ellis and John Addington Symonds, as well as Sigmund Freud's article "Heredity and the Aetiology of the Neuroses," which contains the first appearance in print of the term *psychoanalysis*. Those teaching psychology and gender studies classes recognize that *Dracula's* trafficking in Eros and Thanatos explains, in part, a readership that is fascinated with the novel's fusion of repressed sexuality and fear of death. *Dracula* presents intriguing metaphysical conjecture, now prompted by rapid advances in AI engineering, on what it means to be human in the sense that projecting oneself as being a vampire plays to the posthuman dream of immortality. The essays in this volume offer pedagogical pathways that lead into and out of Stoker's novel by providing language, strategies, and assignments designed to help us as teachers introduce this cultural treasure into the curriculum, to promote new questions and readings, and to animate with new life the scholarship gathering on the horizon.

Part One

MATERIALS

Editions and Translations

The copyright history of Bram Stoker's *Dracula* begins on 18 May 1897, eight days before the novel's publication proper. In order to secure dramatic rights and licensing from the Lord Chamberlain's Office, a staged "copyright reading" was traditional but not legally required. Stoker produced the reading of *Dracula; or, The Un-Dead*, which was performed by fifteen of the resident actors at London's West End Lyceum Theatre and reportedly lasted nearly four hours. The Lyceum was the acclaimed actor Henry Irving's theater—Irving chose the productions, cast himself in the lead roles, and designed the lighting and sets—and Stoker was Irving's manager. Archibald Constable and Company brought out the novel *Dracula* on 26 May 1897, issuing three thousand copies in its first printing. Stoker's friend William Carey registered the book with the United States Copyright Office at the Library of Congress, but the required two copies were never deposited. Upon the novel's publication in the United Kingdom, the Berne Convention for the Protection of Literary and Artistic Works safeguarded the rights for fifty years beyond Stoker's 1912 death; hence, *Dracula* entered the public domain in 1962, and since that time, "666" editions, as Dracula aficionados like to call them, have appeared, including a wealth of mass-market paperbacks from the likes of Penguin, Signet, Pocket, Vintage, HarperCollins, Dover, and a host of independent publishers. Another result of the novel's public domain status is easy access to digital copies. When assigning one of the critical editions listed below, I encourage students to use the *Project Gutenberg* version for electronic searches of the text (www.gutenberg.org/cache/epub/345/pg345-images.html).

Scholarly Editions

Most scholarly editions of *Dracula* provide an apparatus variously consisting of critical introductions, explanatory notes, examinations of the original typescript, biographical information, maps, early reviews, bibliographies, and a chronology of stage adaptations and other remediations of *Dracula* through film, television, opera, ballet, and other modes, such as digital gaming. Many also explore the gothic, the Victorian novel, and selections from the considerable library of vampire fiction. The first notable critical edition is Leonard Wolf's impressive *The Annotated* Dracula, which contains comprehensive explanatory notes and an appendix of manuscript research, maps, and a calendar of the novel's events. Wolf declares that, like "God," who "hides in the details," he has performed "the very closest of close textual, historical, and literary critical readings" (4). Raymond T. McNally and Radu Florescu promote the much debated claim that Stoker's vampire is a descendant of Vlad Ţepeş, or "Vlad the Impaler," in *The Essential* Dracula*: A Completely Illustrated and Annotated Edition of Bram*

4 EDITIONS AND TRANSLATIONS

Stoker's Classic Novel. Leslie S. Klinger, the renowned investigative editor of H. P. Lovecraft, Sherlock Holmes, and Frankenstein, consults Stoker's working papers (with additional research by Janet Byrne) and takes up this historical claim with extensive, speculative notes in *The New Annotated* Dracula, notably endorsed in the introduction by Neil Gaiman, the author of the children's horror fantasy novella *Coraline* and a recipient of the Bram Stoker Award for Best Work for Young Readers. The first British academic edition, prepared by A. N. Wilson for Oxford University Press, contains a sparse collection of footnotes and disparages the novel (xi), as does the later Oxford edition prepared by Maud Ellmann, who declares that the novel lacks "development of character" and "complexity of thought" (vii). Both editors, as well as a certain group of *Dracula* scholars who share this low opinion, invariably point to contemporaneous reviews for support. In his introduction to the Penguin edition, Maurice Hindle discusses nineteenth-century British middle-class anxiety regarding economic decline and challenges from Germany and America. The Artswork *Dracula*, edited by William Hughes and Diane Mason, includes an introduction by Hughes and detailed notes that trace literary allusions, foreign phrases, and British dialects. Roger Luckhurst's Oxford edition offers an expansive and enlightening introduction that details many of the scholarly perspectives on the novel and comprehensive notes. Two other scholarly editions of note are Marvin Kaye's *Dracula: The Definitive Edition*, with surrealist pen-and-ink illustrations by Edward Gorey, and Clive Leatherdale's *Dracula Unearthed*. More recently, Dracula: *The Postcolonial Edition*, edited by Cristina Artenie and Dragos Moraru, makes the calculated claim that it is the first and only postcolonial take on Stoker's novel, ignoring the extensive scholarship on empire, race, and reverse colonization that precedes the edition.

Of the many critical editions available, I have found those published by Norton and by Bedford / St. Martin's to be the two most valuable for scholarly study and use in the classroom. Both reprint the authorized Constable first edition, silently correcting typographical errors and misspellings, and each delivers an informative scholarly apparatus. My experience assigning students the Norton edition one semester and the Bedford edition the following semester has resulted in reliably informed and critically engaged discussions, projects, and essays. Commemorating the novel's one hundredth anniversary in 1997, two eminent *Dracula* scholars, Nina Auerbach and David J. Skal, officially welcomed Stoker's novel into the academic canon with the first Norton Critical Edition. Excerpted works in the "Contexts" section (331–60) include not only Emily Gerard's 1885 essay "Transylvanian Superstitions," Christopher Frayling's "Bram Stoker's Working Papers for *Dracula*," and James Malcolm Rymer's 1847 *Varney the Vampire; or, The Feast of Blood* but also "Dracula's Guest," the allegedly lost first chapter of Stoker's novel that his widow published following his death. Typical of scholarly editions, the Norton offers extensive footnotes to the text and includes a collection of reviews covering the publication's contemporary reception (362–67) and a compendium of the most often cited, essential critical readings from Phyllis

Roth, Carol Senf, Stephen D. Arata, Franco Moretti, Christopher Craft, and Talia Schaffer (411–82). Useful essays covering the film and stage "variations" are accompanied by checklists of significant adaptations (371–407). The second edition, edited by John Edgar Browning and Skal, adds new background pieces and reviews; updates its coverage of dramatic and filmic variations; expands its collection of critical essay excerpts with pieces by Jarlath Killeen, Maurice Richardson, Jack Halberstam, Andrea Dworkin, and others (453–576); and excises from the first edition selections by Frayling, Bram Dijkstra, and Craft. Though the inclusion of the Halberstam piece is a welcome one, the decision to remove Craft's classic, groundbreaking "'Kiss Me with Those Red Lips': Gender and Inversion in Bram Stoker's *Dracula*" is inexplicable and a regrettable loss. The first Bedford / St. Martin's edition of *Dracula* further enhanced the novel's stature in the academy. Edited by John Paul Riquelme, this edition features a well-researched biographical and historical introduction (321), and its collection of contextual documents includes entertaining contemporaneous illustrations with a notable Irish bent (namely, cartoons of an Irish vampire, an Irish Frankenstein, and a self-serving Charles Stewart Parnell equipped with vampire bat wings) as well as excerpted writings that predate the novel's publication from Karl Marx, Friedrich Nietzsche, Walter Pater, and Richard von Krafft-Ebing (370–406). Five scholarly essays written for the edition view the novel through the various lenses of gender studies (Eltis), psychoanalysis (Foster), new historicism (Castle), deconstruction (Riquelme, "Doubling"), and media (Wicke). These essays are prefaced with a comprehensive definition of each discipline. A concise glossary of critical and theoretical terms concludes the volume. The 2016 Bedford / St. Martin's second edition adds excerpts from Joseph Sheridan Le Fanu (382–90) and George Gissing (422–26) and expands its coverage of studies with readings of the novel by way of queer theory (Fox) and cultural criticism (Monk), as it assigns the combined perspective to a different author (Valente, "Stoker's Vampire"), leaving out Riquelme's essay. See also Dracula, *by Bram Stoker: The Mystery of the Early Editions* (Berni).

Translations

Dracula has been translated into forty-four languages, including Chinese, Czech, Gaelic, Greek, and Hebrew. Many of the translations are listed with linked descriptions at the *Internet Speculative Fiction Database* ("Series: Dracula"). Another informative list, compiled by J. Gordon Melton, may be found on the *All Things* Dracula site (www.cesnur.org/2003/dracula). Although the unauthorized Hungarian *Drakula: Angol regény: Harker Jonathan naplója* (*Dracula: English Novel: The Journal of Jonathan Harker*) is sometimes said to be the first translation, other scholars point instead to the anonymous Swedish adaptation *Mörkrets makter* (*Powers of Darkness*) and its Icelandic translation by Valdimar Ásmundsson, *Makt Myrkranna*, as of more interest because their introduction is attributed to Stoker.

6   CRITICAL SOURCES

Critical Sources

Owing to the cultural dominance wielded by the Count and the coalescing of the centennial of the book's publication, the academy has produced a wealth of literary criticism on *Dracula* that affords teachers an opportunity not only to facilitate students' individual close readings but also to critically examine specific approaches in the classroom. Such scholarly works range from source studies and formalist textual examinations to considerations of genre and narrative technique. Symptomatic readings of the novel from Marxist, pop-cultural, new historicist, feminist, sociohistorical, psychoanalytic, and other perspectives continue to proliferate, given the treasure trove that is *Dracula*. Such scholarship often finds itself tapping into the novel's paradoxical dead/undead vein to explore the poststructuralist both/and constructions of colonizer/colonized, Anglo/Irish, highbrow/lowbrow, repressive/liberating, and gender fluidity. *Dracula* scholarship began in earnest in the mid–twentieth century, and inspired scholars of all stripes were soon off and running as English departments inaugurated courses in gothic studies and annual conferences were sponsored by organizations such as the International Association for the Fantastic in the Arts. Not unlike the multitude of Dracula films, the sheer volume of learned texts devoted to a novel that Halberstam called a "meaning machine" is stunning (*Skin Shows* 21). Designed to assist students and teachers of the novel, other noted interpretations and groundbreaking approaches are discussed in the limited survey below.

Bibliographies

As Robert Eighteen-Bisang puts it, "*Dracula* is a bibliographic nightmare" ("Hutchinson's Colonial Library Edition"). *The Vampire in Folklore, History, Literature, Film and Television: A Comprehensive Bibliography* cites over six thousand entries on "vampire studies" in general and upwards of 650 devoted solely to Stoker and his book (Melton and Hornick). The online resource *All Things* Dracula: *A Bibliography of Editions, Reprints, Adaptations, and Translations of* Dracula, compiled by J. Gordon Melton, lists the many translations of *Dracula* and includes a description of the *Dracula* manuscript by Christie's auction house, the novel's publication history, and Eighteen-Bisang's introduction to the Hutchinson edition, which was "issued for circulation in India and the British Colonies only" (Eighteen-Bisang, "Hutchinson's Colonial Library Edition"). In addition to notable collections such as Dracula: *A Century of Editions, Adaptations and Translations*, compiled by Eighteen-Bisang and Elizabeth Miller; Browning's *Bram Stoker's* Dracula: *The Critical Feast: An Annotated Reference of Early Reviews and Reactions, 1897–1913*; and Richard Dalby's *Bram Stoker: A Bibliography of First Editions*, devoted scholars will also consult, through subscription, the more comprehensive *Oxford Bibliographies* research guide (Townshend).

CRITICAL SOURCES 7

Book-Length Studies

In the groundbreaking *Our Vampires, Ourselves*, Auerbach distinguishes Stoker's Count from preceding vampires—namely, Le Fanu's Carmilla and John Polidori's Lord Ruthven—in order to present a conservative Count who follows rules and enforces more hierarchies than he challenges. Auerbach goes on to argue that the novel's fascination with technology and Dracula's isolation and urbanization have the potential to mirror the modern condition. Part of the Twayne's Masterwork Studies series, Senf's *Dracula: Between Tradition and Modernism* is geared a bit more toward the high school classroom. Single-author books dedicated solely to *Dracula* are relatively few (see below), but all books on the literary vampire acknowledge the central place Stoker's novel holds, as in Frayling's *Vampyres: Lord Byron to Count Dracula*. David Glover's *Vampires, Mummies and Liberals: Bram Stoker and the Politics of Popular Fiction* does not limit its sights to *Dracula* but considers Stoker's often-overlooked other novels, stories, nonfiction, journalism, and correspondence in their Anglo-Irish, Victorian context. *A Dracula Handbook*, from the *Dracula* expert extraordinaire Miller, delivers a wealth of information about vampires, Stoker, and the novel. Klinger's *In the Shadow of Dracula* is a valuable illustrated collection featuring classic gothic vampire tales that have been "overshadowed" by *Dracula*, including those from Polidori, Leo Tolstoy, Théophile Gautier, Le Fanu, and Rymer. See also Leonard Wolf, *A Dream of Dracula: In Search of the Living Dead*.

Essay Collections

Teachers should consult the superb introduction to the field of *Dracula* scholarship by William Hughes, whose *Bram Stoker: Dracula* delivers a far-reaching descriptive survey of scholarly readings of the novel, some of which are noted below. For another summary of scholarly approaches, consult Riquelme's "A Critical History of *Dracula*." A collection of the standard, oft-cited scholarly essays can be found in Margaret L. Carter's *Dracula: The Vampire and the Critics*. There teachers and scholars can access publications that appeared between the 1950s and the 1980s, beginning with Bacil F. Kirtley's original source essay and continuing with scholarship from Carrol L. Fry, Joseph S. Bierman, Roth ("Suddenly Sexual Women"), Senf ("*Dracula*"), James Twitchell, Craft ("Kiss Me"), and David Seed. A representative grouping of essential essays is also assembled in the Norton Critical Editions. Senf's *The Critical Response to Bram Stoker* includes criticism of other works by Stoker. *Bram Stoker's Dracula: Sucking through the Century, 1897–1997*, edited by Carol Margaret Davison, delivers new essays from the likes of Patrick McGrath, Senf, Carter, Auerbach, and Miller. Dracula: *The Shade and the Shadow*, edited by Miller, collects essays by Auerbach, Hughes, Leatherdale, Florescu, and Jimmie E. Cain, Jr., among others. In addition to the canonical essays by Roth, Craft, Arata, Auerbach, and Halberstam, Glennis Byron's Dracula: *Contemporary*

8   CRITICAL SOURCES

Critical Essays has essays by Moretti and Glover. Jack Lynch's *Critical Insights: Dracula, by Bram Stoker*, arranges some familiar critical approaches along with a variety of contributions by Matthew J. Bolton, Beth E. McDonald, and Nancy Armstrong. In *Dracula: An International Perspective*, the editor, Marius-Mircea Crişan, presents essays from a global perspective. See also *Bram Stoker: Centenary Essays*, edited by Jarlath Killeen.

Scholarly Journals and Articles

Growing out of the Canadian chapter of the Transylvanian Society of Dracula, the peer-reviewed *Journal of Dracula Studies* began its publishing in the mid-1990s and experienced a number of reconfigurations and locations. Until her passing in 2022, Miller, the founder of the Dracula Research Centre and author of several articles and books of *Dracula* scholarship, edited the journal, which featured international scholarship on Stoker and his novel and cultural depictions of vampires in general. Essays devoted to *Dracula*, some noted above, have appeared in a wide array of academic journals such as *Modern Fiction Studies*, *Victorian Review*, *Jewish Culture and History*, *Victorian Studies*, *Texas Studies in Literature and Language*, *Philosophy and Literature*, *Framework: The Journal of Cinema and Media*, and, with particular frequency, *English Literature in Transition, 1880–1920* and *ELH*. In 1999 the *Journal of the Fantastic in the Arts* published the special issue *A Century of Draculas* (Holte), featuring James Craig Holte's introduction ("Century") and such essays as "High Duty and Savage Delight: The Ambiguous Nature of Violence in 'Dracula'" (Harse), "Bram Stoker and the London Stage" (Moss), "'If I Had to Write with a Pen': Readership and Bram Stoker's Diary Narrative" (Cribb), "Madame Dracula: The Life of Emily Gerard" (Heiss), and "Back to the Basics: Re-Examining Stoker's Sources for 'Dracula'" (Miller).

What follows are brief descriptions of several of the enduring scholarly essays mentioned above, followed by a sampling of some more recent articles and a mention of others. Like the fluid features of Stoker's novel and its titular character, along with the blurring and eliding embraced by the gothic in general, the essays categorized below are rarely limited by convenient (or inconvenient) disciplinary boundaries.

Source Studies

Within the greater market of *Dracula* scholarship, McNally and Florescu have created a cottage industry. Taking up the historical source studies thread begun by Kirtley, who in "Dracula, the Monastic Chronicles and Slavic Folklore" promotes a connection between Stoker's Transylvanian Count Dracula and the historical Wallachian Prince Ţepeş, better known as "Vlad the Impaler" (a claim dismissed by most Romanian scholars, whose refutation Klinger seconds in *In the Shadow of Dracula* [xv]), their research focuses on Romanian vampire

CRITICAL SOURCES   9

legends. They have produced several books that emphasize the Vlad III connection to Stoker's creation (see McNally and Florescu; Florescu and McNally, *Dracula: A Biography of Vlad the Impaler* and *Dracula: Prince of Many Faces*), as does their own edition of the novel proper (Stoker, *Essential* Dracula). The collection of Stoker's manuscripts held at the Rosenbach Museum and Library since 1970 not only contains handwritten and typed notes for the novel composed in Dublin between 1871 and 1881 but also is a trove of photographs, newspaper clippings, and research on vampires, werewolves, shipwrecks, the history and geography of the Carpathians, "dream theory," and Whitby language and tombstones ("Guide"). This material was collected, annotated, and published with a transcribed facsimile edition by Eighteen-Bisang and Miller as *Bram Stoker's Notes for* Dracula; the revised edition is titled *Drafts of* Dracula. Leatherdale's *Dracula: The Novel and the Legend* features historical, biographical, and theoretical frameworks relevant to the study of Stoker's novel and background on the author and the origins of the work, including information on the figure of the vampire in history, folklore, and literature. Glover's "Travels in Romania—Myths of Origins, Myths of Blood" and Clemens Ruthner's "Bloodsuckers with Teutonic Tongues: The German Speaking World and the Origins of Dracula" continue these investigations. More recently, in Dracula *Invades England*, Cristina Artenie points out the neocolonial reach of the British Empire into Dracula's homeland and sees as inspiration Stoker's interest in the 1893 marriage of Vlad Țepeș's descendant Mary of Teck to Queen Victoria's grandson, soon to be George V of England.

Ethnicity and Colonization

In "The Occidental Tourist: *Dracula* and the Anxiety of Reverse Colonization," Arata explains that, unlike the British invasion-scare novel, which expressed the threat posed by political radicals or by other industrial nations, the *Dracula* novel reflects the vexing "Eastern Question" in its staging of a confrontation with the perceived Gothic savagery of the Slav and the Hun (627). Unlike earlier aristocratic, idle vampires, such as Carmilla or Lord Ruthven, Dracula acquires his noble status from a Székely military past that serves him well in his conquest of his British adversaries. Arata explains how the anxiety of reverse colonization—historically colonized people colonizing earlier invaders—is inextricably linked to race. He shows how, with the example of the monstrously sexualized Lucy Westenra, the Count causes fear that miscegenation will replace the status quo with a dominant new racial identity. Arata also reads the novel's narrative trajectory as one that moves from a British travel guide to a threatening encounter with the gothic and points to how, in the book's final "Note," Jonathan Harker tries to undermine the authenticity of what he claims was fantasy. Maria Todorova's *Imagining the Balkans* provides a broader context for Jonathan's (and late Victorian readers') impression of Dracula's homeland, the place Stoker's young solicitor describes as "the horseshoe of the Carpathians,

10   CRITICAL SOURCES

as if it were the centre of some sort of imaginative whirlpool" (Stoker, *Dracula* [Browning and Skal] 13), specifically contextualizing the Gothic nightmare that allegedly transformed the historical Vlad Țepeș into the mythic Dracula. In *Bram Stoker and Russophobia: Evidence of the British Fear of Russia in* Dracula *and* The Lady of the Shroud, Cain continues the investigation into late Victorian anxieties regarding reverse colonization and the threat posed by Russia as played out in the Crimean War in concert with perceived Balkan and Slavic threats to Britain (118–49). Acknowledging the productive scholarship on the novel's anti-Semitic thread, Thomas McLean's "Dracula's Blood of Many Brave Races" meticulously lays out this xenophobic anxiety by aligning it with the influx of political refugees to Victorian Britain and by viewing Count Dracula as a historical nationalist warrior. For a more comprehensive understanding of this racial tension, McLean urges us to acknowledge the complex political circumstances of nineteenth-century eastern Europe by taking into account how Stoker "associates the Count with a remarkable variety of nations and peoples, from China and South America to Scotland and Ireland" (333). For an African American studies reading, explore Kendra R. Parker's *Black Female Vampires in African American Women's Novels, 1977–2011: She Bites Back.*

Anti-Semitism

In "Technologies of Monstrosity: Bram Stoker's *Dracula*," Halberstam relates having been struck when reading Stoker's novel for the first time by the Count's resemblance to stereotypical anti-Semitic representations of the Jew such as those found in Britain's late-nineteenth-century discourse of anti-Semitism, not unlike the xenophobic diatribe *The Jew, the Gypsy, and El Islam* written by Stoker's good friend Richard Burton. Moving beyond Dracula's physique, his parasitical bloodsucking, his aversion to the cross, and his "avaricious relation to money," the essay broadens its scope by applying Michel Foucault's combination of monstrosity and sex to show how the novel's presentation of the Count's perverse sexual identity is that of a Semitic other and provides a "discursive arena" that transforms "metaphors of otherness into technologies of sex, into machinic texts" (334). My "Dracula and Mephistopheles: Shyster Vampires" cites the six-pointed star of David spilling out from behind Bela Lugosi's cape in Tod Browning's 1931 *Dracula* and notes that Stoker matches Immanuel Hildesheim's clichéd Semitic physiognomy and money-mindedness with the Count's in order to cast Dracula as a monstrous mohel duping innocent goyim into a demonic blood pact for a kind of Faustian immortality. Stoker thus inverts Genesis 22.10 when at the end of the novel, rather than the intended Isaac, it is Dracula as a crypto-Abraham who is slain (McBride). In "Nazis, Jews and *Nosferatu*," Marie Mulvey-Roberts examines *Dracula* in terms of Jewishness and blood by pointing to F. W. Murnau's Nosferatu character as conspicuously a Jew (*Dangerous Bodies*, ch. 4). Also see chapter 5 of Davison's *Anti-Semitism and British Gothic Literature* (120–57); "Blurring the Boundaries of Difference:

CRITICAL SOURCES 11

Dracula, the Empire, and 'the Jew,'" by Hannah Ewence; and "How Vampires Became Jewish," by Peter Dan.

Psychoanalysis

Whether endorsing or dismantling this school of thought, most gendered, feminist, and queer readings of *Dracula* use psychoanalysis as a starting point. Craft and Jennifer Wicke, respectively, affirm and reaffirm that Stoker's novel (and vampirism in general) delivers up an intriguingly perverse sexual energy that its readers desperately seek. Scholarly analysis of Stoker's novel along these lines begins in earnest with "The Psychoanalysis of Ghost Stories," by Richardson, who unveils the logic of forbidden desire in *Dracula*, for example, through the psychoanalytic resonance of the confluence of semen and blood. Senf's "*Dracula*: The Unseen Face in the Mirror" looks at the erratic behavior of the small group of privileged vampire hunters who are working in and around Dr. Seward's London mental institution. As the hunters' confusion is compounded by Jonathan's nervous breakdown and Lucy's schizophrenia, Senf leads the reader to question the sanity of the group of professionals who break the laws they have vowed to uphold. David Punter, in "Dracula and Taboo," depicts Dracula as another example, like Polidori's Lord Ruthven, of an aristocratic, antibourgeois figure who (unlike Jesus, whose blood is shed and expiates) supplements his own blood by draining the professional class. In keeping with the gothic tradition that undermines set boundaries, such as the fascination/repulsion dynamic, Dracula breaks several taboos, including socio-moral codes, by blurring lines, variously, between man and beast, "thus echoing fears of degeneracy"; between man and God, "by daring to partake of immortal life"; and between man and woman, "by demonstrating the existence of female passion" (Punter 28). In his essay "'The Little Children Can Be Bitten': A Hunger for Dracula," Dennis Foster provides a post-Freudian reading of the novel's several displaced family romances that depicts Dracula as mother, as child, and as the primal and anal father.

Gender

An early feminist critique, Roth's "Suddenly Sexual Women in Bram Stoker's *Dracula*," extends the work of C. F. Bentley's "The Monster in the Bedroom: Sexual Symbolism in Bram Stoker's *Dracula*" and Fry's "Fictional Conventions and Sexuality in *Dracula*." Using Fry's idea that female vampires are stand-ins for fallen women, Roth helps the reader understand the appeal of the savage staking of Lucy by the rejected suitor Dr. Seward as evidence of hostility toward female sexuality during the Victorian era and into the late twentieth century. Craft extends gothic ambiguity to an ambiguity of sexual desire and fear, in itself a fundamental nonbinary characteristic of the gothic. He begins "'Kiss Me with Those Red Lips': Gender and Inversion in Bram Stoker's

12   CRITICAL SOURCES

Dracula" with a close reading of Stoker's multiple use of *trans* words—such as *Trans*ylvania, *trans*cribing, and *trans*fusion—as a jumping-off point for his queer reading. In an erasure of the boundaries of self and of typical Victorian gender roles that is spelled out by Lucy's sexual aggression following her seduction by Dracula, Craft discusses Jonathan's swooning, "feminine" desire to be penetrated by the Count's ambiguously defined brides, daughters, and lovers (Craft, "Kiss Me" 109). Talia Schaffer's deeply engaged hunt for a closeted Stoker in "'A Wilde Desire Took Me': The Homoerotic History of *Dracula*" finds the logic of triangular desire in (as one example among many) the homosocial scene in which Mina Harker serves as the placeholder between the sexually ambiguous Count and Jonathan. Dracula sucks Mrs. Harker's blood, then forces her to suck his from his breast, all the while with her husband asleep in bed next to them. Schaffer argues that this sequence is one of many displacements wherein Mina's role parallels that of Stoker's wife, Florence Balcombe (who was the former sweetheart of Stoker's friend Oscar Wilde, famously convicted of gross indecency for his relationships with men) and, further, demonstrates that Jonathan's fascination and repulsion toward the monstrous Count are drawn from Stoker's feelings about Wilde ("Wilde Desire"). In "Feminism, Fiction, and the Utopian Promise of Dracula," Armstrong goes over several feminist approaches to the Count and the novel and cites Georg Lukács and Judith Butler, among others, in discussing the complex "inward turn" of the Victorian novel and the "class-specific model of the household" at its center (7). Renée Fox in "Building Castles in the Air: Female Intimacy and Generative Queerness in *Dracula*" looks at the queer female intimacy shared by Mina with Lucy. Also consult "A Vampire in the Mirror: The Sexuality of Dracula," by John Allen Stevenson.

Technology

Friedrich A. Kittler's "Draculas Vermächtnis" ("Dracula's Legacy"), written on the occasion of the death of Jacques Lacan, is an amusing, insightful, and notoriously dense essay perhaps best suited for advanced undergraduate and graduate study. Pointing to a history of men writing with quills and women quilting with needles, the renowned poststructuralist media and literature philosopher characterizes Mina as exemplifying the trend of the woman replacing the man in the front office. She is now armed with her mass-produced Remington typewriter, whose typebars effectively battle the Count's bite marks with their own repeated impressions. Kittler also presents an engaging equivalency between Guglielmo Marconi's contemporaneous radio technology and Mina's weaponized telepathic circuit with Dracula. Wicke engages this aspect of the novel as well. On the subject of recording methods and the questions they provoke, also see John M. Rider's "The Victorian Aura of the Recorded Voice" and Leah Richards's "Mass Production and the Spread of Information in *Dracula*: 'Proofs of So Wild a Story.'" In keeping

CRITICAL SOURCES   13

with an such an analysis, Caryn Radick in "'Complete and in Order': Bram Stoker's 'Dracula' and the Archival Profession" concentrates on the role of the literary archivist and the ways in which the late Victorian interest in record-keeping affects the narrative.

Marxism

Both rigorous and tongue-in-cheek, Moretti's "A Capital *Dracula*," excerpted from *Signs Taken for Wonders: Essays in the Sociology of Literary Forms*, claims that the Count has read Adam Smith in the sense that he is an enlightened exploiter of capitalism and a practitioner of the Protestant work ethic (he drives his own carriage, has no servants, and cooks and serves Jonathan dinner but does not himself eat). He also employs Marx's analogy that capital thrives by sucking up "living labor" (508). From his Marxist insights Moretti moves on to psychoanalytic ones. Citing a slew of writers, including Charles Baudelaire, Edgar Allan Poe, Stendhal, John Keats, Georg Wilhelm Friedrich Hegel, and Sigmund Freud, he points up the ambivalent nature of fear and desire at work in both Stoker's and Mary Shelley's novels. While drawing from Neil Smith's critique of capitalist expansion and building on a network of commentators, notably Arata, Moretti, and Joseph Valente, Patricia McKee casts the vampire hunters as sharing the Count's "unsettled behavior," a possibility granted them by their capitalist privilege, whiteness, and "power to capitalize upon mobility" (42), thereby resurrecting an ideology of racial superiority over the animalized Dracula, with his "child brain" (Stoker, *Dracula* [Browning and Skal] 311). See also "Marxferatu: The Vampire Metaphor as a Tool for Teaching Marx's Critique of Capitalism" (Morrisette).

Formalism

The psychoanalytic approach of Senf's "*Dracula*: The Unseen Face in the Mirror" includes a formalist and reader-response analysis of the relative silence and absence of the Count in comparison with the manic writings of the vampire killers. Reading the rhetoric of Stoker's composition, Seed explains in "The Narrative Method of *Dracula*" how the tale's multiple perspectives involve readers in the narrative, asking them to piece together corroborative evidence of the Count's strange doings from the written records. Alan Johnson's "Bent and Broken Necks: Signs of Design in Stoker's *Dracula*" considers the uncanny doubling structure of men and women whereby the novel delivers a critique of rigid gendered boundaries. In "Doubling and Repetition / Realism and Closure in *Dracula*," Riquelme explicitly thematizes the boundary-blurring anti-logic of Stoker's novel. He points to the encryption in *Van Helsing*, as an anagram of *English*, of a disguised Saint George and Stoker's matching of Dr. Seward's triple commitment to "work, work, work" with Renfield's desire to "feed—and feed—and feed." He further sees an upending of opposites at the heart of any concept of the undead in the chiastic crossing of sleep and dying performed by

14   CRITICAL SOURCES

the two lines of poetry that Dr. Seward records in his diary. Rebecca Pope's "Writing and Biting in *Dracula*" champions the many voices that Stoker creates as the novel invites the reader, through Mina's effective editing, to incorporate each narrative yet leaves its audience with an unresolved story.

Irish Studies

Echoing a group of critics who dismiss the literary quality of *Dracula*, W. J. McCormack's "Irish Gothic and After, 1820–1945" does allow consideration of Stoker's novel within the terms of literary Irish studies, a broad designation that examines the Irish political, cultural, religious, and historical character from the early Celts to the diaspora and the modern era. Given that the Stoker novel makes no explicit mention of Ireland, interpreting *Dracula* under the designation of Irish studies requires a certain dedicated reading of the novel. Most often, such an approach necessarily combines the biography of the brogue-inflected, Protestant Irish author in London with an engaged historicopolitical allegory. As with most approaches to the novel, such recourse to the biography presents teachers with an opportunity to discuss New Criticism and the caution by W. K. Wimsatt and Monroe Beardsley against affective, intentional, and biographical "fallacies." "The Irish Vampire: *Dracula*, Parnell and the Troubled Dreams of Nationhood," by Michael Valdez Moses, sees the Count as both an Irish revolutionary and a ruthless landlord who shares with Parnell a certain hypnotizing, threatening, aristocratic positionality as the foreigner bent on upsetting staid Victorian centers of power. Alison Milbank's "'Powers Old and New': Stoker's Alliances with Anglo-Irish Gothic" gets at Stoker's ambivalence toward his Irish identity with recourse to several elements in his biography, from his Trinity College schooling and the influence of his fellow Irish writers Le Fanu and Charles Maturin to his attempt to reconcile Irish religious factionalism in portraying the destruction of an invading monster by a unified Catholic and Protestant front. Riquelme effectively groups together the modernists Wilde, William Butler Yeats, James Joyce, and the postmodern Samuel Beckett as he identifies an Irish gothic thread in Stoker's work along with the novelist's predilection for doubling in "Toward a History of Gothic and Modernism: Dark Modernity from Bram Stoker to Samuel Beckett." Such doubling is further elaborated by Valente in *Dracula's Crypt: Bram Stoker, Irishness, and the Question of Blood*. He expands this notion into a sustained discussion of the novel's doppelgänger interplay that is constitutive of Stoker's double Anglo-Irish identity as both the conquering imperialist and the conquered subaltern (15–41). In addition to an extended historicocultural analysis of the novel and its canonical status, the book provides teachers and students with a helpful recounting of the previous decade's analysis of the "Irish *Dracula*" (1). See also "Was Dracula an Irishman?," by Bob Curran, and "Gothic Genealogies: Dracula, Bowen's Court, and Anglo-Irish Psychology," by Raphaël Ingelbien.

Medical Science

Taking up Van Helsing's invocation of the criminologist Cesare Lombroso and his student Max Nordau (highlighted by Wolf in *The Annotated* Dracula, 300n23), Ernest Fontana's "Lombroso's Criminal Man and Stoker's *Dracula*" launches an investigation into degeneracy and evolution in Stoker's novel, linking together Renfield and Dracula as criminals, Lucy as possibly evidencing epilepsy, and the role played by Charles Darwin's evolution theory. In *Horror Fiction in the Protestant Tradition*, Victor Sage analyzes aspects of Christian transubstantiation of blood in the novel and the pairing of the Count and Dr. Van Helsing as studies in deviance. In "'So unlike the Normal Lunatic': Abnormal Psychology in Bram Stoker's *Dracula*," Hughes reaches back to William B. Carpenter's 1874 *Principles of Mental Physiology with Their Applications to the Training and Discipline of the Mind, and the Study of Its Morbid Conditions* to support his close-reading corrective regarding the cause of Renfield's lunacy in that it predates the Count's arrival. Aligning with the critical consensus that the novel supplies a doubling of narrative and character, he shows a commonality between the alienist Dr. Seward and his patient that demonstrates as mere surface the division between mental illness and mental health. Hughes continues his research in *Beyond* Dracula*: Bram Stoker's Fiction and Its Cultural Context* with a historicobiographical look at other books by Stoker and their reflection of late Victorian medical language and practice regarding blood, genealogy, and race so as to open up such readings of *Dracula*. Glover's "'Our Enemy Is Not Merely Spiritual': Degeneration and Modernity in Bram Stoker's *Dracula*" takes up Carpenter as well and finds the novel reflecting the middle-class Victorian fear of the liberal human being descending back down Darwin's evolutionary ladder, detecting a reading public "transfixed by the findings of the modern sciences and parasciences." Following David Hume Flood's thematization of the novel that assigns a gender valence to blood, Mulvey-Roberts shows how Stoker's novel associates blood with menstruation and women with disease, notably syphilis, the putative killer of Stoker, and the threat posed by another so-called invasion, that of the suffragettes, who are pathologized as victims in need of treatment by the male medical establishment ("*Dracula* and the Doctors"). See also "'Terrors of the Night': *Dracula* and 'Degeneration' in the Late Nineteenth Century," by Daniel Pick.

Film and Theater

The films spawned by Stoker's novel are legion. Donald F. Glut's well-illustrated *The Dracula Book* is one of the first to assess the many appearances of Stoker's Count in films and other media. Skal's scholarship provides the most comprehensive account of these reimaginings, significantly in *The Hollywood Gothic: The Tangled Web of* Dracula *from Novel to Stage to Screen*. Skal investigates

George Melford's 1931 Spanish-language film in "The Spanish *Dracula*" and gives a history of his involvement in promoting the film in a 2021 interview ("Ninetieth Spanish *Drácula* Anniversary"). He discusses *Drakula İstanbul'da (Dracula in İstanbul)*, produced by the Turkish studio And Film, in "*Dracula* Unearthed" and lays out a discursive history of dramatic adaptations in "'His Hour upon the Stage': Theatrical Adaptations of Dracula," followed in the second Norton Critical Edition by a checklist of dramatic adaptations (380–81). See also *Dracula in Visual Media*, by John Edgar Browning and Caroline Joan Picart; "Dracula on Film and TV from 1960 to the Present," by Stacey Abbott; and "Untold Draculas: Textual Estrangements, Cinematic Reincarnations, and the Popular *Dracula* Legend," by Matthew Crofts.

Other Works by Stoker

Fiction

The Chain of Destiny (1875)
The Primrose Path (1875)
Under the Sunset (1882)
Gibbet Hill (1890)
The Snake's Pass (1890)
Miss Betty (1891)
The Shoulder of Shasta (1895)
The Watter's Mou' (1895)
The Mystery of the Sea (1902)
The Jewel of the Seven Stars (1903)
The Man (1905)
Lady Athlyene (1908)
The Lady of the Shroud (1909)
The Lair of the White Worm (1911)

Fiction Collections

Snowbound: The Record of a Theatrical Touring Party (1908)
"Dracula's Guest" and Other Weird Stories (1914)
The Bram Stoker Bedside Companion (1973)
The Bram Stoker Omnibus (1992)
The Complete Short Stories of Bram Stoker (2015)

Nonfiction

A Glimpse of America: A Lecture Given at the London Institution (1886)

"Lecture on Abraham Lincoln" (1886)

"The Great White Fair in Dublin" (1907)

"The World's Greatest Ship-building Yard: Impressions of a Visit to Messrs. Harland and Wolff's Ship-building Yards at Belfast" (1907)

"The Censorship of Fiction" (1908)

"The American 'Tramp' Question and the Old English Vagrancy Laws" (1909)

Famous Impostors (1910)

Nonfiction Collections

Bram Stoker and the Stage: Reviews, Reminiscences, Essays and Fiction, 2 vols., edited by Catherine Wynne (2012)

The Forgotten Writings of Bram Stoker, edited by John Edgar Browning (2012)

The Lost Journal of Bram Stoker: The Dublin Years, edited by Elizabeth Miller and Dacre Stoker (2012)

Biographies

Working with papers made available by Stoker's son, Noel, Harry Ludlam's *A Biography of Dracula: The Life Story of Bram Stoker*, appearing in 1962, was the first biography of Stoker. Subsequently, Bierman published on the mysterious illness that kept Stoker bedridden for the first seven years of his childhood. *The Man Who Wrote* Dracula: *A Biography of Bram Stoker*, by a great-nephew of Stoker's, Daniel Farson, emphasizes the relationship with Irving and the London theater scene, in which Stoker participated as a critic and theater manager. Phyllis Roth's biography of Stoker is an early example of viewing Stoker's life and novel through a Freudian lens; Barbara Belford's *Bram Stoker: A Biography of the Author of* Dracula follows suit. The twenty-first century has seen a slew of biographies. Paul Murray's *From the Shadow of* Dracula: *A Life of Bram Stoker* treats the family dynamic with Stoker's children and looks at his other writings. Andrew Maunder's *Bram Stoker* addresses the writer's career as a commercial novelist and the anxieties and challenges of fin-de-siècle London. Lisa Hopkins's *Bram Stoker: A Literary Life* places the novel within the Stoker oeuvre to reveal insights into the author's entire literary career. And Skal's recent, monumental *Something in the Blood: The Untold Story of Bram Stoker, the Man Who Wrote* Dracula is a

18   CLASSROOM GUIDES

learned and speculative entry that advances the thesis that Stoker was gay by highlighting Stoker's love letters to Walt Whitman and spends roughly a quarter of its six hundred pages devoted to the comings and goings of Oscar Wilde, including a forty-page side trip entitled "Undead Oscar" (379–421).

Classroom Guides

Dracula: A Study Guide, by Roy Johnson, includes resource guides, an introduction to the main themes addressed in *Dracula* criticism, and a brief bibliography of scholarly essays and web links. "How Did Dracula Become the World's Most Famous Vampire?" is a well-produced five-minute TED-Ed talk that is accompanied by additional resources and discussion questions (Stepanic). A helpful resource for teachers of upper-level high school students is *Bram Stoker's* Dracula: A Critical Study Guide, by Lilith Steinmetz, which contextualizes the novel's place in the gothic genre as it presents *Dracula*'s central themes, passages, and literary terms along with designs for exams. Published by Gale, *Study Guide for Bram Stoker's* Dracula provides a Stoker biography, historical contexts, plot summaries, analyses of main characters, themes, quotes, symbols, study questions, and suggestions for further reading.

Additional Online Resources

The following additional resources are recommended:

> *A Hyper-concordance to the Works of Bram Stoker,* by Mitsuharu Matsuoka, at Nagoya University (victorian-studies.net/concordance/stoker/)
>
> *The Leslie Shepard Bram Stoker Collection at Dublin City Library and Archive* (dublincity.ie/sites/default/files/media/file-uploads/2018-06/ leslie_shepard_bram_stoker_collection.pdf)
>
> The "Modern Criticism" section of *Bram Stoker,* a research guide compiled by Hughes, which contains nearly two hundred entries, including several French titles (victorianfictionresearchguides.org/bram -stoker/modern-criticism/)
>
> *Bram Stoker (1847–1912),* which offers a descriptive bibliography of Stoker works and critical apparatus with separate files of commentary, quotations, and ancillary books (ricorso.net/rx/az-data/authors/s/ Stoker_B/life.htm)
>
> A scan of the first American edition of *Dracula* (archive.org/details/ draculabr00stokuoft/mode/2up)

Part Two

APPROACHES

Introduction

William Thomas McBride

> Nothing is too small. I counsel you, put down in record even your doubts and surmises.
> —*Van Helsing to Dr. Seward,*
> *in Bram Stoker,* Dracula

In this collection of pedagogical essays, diverse and distinguished *Dracula* scholars with experience teaching the novel from a variety of interpretive positions and approaches invite us into their classrooms to share successful strategies and creative assignments. The essays are designed for instructors of students at different stages of their schooling as they take into account the novel's unendingly visible, premier place in popular culture. While the following essays are thematized under discrete headings, such rigid categorizing belies their scope, and soon the reader will appreciate the ways in which one theoretical approach bleeds into another while certain strategies reappear. As with the Dublin of James Joyce's *Ulysses*, one can enter anywhere and skip around; therefore, there is no recommended reading sequence. In addition to historicizing and looking at narrative technique and genre, contributors consider the novel alongside Bram Stoker's varied life experiences so as to make observations regarding his relationships with Henry Irving, Oscar Wilde, and Walt Whitman, all set against a fin-de-siècle, Anglo-Irish Protestant anxiety regarding fluid sexual agency and reverse colonization. In addition to pedagogical approaches from teachers throughout the United States, the volume offers contributions from the Netherlands, Canada, England, and India.

Some of the main challenges that teachers confront when assigning *Dracula* arise from students' unfamiliarity with the epistolary genre and their resistance to the novel's length. An instructor needs to help students navigate through Stoker's novel, including its depictions of racism and sexual violence, and locate it within a context of shared associations that encompasses a broad range of kindred works and creators, known as the Dracula "megatext." A handful of contributors discuss teaching during the pandemic, recounting how they restructured their face-to-face courses for online platforms and how they judiciously used the uncanny parallel between the novel's express concern over a foreign infectious invader appearing as a vampiric "big bat" (Stoker, *Dracula* 111) and the Wuhan wet market bat that early on was named as the speculative cause of COVID-19. There are contributors who demonstrate the benefit of processing the novel through *Project Gutenberg* and how, in general, to use digital humanities to process the complex media patchwork that is *Dracula*. Citing rapid full enrollment, teachers of *Dracula* attest to the popularity of large lecture classes, particularly when film adaptations are part of the syllabus.

22   INTRODUCTION

A series of questions posed by instructors arise: What is Dracula's threat? What is abjected in Stoker's original novel? What do new media reveal about cultural anxieties and modern innovation? Do games and interactive videos humanize Dracula, and if so, how might sympathy for the monster impact our reading? Does Stoker violate or uphold the morality he seems to advocate? And how might a Me Too awareness of pervasive sexual violence, inside and outside the academy, facilitate our teaching of *Dracula*?

The "Critical Reading" section begins with Ana Raquel Rojas's account of an introductory theory course in which students write three separate papers on *Dracula*, each time deploying a cluster of different interpretive methodologies in order to answer the question, What is Dracula's threat? Rojas shares her technique that challenges students to suspend, however "inconceivable" it might seem, references to race, gender, class, or history in order to attend to the epistolary structure of *Dracula*. The semester-long exercise results in students' acquiring the language of critical theory, a fluency in *Dracula* scholarship, and an enriched appreciation of the novel. Agnes Andeweg describes how, in undergraduate gothic fiction courses taught to a diverse and international group of students in the Netherlands, students read four very different critical approaches to the novel, improve their comprehension of the interpretations, and gain confidence in how their own knowledge is acquired and shared. Joshua Gooch uses *Dracula* and scholarship by Friedrich Kittler and Franco Moretti in a special topics course that examines the New Woman's secretarial labor, the professional consortium of white-collar vampire hunters, and Jonathan Harker's work anxiety, an approach that can speak to students grappling with the real-life prospect of an underpaid job made even "more fraught" given the previous pandemic's focus on "infection and death."

In the next section, "The Gothic," Jerrold E. Hogle relates how he begins his course teaching Horace Walpole's *Castle of Otranto*, John Polidori's *The Vampyre*, and Mary Shelley's *Frankenstein* so as to ensure that his students arrive at a clear definition of the gothic. He then applies Julia Kristeva's notion of abjection to help students reach a greater understanding of just "what is abjected . . . in Stoker's original novel." Richard Haslam asks students to interrogate the "wishful linking" of allegoresis that leads to an inevitable positing of an Irishness in Stoker's novel. Students identify key elements of the Irish gothic in *Dracula* and in more recent Irish fiction and read excerpts from two groups of allegorizing critics—one that figures the Count as an oppressive Anglo-Irish landlord and one that sees Dracula as a nationalist leader à la Charles Stewart Parnell—in order to judge for themselves the strength of these arguments. While such a challenge puts into question the critical positioning of several of the essays in this volume, Haslam's essay serves as an effective balance. I can vouch from my own classroom experience that interrogating traditional, symptomatic approaches has the potential to spark productive discussions regarding argument and textual evidence so as to make space for formalist considerations.

To successfully position *Dracula* as pertinent and accessible to BIPOC students in general and to Latinx students specifically, Lisa Nevárez, in the "Ethnic Studies" section, asks instructors to consider current demographics when teaching Stoker's novel of migration and border crossings and to see how these aspects of the novel can connect with readers' own family histories. Exploring non-European themes in *Dracula* and Latinx vampire texts, Nevárez offers activities, analogies, and discussion prompts along with suggestions for research and reflection projects. After briefly reviewing the history of vampire myths from Africa and the African diaspora, Jerry Rafiki Jenkins turns to Stoker's novel in an upper-division course on African American vampire fiction and also in a literature-focused composition course. Investigations into, for example, *Dracula*'s resurrection vampirism and cultural fears of miscegenation shed light on the novel's absence of Black characters and on the rise of Black vampire speculative fiction in response to that void. Srirupa Chatterjee shares her experience teaching a course on popular fiction to undergraduate engineering students in India. After introducing them to differences in Indian and European aesthetic conceptions of fear, Chatterjee helps her students explore how the figure of Dracula becomes multivalent and invested not only with many qualities that British colonists thought showed their "racial supremacy" but also with an ironic character that "deftly deconstructs the racial pride that lay at the heart of the imperialist mission."

Elizabeth Way teaches *Dracula* in a first-year seminar on the science of nineteenth-century gothic fiction in both her Introduction to British Studies course and in a gothic course for adult learners. Way details in the "Medical Science" section how students research late-nineteenth-century medical discourse, the "nervous systems" of fin-de-siècle England, and the attendant gender anxieties and fear of gender inversion that contribute to the horror at the core of Stoker's novel. Ess Pokornowski, who has taught *Dracula* in lower-division literature and first-year writing courses that thematized contagion, otherness, outbreak narratives, and an "equity-minded pedagogy of care," discusses the impact of COVID-19 and provides assignment suggestions designed for remote instruction. William Hughes presents as a worthy model Professor Van Helsing and his Victorian fin-de-siècle diagnosis and prognosis of "contemporary pathologies," whether physical or psychological, and opens up classroom discussions with tools used by queer studies, psychobiography and cultural history.

In the "Sexuality and Gender" section, Jolene Zigarovich tasks students with collecting textual evidence to apply an approach to *Dracula* that both engages and disrupts queer gothic readings. To that end, Zigarovich demonstrates, as do other contributors in the volume, the utility of electronic word searches to support students' theses—for example, the prevalence of terms like *Trans*ylvania, *trans*cribing, and *trans*fusion as evidence of the novel's language of "fluid gender subjectivities," which enables a liberating potential for "mortal humanity." Andrew Smith teaches the novel in a final-year undergraduate module on the fin-de-siècle gothic. He provides students with a way of thinking about how the

24   INTRODUCTION

novel aligns "constructions of national identity" with representations of masculinity alongside accounts of degeneration that draw on medical science and Darwinism. Patrick R. O'Malley teaches *Dracula* in a number of courses dedicated severally to Victorian sexualities, nation and empire, and the gothic as well as offering a course that explores methodological approaches to literary analysis. He reports on a recent widening of his classroom focus beyond the delimiting concentration on the novel's "tableaux of spectacular gender and sexual anxiety" toward a wider "range of ways of inhabiting—and querying—gendered and sexual identities" of Stoker's novel. Applying Eve Kosofsky Sedgwick's "reparative reading" helps students see Mina's ambivalent position vis-à-vis the "New Woman" and Mina and Lucy's participation in a female erotics that can be obscured from the view of the male characters.

In the "Film and Television" section, Jeffrey Andrew Weinstock writes about how his classes revisit their prior knowledge of Stoker's creation through the lens of key cinematic adaptations—that is, the four films out of the hundreds of Dracula movies that he convincingly argues have shaped "the contours" of the Dracula megatext: F. W. Murnau's *Nosferatu*, Tod Browning's *Dracula*, Terence Fisher's *Horror of Dracula*, and Francis Ford Coppola's *Bram Stoker's* Dracula. Through this exercise, students come to understand the composite nature of the Dracula multiverse and how to situate Stoker's novel within it. Peter Gölz, having adapted his large lecture course, A Cultural History of Vampires in Literature and Film, to a synchronous online format, thus opened up enrollment of students from Asia, Europe, and North America in his three film modules, "The Classics," "Remakes and Retakes," and "New Generations." Gölz recounts *Zoom* visits from scholars and walks readers through the components of the revamped course in a "virtually flipped classroom."

Christopher G. Diller, in the "New Media and Digital Humanities" section, details how he introduces upper-division literature majors to ways they can perform textual analysis by applying *Voyant Tools* and *ZeeMaps* and by looking at collocations, statistical correlations, geospatial mapping, and word frequencies in *Dracula*. Small-group peer reviews create a teamwork atmosphere as students discover the benefits of sharing a single primary text and the importance of place and movement in literature, a practice designed to encourage students to arrive together at a middle ground between "close" and "distant" reading. Zan Cammack teaches the novel as an "experiment in hypothetical, pre-Internet multimodality." After collaboratively identifying the various technologies in *Dracula* and tracking the ways they are used, students can explicate the relative importance of the role each plays and consider what information is yielded. This multimodal reading of *Dracula* encourages students to understand the media in the novel as bearers of meaning. As Weinstock incorporates the Dracula megatext generated by the film industry, Shari Hodges Holt asks students in her gothic fiction courses to engage with the transmedia storytelling of the *Dracula* "culture-text," which can include graphic novels, streaming video, fan-produced adaptations, television series, and video games. By exploring the way these new works open up Stoker's novel, students have the opportunity to learn how adaptation and interactivity enable users, viewers, and writers of digital posts to humanize the monster so as to reinterpret the novel's themes.

Closing out the volume, the "Board Games and Study Abroad" section sparks participation and immersion through gaming and location-based courses. David Smith demonstrates the pedagogical efficacy of the board game *Fury of Dracula* for breathing life into the novel's historical settings and demonstrates how, in the age of COVID-19, instructors can address "themes of contagion and miasma . . . through various cards and abilities in the game." Further, Smith argues, board games can be used to teach socialization, multicultural awareness, and sympathy. Dragan Kujundžić teaches the novel in London to American students who visit historic locations set in Stoker's novel. In course offerings supplemented by invited talks by noted British scholars, historians, and artists, Kujundžić uses Stoker's novel, and in particular Coppola's film, to make a space for play. He allows creative projects and encourages students to seek contemporary valences by using *Dracula* as an interpretive tool when applied to political events.

All references to *Dracula* throughout this volume cite the second Norton Critical Edition, edited by John Edgar Browning and David J. Skal.

CRITICAL READING

Teaching Critical Theory with *Dracula*

Ana Raquel Rojas

"How can we possibly write three different papers on the same novel?" My students tend to ask some version of this question at the start of Critical Analysis, an introduction to literary and critical theory for undergraduate majors in English and comparative literature. The goal of the course is to teach students about the major interpretive methodologies of the twentieth and twenty-first centuries and how they can be applied to literary analysis. Because the critical readings in this class can be quite challenging, I aim to simplify the process by assigning only one literary text for the semester. Students write three papers on a single novel, each time taking a different interpretive approach in their analysis. Bram Stoker's *Dracula* is excellent for this purpose. Students typically find it engaging, and they are all familiar with the character of Dracula; even if they have never read the novel before, they still enter the class with some knowledge of the text, which is a benefit, given that so much of the other course material is new to them. *Dracula* is also effective for teaching critical theory, because as the students become familiar with different methodologies, it becomes fairly evident how they can be employed to analyze the novel.

All three papers have the same prompt question: What is Dracula's threat? The answer seems rather obvious at first, since Dracula's threat would appear to be his vampirism. Faced with the task of responding to this question in three different ways, students worry about running out of things to say. Even though they have been taught that a text can sustain multiple interpretive possibilities, they also tend to believe there is a finite limit to the amount that can be said about any text—and certainly to what they have to say about it. As they learn more about critical theory, students start to recognize that the answer to the question of Dracula's threat varies depending upon which approach they use to examine the novel. They start to see how vampirism becomes a way of representing any number of threats: sexual, racial, economic, cultural, and so on. As they engage more with the wide body of scholarship on the novel, they learn to see Dracula's threat in more nuanced terms and become more attuned to details to which they might not have paid much attention initially.

When teaching *Dracula* in a critical theory course, I prefer the Norton Critical Editions, whose criticism sections offer a variety of scholarly perspectives. Another edition of *Dracula* effective for this purpose is edited by John Paul Riquleme and published in the Bedford / St. Martin's Case Studies in Contemporary Criticism series. The principal text I use for teaching theory is *How to Interpret Literature: Critical Theory for Literary and Cultural Studies*, by Robert Dale Parker, which provides the organizing structure for the course by offering a broad historicist survey of the major movements in literary study across the twentieth and twenty-first centuries. Its twelve chapters, each on a different methodology, offer a useful way of organizing the semester. In a typical week, students are assigned a chapter from *How to Interpret Literature* that introduces them to the history and key concepts behind a given critical approach, then a foundational theoretical reading that allows them to engage directly with critical theory, and finally an essay that offers an analysis of *Dracula* through the lens of that particular methodology.

One of the challenges of teaching critical theory with *Dracula* is the novel's length. Assigning a three-hundred-page novel alongside other readings, some of them quite difficult, can easily overwhelm students. To make the workload manageable, I assign about five chapters of *Dracula* for each class session, meaning that it takes approximately three weeks to get through the novel. During that time, students are also beginning to learn about formalist methodologies of interpretation. Because few of my students have ever thought consciously about how they approach an analysis of literature or why they do so, the first weeks of class focus on tracing a history of literary interpretation. We do not typically discuss *Dracula* until everyone has finished reading the novel in its entirety, at which point I ask students to write a brief response addressing what they are interested in exploring within the novel. Our first discussion of *Dracula* therefore tends to be wide-ranging, touching on a number of topics that we will later consider in greater detail. This approach sets the stage for what follows: a deep dive into the wealth of interpretive possibilities that critical theory enables.

Our first unit focuses on New Criticism, structuralism, and deconstruction, and generally my students find this the most challenging. Millennial undergraduates are accustomed to seeing a literary text as a cultural product, even though they may not be familiar with the theoretical underpinnings that inform their perspective. Reading a text largely without reference to race, gender, class, or history is fairly inconceivable to them. This unit, however, allows students to focus intently on the text itself as we explore the epistolary structure of *Dracula* and the implications of its metanarrative. I often begin with a lame joke: "Spoiler alert: Dracula is a vampire." Students' cultural knowledge of the text ensures this disclosure comes as no surprise, but the point is to emphasize the fact that Dracula's identity as a vampire is not something that is discovered and revealed until midway through the novel. This allows students to see how *Dracula* begins as a series of disparate and seemingly unconnected documents that only start to cohere into a single narrative once Dracula's identity and nature are understood

28   CRITICAL THEORY

by the other characters. Students readily see how Dracula forms the point of connection between the various plotlines, but in learning more about New Criticism, they begin to think about the form and content of the novel together and start to recognize how *Dracula* is structured so that initially distinct narratives eventually get woven together. Ordinarily, my students might have taken the novel's structure for granted, but the New Critical focus on the necessary relationship between the events of the plot and the way they are recounted provides them with the means to analyze narrative form.

We also consider the implications of the novel's metanarrative about how this manuscript came to be by discussing the brief editorial preface to *Dracula*: "How these papers have been placed in sequence will be made manifest in the reading of them . . ." (Stoker, *Dracula* 7). As students learn more about structuralism and narratology, they begin to consider how the novel is composed of a series of dated documents that create the impression of events unfolding contemporaneously but are revealed to have been gathered, organized, and typed by Mina; as Jonathan's final note makes clear, these events turn out to have taken place seven years earlier. This process allows students to consider how the narrative may function as the heroic characters' ex post facto attempt to make sense of Dracula's effect on their lives and create a sense of control over Dracula.

In addition to recognizing the narrative power that the characters exert, students also reflect on the notable absence of Dracula's own voice in the novel. Deconstruction provides a useful framework for considering Dracula's simultaneous absence and presence within the text as a kind of absent center who is discursively created while also being held in abeyance by the narrative. By the end of this unit, students have come to see Dracula's threat in textual terms and to analyze how the novel's characters turn to narrative as a means of fixing in place something they fear is becoming destabilized. Although the students initially express some concern about writing a purely formalist analysis, they ultimately come to appreciate the ability to write an entire paper on a single scene, passage, or even word.

The second unit focuses on poststructuralism and includes psychoanalysis, feminism, queer theory, Marxism, new historicism and cultural studies, and postcolonial theory and critical race studies. Many students gravitate toward these methodologies in their initial response to *Dracula*, and this unit enables them to gain a greater awareness of the ideologies that informed their preliminary readings. Students are most frequently attuned to the sexual dynamics of the novel; by learning more about psychoanalytic, feminist, and queer theory, they acquire a richer and more precise vocabulary for examining the elements of the text they find most compelling. The wealth of scholarship on the erotic dimensions of the novel also helps students see the greater complexity of the text's details. Students start to recognize how the formalist methodologies of the first unit continue to enrich their understanding of the novel in the second unit. For example, Phyllis A. Roth's claim that "Lucy and Mina are essentially the same figure: the mother" and that *Dracula* is therefore "the same story told twice with different outcomes" ("Suddenly Sexual Women" 549) enables students to see how a psychoanalytic reading of the novel's oedipal dynamics is imbricated in the novel's narrative structure. *Dracula* pairs well with Sigmund Freud's essay on the uncanny, and the idea that Dracula operates as the return of any number of repressed desires offers students multiple productive avenues for interpretation. Students are also intrigued by Freud's notion of ambivalence; while they readily see the violence involved in the novel's expressions of desire, students also learn to recognize how the text's many expressions of friendship, love, admiration, and devotion can betray repressed hostility and aggression, not only toward women but most especially between and among the men.

Students often begin their psychoanalytic readings of *Dracula* by focusing on Lucy and Mina, but learning more about queer theory enables them to see the significance of the rivalries and bonds between the male characters. Because students often initially focus on the sexual dynamics at play in the many blood transfusions that Lucy receives and the gruesome violence inflicted on her body, they tend not to pay much attention at first to the significance of the conversations and interactions between the men as they struggle to save Lucy's life and soul. I assign excerpts from Eve Kosofsky Sedgwick's *Between Men*, and the idea of erotic triangles provides students with new insights into ways of analyzing the complex and overlapping dynamics of desire and violence. Once students learn about homosocial bonds, they become much more attuned to the repeated articulations of solidarity between the men and begin reconsidering these dynamics through the lens of the fact that Arthur, Seward, and Quincey were all rivals for Lucy's hand in marriage. As students read the essays collected in the first and second Norton Critical Editions, they see how Roth and Christopher Craft offer contrasting interpretations of these homosocial bonds: Roth argues that the repeated professions of friendship and trust between the men "mask a deep-seated rivalry and hostility" ("Suddenly Sexual Women" 547), whereas Craft interprets these bonds as homoerotic and displaced onto Lucy as an acceptable heterosexual object of desire: "only through women may men touch" (Excerpt 448). In looking at these readings together, students perceive how the same set of circumstances in a text can be interpreted in different ways depending upon the critical theories used for analysis.

Although students begin this unit eager to analyze issues of gender and sexuality, what typically sparks the greatest interest are the discussions on Marxism, new historicism and cultural studies, and postcolonial and critical race theory. My millennial students are particularly invested in topics of race and class, and their interest in contemporary social justice movements fuels their enthusiasm for learning more about the ideological foundations of the issues they see as most pressing and relevant. Students become most excited by these discussions because they open up avenues for interpreting *Dracula* they had not considered before. Just as students begin to think that we may have exhausted topics for discussion, these methodologies open new horizons for exploration.

Since most of my students are from the United States, their understanding of English aristocracy and Britain's class system is somewhat limited, so

30   CRITICAL THEORY

we discuss the significance of the fact that midway through the novel, Arthur Holmwood becomes Lord Godalming, inheriting his father's title and property. Students quickly recognize that Arthur's money enables the fight against Dracula and that his aristocratic position shields him and, by extension, the others from questions about the legitimacy of their actions. His title opens doors for them, literally and figuratively, from an estate agent's willingness to provide Jonathan—ostensibly on Lord Godalming's behalf—the details of Dracula's purchase of a house in Piccadilly to the locksmith's willingness to let them into the house in broad daylight, in full sight of a policeman. Students explore how the ability to track down and defeat Dracula depends in large part on the position of social privilege that Arthur gains upon his accession to the peerage. Our discussions of wealth and class are also informed by Franco Moretti's analysis of capitalism in *Dracula* ("Capital *Dracula*"). Moretti's reading fascinates students in its focus on all the ways in which Count Dracula does not conform to the expectations of his class position: he appears to employ no domestic servants, seemingly doing all the cooking and cleaning himself as well as driving his own carriage. This detail becomes particularly striking once I point out that even Jonathan and Mina, perhaps the least economically privileged of the novel's main characters, employ a servant. Moretti's analysis of capitalism in *Dracula* draws attention to textual elements to which my students, who until this point have been largely focused on issues of gender and sexuality, have not paid as much attention. The idea that Dracula can function at once as the threat *of* capitalism and a threat *to* capitalism is one that many students become keen to explore further in their papers.

As we move on to new historicism and cultural studies, students are eager to analyze *Dracula* within its wider historical context. Discussions on this topic are varied, from the role of religion in the story to the role of science and technology. We discuss the significance of *Dracula*'s date of publication—1897—and analyze how the narrative at once looks forward to the dawning new century and backward to a medieval past. We consider the tensions in the novel not simply against the backdrop of history but in relation to history, a battle over past and future simultaneously. Having considered Dracula's threat in terms of narrative time earlier in the semester, now we examine his threat to historical time. Raymond Williams's concepts of the dominant, residual, and emergent as counterpoints to an epochal analysis of history provide a helpful framework for analyzing Dracula's position in relation to history and time, revealing how Dracula's existence challenges the very notion of history as a progression of stages. As Jonathan notes when Dracula regales him with stories of the family's history and the many battles fought against invaders, "[H]e spoke as if he had been present at them all" (Stoker, *Dracula* 37). Students are apt at first to see Dracula as the threat of the past and the novel's heroes as the promise of the future, but their knowledge of deconstruction enables them to look beyond this binary and to consider Dracula's ability to collapse time. Dracula may live in a crumbling medieval castle, but he also easily blends in with London's bustling modernity.

Even in our first discussion of *Dracula*, students frequently note the stark contrast the novel draws between Transylvania and England, particularly in the opening chapters, so learning about postcolonialism and critical race theory provides them with the means to analyze these details more thoroughly. Assigning excerpts from Edward Said's *Orientalism* enables students to see how Dracula's apparent racial and cultural threat is discursively constructed by the narrative through distinctions made between East and West, and a close reading of the opening pages of *Dracula* provides abundant examples, including the way Jonathan exoticizes the food he eats and describes the region surrounding the Carpathians as an "imaginative whirlpool" of "every known superstition in the world." Students are quick to draw connections between Said's argument and Jonathan's comments, including the assertion that "there are no maps of this country . . . to compare with our own Ordnance Survey maps" and the expression of frustration "It seems to me that the further East you go the more unpunctual are the trains. What ought they to be in China?" (Stoker, *Dracula* 13). They are, however, initially less attuned to the way the scenes that take place in England are equally examples of a discursive construction of the West, so as they learn more about postcolonial theory, they become increasingly skeptical of the way location appears to become naturalized once the narrative returns to England. Students recognize how Dracula is cast as an invasive threat because he is foreign, but critical race theory also provides them with the means to interrogate how Dracula, who is white and European, is presented more specifically as a racial threat. Students find illuminating essays by Bram Dijkstra and Stephen D. Arata excerpted in the Norton Critical Editions, particularly Dijkstra's analysis of Dracula's Semitic appearance (Stoker, *Dracula* [Auerbach and Skal] 460–62) and Arata's arguments about vampirism and reverse colonization (*Dracula* [Browning and Skal] 499–507). While my students may have initially worried about having to write a second paper on Dracula's threat, by the end of this unit they eagerly seek to combine multiple methodologies in their analysis of how Dracula's threat operates at the intersection of gender, class, and race.

The third unit encourages students to draw connections between *Dracula* and more recent scholarly developments. As much as I find both Norton Critical Editions of the novel useful tools for teaching theory, the critical excerpts they include represent foundational texts in the study of the novel rather than the most current scholarship. The final chapter in Parker's book focuses on ecocriticism and disability studies as examples of emerging fields in literary analysis (379–410); even though it is abbreviated in comparison to the other chapters, my students are particularly intrigued by the interpretive possibilities this opens for them. Once again, these are issues to which they feel a personal connection, and the idea that a study of the environment or of disability can form the basis of substantive literary analysis is eye-opening for most of them. This chapter

32   CRITICAL THEORY

leads to a lively discussion as my students, who in many cases were certain that they had exhausted all the different ways that *Dracula* could be interpreted, suddenly realize that there is still more that can be explored. Our discussions of East and West from our lesson on postcolonialism start to extend to a discussion of the environment and the way Transylvania is presented as a wild and untamed space in contrast to the largely urban and interior spaces that become the backdrop for the novel in England. Earlier discussions about the binary opposition between sanity and insanity lead us to a discussion of disease and disability, and we explore not only the debilitating effects of vampirism in the novel but also the new powers of mobility and ability it seems to grant women. Although I do not assign any readings that analyze *Dracula* through the lens of ecocriticism or disability studies, I encourage students to pursue these possibilities in their final research paper. Students who were especially excited by new historicism and cultural studies have the opportunity in this assignment to conduct further research on the social, cultural, and historical contexts that most interest them. Topics have included how the Oxford movement and Tractarianism in the late nineteenth century relate to the novel's depiction of Catholic symbols and rituals, how the Me Too movement can inform an analysis of the physical assaults Lucy and Mina experience, and how Francis Ford Coppola's film adaptation (*Bram Stoker's* Dracula) inserts a heterosexual origin story for Dracula's character that serves to efface the queer dynamics of the novel.

As a culminating assignment, I ask students to reread what they first wrote about *Dracula* at the start of the semester and to write a brief reflection on what larger insights they have gained since then. Many students marvel at their initial doubts about having enough to say in response to the question, What is Dracula's threat? Given that what undergraduates usually read in literature classes is within the framework of some specific topic, such as the Victorian novel or gothic literature, my students eventually come to find it a great luxury to have spent the entire semester focusing so intently on one book and using it as the means to explore a variety of topics. The benefit of teaching critical theory with *Dracula* is that students not only gain an appreciation for how theory helps them analyze literature but also gain a richer appreciation for the novel itself.

Navigating *Dracula* Criticism in the Classroom

Agnes Andeweg

For many years I have taught *Dracula* as part of an advanced undergraduate course in gothic fiction to students in a liberal arts and sciences program in the Netherlands. This institutional context implies that my diverse, international students are never solely students in literature. Rather, they come with a variety of disciplinary backgrounds and interests. Often, our discussions are enriched by comparisons the students bring in from their other courses in politics, history, or philosophy. All will have had some previous training in the study of literature by the time they arrive in my course, but hardly more than two or three courses. So this course in gothic fiction functions as a prism to address key debates they may not yet have encountered in much depth: about Romanticism and realism, high and low culture, and literature in relation to other media and technology, from phantasmagoria to film. Because students' familiarity with the gothic as a cultural mode widely varies, I make sure to build ample room for student questions and discussion into the course.

One of the objectives of the course is to guide students to reflect on literature's potential to function as a form of cultural critique and to help them develop their critical capacities, specifically in the context of doing research. More often than not, my students will be writing their undergraduate thesis, be it in literature or in another discipline, the semester after they take my course. My experience as a thesis supervisor is that many students find it difficult to write a good literature review; their efforts often read as a rambling list of summaries (in Dutch proverbially called "the toppled bookcase") rather than a discussion of secondary sources, guided by a research question, in which the student's authorial voice is clearly audible. Therefore, I aim to prepare my students in the gothic fiction course for assessing secondary literature on their own and to let them find their academic voice. For this, *Dracula* is an ideal case study.

The vast body of academic literature on classics like *Dracula* can be daunting to undergraduate students, but I consider this a great pedagogical opportunity. My main goal in teaching *Dracula* and its criticism is exposing students to the wide variety of interpretations that they can consider as a starting point for developing their own analytical skills and their ability to speak with some authority about the material they have studied closely.

Because I strongly believe that students' judgments can be well informed only if they know the novel firsthand, I directly address the reading experience in class. Especially in the context of gothic fiction, the affective dimension is important, and discussing students' responses to *Dracula* also offers many pedagogical opportunities. The question of whether students enjoyed the novel

34 *DRACULA* CRITICISM

can easily be turned into a discussion of the historically changing techniques that affect or disturb readers: To what extent are style and composition still effective? Therefore, I spend two sessions on *Dracula*, in the first of which we discuss reading experiences with the whole group. Students generally report that they enjoy reading the action-packed novel (whereas they tend to find *Frankenstein*, which we also study, tedious or too abstract). We reconstruct the plot and discuss the way our textbook, Andrew Smith's *Gothic Literature*, presents *Dracula*. Smith observes that the novel can be read in conflicting ways, a few of which (by Franco Moretti, Robert Mighall, William Hughes, and Stephen D. Arata) he examines in more detail, pointing out, among other things, the fundamental ambivalence surrounding masculinity in *Dracula*. Smith is critical of Moretti's Marxist reading and of all-too-symbolic psychoanalytic readings; he clearly favors a more contextualized, historical approach to the novel (109–21). At this point in the course, these critical disagreements do not really seem to resonate with students, who seem either to take them for granted, not engaging critically with different viewpoints, or to take on an "anything goes" attitude. Usually I end this first session by asking students to nominate themes or perspectives they would find interesting to explore further or, alternatively, to come up with at least ten different themes or perspectives to use for reading *Dracula*.

Then we spend a second session on four widely different interpretations of *Dracula*, by Anne Williams ("Dracula"), Barry McCrea, Robert A. Smart, and William Hughes ("Singular Invasion"). The secondary texts help me make students aware of changing critical perspectives in the discipline of literature in general and gothic criticism in particular and discuss what (textual or other, internal or external) "evidence" various authors use to make their arguments. Together, the articles show a plurality of critical perspectives and demonstrate that there is not one "correct," or final, interpretation. Because students often take the authority of the texts in the syllabus for granted, this exercise is valuable in training them to become critical readers. Without being dismissive about gothic or literary criticism in general (as some academics are or have been), it is possible to venture criticism of specific interpretive moves as long as this is well-motivated, and I deem it important to teach this to liberal arts students who in their major often have to negotiate the expectations of a "hard," evidence-based science perspective with a humanities approach that inevitably involves judgments. I hope this exercise teaches them to navigate ambiguity without falling into relativism.

I chose these four articles not necessarily because I agree with the arguments they make—in some cases, to the contrary—but because they offer clear approaches and positions, which I discuss in more detail below. Because of time constraints, it is hardly feasible to ask students to prepare four articles in depth for one class. Therefore, I assign one article to each student, to be read and prepared individually using the following questions: What is the argument your author makes about *Dracula*? How does the author support this argument? Does the author leave out relevant parts or contexts? In class, students first briefly discuss their answers with others who read the same article. This helps them attune their answers and identify their author's main points. Next, each group presents their findings to the other three groups. This always produces great surprise about the highly different readings of *Dracula* the four authors offer and the great variety in textual and external evidence they use for support. It results in a lively discussion about textual evidence and interpretive license.

This setup is to some extent comparable to the "jigsaw method," as it is called in didactics. The idea behind this teaching approach is to let students engage with material in small groups. By giving each member a specific task with specific information, the individual student becomes an "expert" on their part of the puzzle. Ideally, students gain in confidence when they realize others rely on knowledge only they possess. The difference with my setup is that I let groups, rather than individual group members, work on different tasks. The reason is that I think my advanced bachelor students, in order to process complex arguments, first need practice in paraphrasing these arguments, which happens when they first discuss their article with peers who read the same text. The stage of bringing the different groups together, however, does have the jigsaw effect: each group has become an expert on their article, and only by comparing the argumentation of "their" author to the others' can they arrive at a higher-level analysis. It is certainly possible to do the second stage of this exercise according to the jigsaw method and then reshuffle the groups with one student representing one article. I was fortunate enough to be able to teach this class in person, despite COVID-19, to a small group of twelve students, so we could easily have a plenary discussion in class. With a larger group, the setup with a reshuffle of the groups instead of a plenary discussion may be preferable. Of course, this could also be done in an online rendition of the course: in *Microsoft Teams* or *Zoom* this would entail preparing breakout rooms in advance and letting students enter these of their own accord rather than allowing *Teams* to assign students to a room randomly.

The four articles by Williams, McCrea, Smart, and Hughes present students with widely different interpretations of *Dracula*—informed by psychoanalysis, queer theory, and postcolonialism. Williams reads the novel psychoanalytically yet contra previous psychoanalytic interpretations of Dracula as a primal father figure. Reading *Dracula* as a "public nightmare" (446), she interprets the Count as an embodiment of the repressed feminine principle, referring to the novel as dream at various moments in her article. She explicitly refrains from biographical criticism: "we need not search for personal neuroses, for this conquest of the disguised mother is one of patriarchy's favorite stories" (455). Williams compares *Dracula* to myths like the *Odyssey* and the legend of Saint George—after all, Harker arrives at Dracula's castle on Saint George's day, a detail easily missed by students (and, strangely enough, not referred to explicitly by Williams). Williams reads symbolically with a keen eye for textual details like the feminine names of Dracula's ships—*Demeter* and *Czarina Catherine*—or the scene where Mina is "soiled" by acting motherly when she rescues Lucy. When

36   *DRACULA* CRITICISM

Mina lends Lucy her own shoes and gets her feet dirty, Williams interprets this as the "proximity of the human mother and Mother Earth" (451). The students and I discuss whether they would attribute as much analytical weight to these details as Williams does and what the advantages and disadvantages of using such a grand analytical scheme are. We note, for example, that in Williams's analysis historically specific elements such as modern technologies, like trains and typewriters, or geographical distinctions between Western and Eastern Europe receive no attention.

When we turn to McCrea's article, we find he takes a very different approach. Much more than Williams, McCrea analyzes the plot structure of the novel, which leads him to see parallels between Jonathan's journey to the Count and the developing romantic engagements of Mina and Lucy at home. Instead of searching for latent meanings like Williams, he stresses "the more obvious and overt ways in which the text is centered on courtship and matrimony" (254). And rather than myths and legends, the domestic comedy of manners serves as McCrea's genre of comparison. Taking a stance against "oppositional" readings of Dracula as the ultimate other, McCrea discerns an "uncanny continuity between Castle Dracula and the happy English home" (253), in which Jonathan comes to experience the horrors and exotic foreignness of heterosexual marriage from the vantage point of the closeted gay man. McCrea's rather complicated argument raises a number of questions: Is Jonathan's relation to Dracula a "terrified fantasy of heterosexuality as imagined from the closet" (266)? How is one to read the scene where Jonathan is seduced by the vampiric women? And what are we to make of Jonathan's loving remarks about Mina in his diary and the letters he writes home? Students tend to observe that McCrea bases his argument mostly on the first part of the novel, when Jonathan is trapped in Dracula's castle, and pays little attention to the events related to Van Helsing and his band of men chasing the vampire.

The articles by Smart and Hughes take a postcolonial perspective. Both are in conversation with the influential essay by Arata—also a point of contrast for McCrea, by the way—that reads Dracula as reversing the horror of colonialism and bringing gothic terror home, but they do so in very different ways: whereas Hughes focuses on the difference between one and many invaders and refutes Arata's argument, Smart shifts the geographical focus to English-Irish colonial relations. Students are often surprised to read a postcolonial analysis that does not involve race; their relative unfamiliarity with Irish history leads to questions about Catholicism and Protestantism, British-Irish relations, and Stoker's Protestant Irish descent. In his analysis, Smart makes much of the fact that Mina, Jonathan, and even Lucy—after her mother's death—are orphans. He reads their orphaned status as a symbolic rendering of their Anglo-Irish position. When I ask whether students have noticed that Jonathan and Mina are orphans, no one has ever answered in the affirmative. So we talk about textual evidence: How much support do we need for our interpretive claims? What does Smart base his statement on? A quick search of the digital text on *Project*

Gutenberg (www.gutenberg.org/cache/epub/345/pg345-images.html) does not produce the word *orphan*, and this allows me to talk about search strategies: If the word *orphan* is not there, what else can we search for? Using *parents* (one result) or *father* (twenty-eight results) and *mother* (fifty-three results), we find that Mina's status as orphan is mentioned once, when she writes to Lucy about the death of Mr. Hawkins, Jonathan's employer:

> Such a sad blow has befallen us. Mr. Hawkins has died very suddenly. Some may not think it so sad for us, but we had both come to so love him that it really seems as though we had lost a father. *I never knew either father or mother*, so that the dear old man's death is a real blow to me. Jonathan is greatly distressed. It is not only that he feels sorrow, deep sorrow, for the dear, good man who has befriended him all his life, and now at the end has treated him like his own son and left him a fortune . . .
> (153; emphasis added)

Jonathan calls Mr. Hawkins his "'second father,'" but one might wonder whether that implies his first has died.

Smart also states without further support that Mina Murray is "an Irishwoman" (28), like Lucy Westenra, who is "also Irish, by the way, from County Roscommon" (28). To be sure, the name Roscommon is never mentioned in *Dracula*—nor is Mina's youth or background, or Ireland, for that matter—so we delve into the provenance of surnames to see if we can accept Smart's bold claim (and note in passing that McCrea reads the name Westenra in a symbolic way, as representing "western," and calls it "especially striking" (267)). Referring to Stoker's "clearly mixed'" feelings about the Irish appeal for home rule, Smart reads Mina, Jonathan, and Lucy as Anglo-Irish orphans and Dracula as a manifestation of Anglo-Irish fears, a Catholic who seeks out these "orphaned" children, in a symbolic reversal, on English soil (32). Both McCrea's and Smart's readings engage with an aspect of Stoker's biography—Stoker's presumed homosexuality and his Irish background, respectively—and both take that as their main cue into the novel. This allows us to discuss how biographical information can or cannot serve as a valuable source of information.

Like Smart, Hughes reads *Dracula* in a postcolonial vein, but he takes a very different direction. Questioning earlier readings of the Count's Transylvania as a stand-in for a British imperial sphere of interest like India, China, or Africa, Hughes states, "Harker is no colonist, Count Dracula no subaltern subject ready for exploitation" (W. Hughes, "Singular Invasion" 92). Likewise, he refutes the interpretation of Dracula as a synecdoche for a colonizing army of invaders, returning to the metropole, the heart of empire. While the invasion script is explicitly there, Hughes stresses Dracula's position as a loner—as operating very much on his own—which sits uncomfortably with the idea of an inverse colonial invasion. Hughes highlights the various comparisons, made by Van Helsing and Mina, between the Count and solitary animals: the fox and the tiger. Instead,

38   *DRACULA* CRITICISM

Hughes interprets Dracula as an "Imperial Hero," embodying the "myth of individual achievement" (96). Dracula's "singular invasion" (99) pushes connotations to a racial invasion to the background, argues Hughes.

This leaves us with four highly different interpretations of the vampire. If we have to choose between Dracula as the embodiment of maternal repression (Williams), the gay seducer (McCrea), the bloodsucking Catholic (Smart), or the colonial entrepreneur à la Cecil Rhodes (Hughes), whom do we choose?

After this second class I let students reflect once more on the article they prepared and discussed in a reading report that compares it to one of the other articles they were presented with in class. They have to discuss to what extent they were convinced by "their" author and what this implies for the other article. I also ask them to build on the work of the author they want to support, or develop their own argument, by close-reading a scene from *Dracula* not discussed by the author they read. Generally speaking, I find students are much more capable of assessing the different ways of argumentation in this reading report than they would have been in a regular plenary class discussion of the articles or after a lecture by me. The contrast with the first session—where we did touch upon different interpretations of *Dracula* by way of discussing Smith—is striking. As always, comparison brings out difference, and thus this comparative exercise raises awareness—awareness of textual details, of different critical perspectives, and of styles of argumentation. While this may be confusing—as some students reported—it is definitely a learning experience. So even the student who sighed after the first session that he would like to get a clear answer on the question "What is *Dracula* really about?" was reconciled to the inevitable plurality of perspectives without necessarily accepting all.

Teaching *Dracula* and the Professions:
Work, Money, and Desire

Joshua Gooch

Dracula is a text crisscrossed by temporalities. The novel's characters themselves sense it. Harker describes his experience early in the novel as "nineteenth century up-to-date with a vengeance" (Stoker, *Dracula* 45); later, Van Helsing saves his companions with his knowledge of "the lore and experience of the ancients" (203). Much of the scholarship on the novel's relation to its economic moment focuses on its embeddedness in the late-nineteenth-century global economy. Yet, as Achille Mbembe suggests, history is perhaps better understood as a set of overlapping and disparate temporalities—much like the novel itself. For this reason, *Dracula's* representation of work and its use of the nineteenth-century professions can offer students ready historical-economic connections to the present and help them recognize how the novel's characters enact ideas about professional white-collar work that resonate with ideas about professional work today.

To ground discussions of work in the literature classroom, I introduce students to scholarship about work in the contemporary world and in the literary text's conjuncture. One of the most striking aspects of work in twenty-first-century postindustrial economies is the ways in which employers have reshaped work into something creative, caring, and fundamentally improvisational. Whether we choose to call the economic system organizing our world late capitalism, neoliberalism, neofeudalism, or, as Mackenzie Wark suggests, something worse than capitalism, the ideology of work that it offers us means to counter critiques of labor as intellectually stultifying (e.g., factory labor) and soul-crushing (e.g., work in bureaucracy's iron cage). This shift in how people understand work may be due to international changes in production and distribution—for example, the movement of industrial production from the Global North to the Global South, the rise of just-in-time production, and the construction of financialized service economies across the Global North—yet it has had real subjective effects on workers. For employers, flexibility and innovation are as important to their conception of a good worker as their understanding of modernized production processes. In their analysis of 1980s management literature, Luc Boltanski and Eve Chiapello show how work became viewed as a space of creative networked projects in which workers must rely on "what are increasingly called 'life skills,' as opposed to knowledge and *savoir faire*" (98). These life skills are as much affective as cognitive. The sociologist Arlie Russell Hochschild terms the exploitation of these affective life skills "emotional labor" (147). Emotional laborers are trained and supervised to evoke specific emotional states in customers and

40   DRACULA AND THE PROFESSIONS

to control their own emotions while they work, what Hochschild calls "emotion work" (253). In 1983, Hochschild speculated that demand for emotional labor would "grow and expand with the spread of automation and the decline of unskilled labor" (160). This expansion, she suggested, would also expand the idea of professionalism beyond the scope of the original professions. *Professionalism* would become what it is today, a byword for a particular kind of emotional management. Paolo Virno describes this focus on life skills as part of capitalism's turn to the general intellect—that is, its move to exploit people's cognitive, linguistic, and affective capacities. Workers who depend upon their life skills are "virtuosos" to Virno: they improvise ceaselessly in their work, drawing on their skills as much as on technical knowledge or expertise (52).

The new prominence given to life skills in contemporary work has important implications for understanding exploitation in capitalism, including Marx's oft-repeated homology of capitalism and vampirism sometimes deployed in analyses of Stoker's novel. Marx focuses on the extraction of labor from workers and the conversion of their lives into value, a process achieved through the dual mechanisms of lived time and socially necessary labor time. His vampiric metaphor represents exploitation as an extractive process that relies on physical discipline, coercion, and the machinic organization of the production process. When applied to twentieth-century white-collar work, as in Harry Braverman's study *Labor and Monopoly Capital*, worker exploitation relies on Taylorist refinements of bureaucratic discipline. By contrast, professional work in the twenty-first century looks different. The exploitation of improvisatory life skills, while certainly affected by layers of bureaucratic discipline, has been reorganized and reimagined by employers as a series of creative interactions across horizontal networks. Exploitation has become less the continual revolutionizing of production for efficiency than a continual stream of projects crisscrossing a firm's organizational chart under the guise of innovation. This shift reveals that exploitation is no longer (or perhaps never was solely) achieved through discipline or control over the organization of production. For Italian Marxists like Mario Tronti, this shift reveals that society itself has become the factory floor. However one interprets this situation, one can recognize that work is a process of exploitation and of subjection. As Boltanski and Chiapello explain, contemporary forms of work "penetrate more deeply into people's inner selves—people are expected to 'give' themselves to their work—and [thus] facilitate an instrumentalization of human beings in the most specifically human dimensions" (98). In place of vampiric exploitation, contemporary capitalism encourages the idea that this work-based humanism is an end to alienation. *Do what you love and you will never work a day in your life*, as American culture encourages itself to believe. One can find in this ideology of a happy unity between work and worker what Frédéric Lordon describes as a demand to become the willing slaves of capital. Or, as Renfield says, "I am here to do Your bidding, Master. I am Your slave, and You will reward me, for I shall be faithful" (Stoker, *Dracula* 105).

The Professions as a Model of the Happy Worker

Although vampiric mind control most directly figures this convergence of work and worker in the novel, the simultaneous desire for and revulsion at one's own subordination appears first in the novel as a problem for Jonathan Harker. In a letter of reference, Peter Hawkins describes his employee to the Count as "a young man, full of energy and talent in his own way, and of a very faithful disposition. He is discreet and silent, and has grown into manhood in my service" (23). Here the novel helps uncover a genealogy of the happy worker that runs through the professions. For Hawkins, Harker's knowledge as a solicitor is of less importance than what Boltanski and Chiapello call life skills—namely, his youth, energy, and talent—as well as the assurance that these skills will be properly inscribed in the paternalist work relations typical of nineteenth-century gentlemanly services. Harker's "faithful disposition"—which Renfield's vow of fealty to the Count echoes—suggests this faith is a kind of filial duty to his employer, a reading underscored by Hawkins's attestation that he has watched over Harker's development as a man.

No wonder, then, that Harker is caught in a prolonged period of adolescence as the novel begins. The history of service work in Britain includes the feudal custom of sending young people to work as servants in other households, a situation that allowed them to gain knowledge, experience, and, through the wage, the means to establish their own households. Wage labor, as David Graeber explains, was understood as part of adolescence. Under capitalism, employers retained this infantilizing of working for money rather than for one's own business in order to make the poor seem "frustrated adolescents" (228). This framing of working for money as adolescence occurs alongside the history of apprenticeship. White-collar work during the nineteenth century operated under conditions akin to guild apprenticeships even though the benefits of formal guild apprenticeships had all but disappeared by the beginning of the eighteenth century (Linebaugh 62–63). While apprenticeship in manual work was no longer a guarantor of economic mobility in the nineteenth century, apprenticeships in white-collar work retained the pretense of mobility through the middle of the century. In the 1850s, it was possible, if unlikely, to begin life as a clerk and work one's way into a partnership; by the 1890s, the possibility of upward mobility had all but disappeared, the result of an expanding workforce, the introduction of new technologies, and the hiring of female clerks. Male clerks blamed women and German immigrant clerks for their loss of status and formed self-help societies in the hope that improved education and social networks would aid them (Anderson 60–62, 89–96).

Dracula appears in the midst of this shift. It is this desire to rise and the certainty that rising isn't possible that Harker's experience suggests in his apparent emasculation as a clerk, a result first of his employment and then of his trauma at the hands of the Count. Although Harker has passed his solicitor's examination before traveling to Transylvania, he continues to think of himself as Hawkins's

42   *DRACULA* AND THE PROFESSIONS

clerk and subordinates his desires to those of his boss to such a degree that he defers his marriage to Mina to do Hawkins's bidding in Transylvania. Like many aspiring workers of the period, Harker makes economic success and sexual activity coeval, an echo not only of Thomas Malthus but also of the exploitation of adolescent sexuality in Mediterranean apprenticeship that Christopher Chitty locates as crucial to the construction of middle-class sexual hegemony (45–48). The Count's sapping of Harker's masculinity after his escape from the Count's home draws a parallel between the Count and Hawkins. To exit from abstinence, adolescence, and domination, Harker must draw on his energy, talent, and faith, the last a recurrent and important word for the narrative. Harker's position at the beginning of the novel models the vampiric relation of master and servant, his life skills supporting his employer. His position at the conclusion, however, shows that he has taken on the position of the master, a shift he achieves only by displacing his economic master with a religious one: God. In this way, Harker's professional calling becomes a religious one, a vocation the novel conjures in its recurrent calls to faith and duty. The "wild work" of vampire killing thus becomes part of Harker's professional calling (232).

Work and Transhistorical Pedagogy

One of the benefits of this cultural studies approach to the novel is its flexibility. I have used it in special topics courses on the gothic, serial killers, and the emergence of the service sector in literature. In part, this flexibility is a result of the novel itself. Reading gothic texts as sociopolitical allegories is one of the few shared aspects of the otherwise highly variable English curriculum offered in the United States. It is also due to the kinds of students I most often meet in the classroom: first-generation students, largely in professional majors. As the majority of my students take my courses to meet general education requirements, I cannot and do not expect that they will have a strong grasp of close reading. Foregrounding our shared experiences of work can help students learn to focus their close reading skills by reflecting on ideas about work that remain recognizable over one hundred years later. One can scaffold writing activities to build close reading skills with a mix of connections journals (that is, short, informal writing exercises in which students make personal connections with course contents), quotation commentary activities (in which students paraphrase and interpret brief passages from scholarly material), and formal research essays. I have found that personal connections tend to make students' use of historical and theoretical material more meaningful while practice working with concepts and passages in short form helps them identify crucial pieces of text that enable them to build stronger arguments.

It also helps that the question of work and our experience of domination is not particularly abstract, especially for students who may be working their way through college while grappling with amorphous cultural ideas about what it means to become a "professional." What is the drive for a professional degree if not one for upward mobility, a desire whose fulfillment one can purchase by deferring other desires according to the demands of superiors—of professors, programs, and employers? When I first began teaching *Dracula* in this way, students resisted examining their implication in these ideas about professionalism. More recently, however, students seem less ideologically captured by the idea of professionalization. Much as one might decry the fact that many students understand their education to be a form of job training, this view has led more students to resent that they must bear the cost of job training in return for vague assurances of future employment. The pandemic and its economic effects are likely to increase these feelings. Students preparing for careers in the health professions now find themselves in a more fraught position. Demands to become or act professional are being redefined by the vulnerability of healthcare workers to infection and death. Much as professionalization relies upon a sense of becoming a happy subject—*Do what you love! Make your care for others pay!*—its costs are now writ large. Fictional anxieties about professionalization, such as those experienced by Jonathan Harker, offer students studying *Dracula* a way to grapple with real and timely fears about professional work, especially professional care work.

To teach *Dracula* through professional work is to try to bind scholarship about the novel to students' concrete experiences of the world. My aim is to help students explore the resonances a text can generate with the present while remaining attentive to the material, historical, and social differences between our moment and the past. To that end, I have found the following material helpful in upper-division courses: Friedrich Kittler's account of the typewriter and secretarial labor in the novel (*Discourse Networks*), Mark Selzer's revision of this account to analyze the role of the serial killer in culture, Stephen Arata's treatment of the text's racism, and Franco Moretti's allegorical reading of the novel in the light of finance capital (*Signs*). The last, I admit, is sometimes more useful as a counterexample, but it is one students enjoy. In addition, other useful sources include Charles E. Prescott and Grace A. Giorgio's examination of the New Woman and secretarial labor in the novel, Nicholas Daly's account of the vampire hunters as a sort of professional consortium ("Incorporated Bodies"), Dejan Kuzmanovic's work on masculinity and professional labor in the novel, and perhaps my account of the novel's account of work as a nineteenth-century vision of cruel optimism in *The Victorian Novel, Service Work, and the Nineteenth-Century Economy*. Learning the history of professional labor through *Dracula* can help students reflect on the work they are called to do and what it means that they feel called to do it.

THE GOTHIC

Gothic Abjection in the Original *Dracula*

Jerrold E. Hogle

Extensive scholarship, in this volume and elsewhere, has shown us how much the title figure in Bram Stoker's *Dracula* becomes, as the novel progresses, a multilayered symbol of numerous social and psychological otherings—and fears connected to them—seething in the cultural subconscious of the West, as well as the personal unconscious as Sigmund Freud was starting to define it. It is therefore vital that we help our students see, analyze, and understand how wide and deep these symbolic suggestions go in the text of Stoker's book. After first showing students how much Count Dracula combines features of the aristocratic vampire as they had multiplied over the nineteenth century on the page and stage (see R. Stuart 41–117 and Hogle, "Mutations"), we should help them grasp for themselves how this multiplicity reveals, when closely examined, what Jack Halberstam has articulated especially well: an "aggregation" of figures for men and women, races, class types, old-time beliefs, and social or sexual behaviors that were regarded as most "foreign and perverse" by the rising Anglo-European middle class that was Stoker's milieu and audience. Dracula is a conflation of these othered beings into one figure set against a "hegemonic ideal" of human identity, all to reinforce that ideological construct by being its frightening antithesis and dark subconscious (Halberstam, *Skin Shows* 88–105). A major challenge in teaching Stoker's *Dracula*, then, is to get students to fully grasp how its vampire is able to harbor and suggest so much at once and to locate evidence of these layered otherings in the text of Stoker's novel, especially in its use of gothic modes of monster-making that hark back not just to John Polidori in the early nineteenth century but also to Horace Walpole's *The Castle of Otranto*, which in its second edition in 1765 was the first romance to be labeled "a gothic story." Here I argue for an approach that I think accomplishes these learning objectives, one that I have found effective with upper-division undergraduates and first-year honors students either in a class on the gothic tradition that includes Bram Stoker or in a course about *Dracula* and what its otherings say about our culture in both the novel and adaptations of it.

This approach should start, not just with a mini-lecture and reading assignment (such as Hogle, "Mutations") on past vampire fictions that feed into Stoker's *Dracula*, but also with an initial orientation by the instructor on what it meant symbolically when the vampire was turned into a Walpolean "gothic" symbol in the early nineteenth century. By the time of Mary Shelley's *Frankenstein* and Polidori's novella *The Vampyre*, both begun at the Villa Diodati near Geneva in June 1816, when Lord Byron challenged his guests to write their own "ghost stories" after they had read multiple texts indebted to Walpole's gothic (see Hogle, "Gothic Image"), the vampire figure, hitherto rarely connected to gothic fictions, was pulled from scattered circulation throughout Europe and reincarnated in wildly contradictory monsters. In each case, Shelley's as well as Polidori's, one or more dead bodies are brought to life to threaten the living while still being at least partly dead; indeed, Shelley's Victor Frankenstein comes to see his living being made from cadavers as his doppelgänger, "my own vampire, my own spirit let loose from the grave," setting out to "destroy all that was dear to me" (Shelley 51). Such living-dead, enlarged, unusually powerful, at least somewhat supernatural, and life-draining figures look directly back, as Shelley admits in her preface to the 1831 reissue of *Frankenstein*, to ghost figures from Franco-German tales read out at Diodati that were pointedly imitative of the specters in *The Castle of Otranto*. The figure Shelley recalls as inspiring her creature the most, in fact, was a "gigantic, shadowy form" of a principality's murdered original ruler, walking forth like a moving statue "in complete armour . . . like the ghost in [Shakespeare's] Hamlet," as if he had stepped out of his portrait to invade his former castle and siphon off the lives of the usurper's descendants (Shelley 166–67). This specter combines two of the ghosts in Walpole's *Otranto*, one of them an armored statue on the tomb of the castle's founder that reappears as enlarged, wandering, haunting fragments of itself, and the other a portrait of the current usurper's grandfather (the poisoner of the founder) that suddenly breathes and walks out of its background and frame (Walpole 21–26).

In being like those ghosts, I point out to my students, such a monstrous shade is actually two-faced, like the old Roman god Janus, by the very nature of the Walpolean gothic (see Hogle, "Abjection" 116–17). Walpole himself defines the "gothic story" in the preface to *Otranto*'s second edition as an "attempt to blend the two kinds of romance, the ancient and the modern" (Walpole 9). The former, "ancient" romance looks backward to medieval tales of chivalry and the supernatural—even as the first *Otranto* preface declares their Catholic foundations "exploded," leaving them uprooted from the belief systems that produced them (6)—and the latter, the "modern," looks forward to the Protestant, Enlightenment worldview of the later eighteenth century and the then-emerging realistic novel, in which "the mortal agents" act "according to the rules of probability" based on their perceptions of their family dynamics and historical circumstances empirically learned over time (9–10). As E. J. Clery has shown in a chapter I assign to my students (*Rise* 68–79), this peculiar combination in monstrous or

46   GOTHIC ABJECTION

ghostly Walpolean figures makes them hark retrogressively toward the allure of old, hollowed-out Catholic icons no longer grounded in solid belief even as, with their past meanings having receded to the point where they are signs mostly of signs (ghosts of a statue or a portrait), they look ahead to newer meanings and conditions, such as their possibly being psychological projections caused by tensions arising from the characters' interpersonal relations (relations as they are rendered in middle-class novels of Walpole's own time by Samuel Richardson and Tobias Smollett). I particularly direct my students to Clery's observation that this symbolic combination allows *The Castle of Otranto* and its imitators to both suggest in their Janus-facedness and conceal in their antiquated features the "contradiction between the traditional [aristocratic] claims of landed property and the new [more bourgeois] claims of the private family," a "crisis in the experience of [*Otranto*'s] eighteenth-century audience" (77–79). Gothic monster-specters, developed from Walpole's "shadowy form" into Shelley's and Polidori's walking dead, now become defined for students as tugs-of-war in one image that can both intimate and hide in anachronistic figures both the underlying and unresolved conflicts of their times between regressive and progressive (and class-based) ideologies and contentions among beliefs about human identity and what must be "othered"—made "monstrosities over there," so to speak, in antiquated specters increasingly disengaged from their older meanings—to affirm the standard identity construction toward which the rising middle class aspired in the eighteenth and nineteenth centuries (and also does today). At this point, I also make sure that students have arrived at a clear definition of the gothic as it has developed out of Walpole. It is an aesthetic medium of terror, they should now realize, in which possibly supernatural, but also psychological, hauntings invade a hyperrealistic, though usually antiquated, setting to confront characters and audiences with manifestations of what they want to remove from themselves but cannot: unresolved contestations between fading, questionable older beliefs and icons that still seem attractive, on the one hand, and, on the other, rising, more modern ideologies and behaviors that strive, but are unable, to leave their predecessors entirely behind.

This basic symbolic process in the Walpolean gothic enacts what Julia Kristeva calls "abjection" in her book *Powers of Horror*, the opening sections of which (3–31) I assign in translation. There, the human subject (think Victor Frankenstein, Polidori's hero-worshipping Aubrey, all the pursuers of Dracula, and, of course, nearly every reader) seeks the illusion of a rising middle-class identity without the anomalies that can make it other-than-itself-within-itself—which, students readily agree, is really what it is at the foundations of itself, rooted as we all are in unconscious, conflicting memories and at least somewhat heterogenous ancestries. Such anomalies include for Kristeva visceral trace memories of the primal "archaism," where the subject being born was half inside and half outside the mother and thus half alive and half dead (Kristeva, *Powers* 10)—a state we always still long for yet must constantly cast away in order to be "ourselves"—as well as dim realizations that we are not automatically or purely one race or one class or even one gender type. All these we seek to expel from ourselves into what seems "foreign," as Kristeva goes on to argue in *Strangers to Ourselves*. The subject, then, in this scheme that accounts for gothic monsters so well, looks for a seemingly "alien" counterpart, an "abject," onto which to throw off (the literal meaning of *ab-ject*) the most inconsistent and nonstandard aspects of its existence, be they preconscious drives, the kinds of beings that it wants to be unlike, or the waning and waxing belief systems of its culture between which it is torn. Abjection means, the students now see, that what we come to fear most in any designated "other" is really what we uncannily harbor and are terrified to face at the most primordial and conflicted levels of our personal and social existence. The gothic, they now see too, is the conflicted symbolic scheme most suited to figuring forth such "abjects" (see Hogle, "Abjection" 113–23), because it confronts characters and readers in their present times with obscure yet suggestive visitations from their personal and cultural pasts that are simultaneously desirable and repellent, anomalies they want to throw off but must face in dark doubles in order to construct a coherent sense of themselves.

Students, I find, can grasp all this securely if it is exemplified first by the gothic monster-vampire with which they are most familiar already: Victor Frankenstein's creature as Shelley wrote him (read in full in a class on the gothic or in part in a course entirely on *Dracula*). Victor creates this being without the participation of a woman in order to avoid his deep unconscious longing for his maternal origins. We see that in the dream he falls into just after his cadaverous creature comes to life, where he embraces his fiancée only to behold her "features" turning into the "corpse" of his dead mother, all of which dissolves into the visage of his "monster" (Victor's first use of that word) looming over him, half dead and half alive (Shelley 36). Right away this gothic image, pulled Janus-like between outdated medieval alchemy and more modern Enlightenment science, can be seen by students as harboring not only a longing for and fear of reabsorption into the dead mother that shows both desire and dread toward the moment of his birth but also a vexed undercurrent of cultural debate over the status of women in the 1810s. This was, after all, a time at which rising industrialism and science, touted as promising an improved "new [human] race," Victor's stated aim (33), threatened to replace human with mechanical reproduction and deprive women of their most undeniable power, the ability to bear children. Once they understand this much, students can readily grasp that Frankenstein's creature as a doppelgänger embodies, first, his creator's unconscious drives, starting with his longing to both rejoin his deceased mother and cast her off, and, second, Victor's immersion in the most underlying and fraught quandaries of his time. Among the latter are the tug-of-war between older and newer scientific technologies, unresolved debates about the status of women, and, as students can sense in the creature's swarthy laborer's body and the several colors (yellow, black, white) in his monstrous face, the anxieties of the middle class over a complex of threats to it: its dependence on and fear of

48   GOTHIC ABJECTION

the rising working classes (see O'Flinn) and its desire for the perfect human race to be white, countered by the knowledge that humanity is made of many colors—the bases of both a classicism and a racism, two of many noxious reactions to the creature's anomalies, that Victor and much of his culture abject into his "monster" and "vampire." From here on, then, any figure that gothically assumes such a role can be seen by students as an "abject" in Kristeva's sense of that word (depending on how symbolic authors or filmmakers choose to make it), harboring multiple conflicts among beliefs and emotions cast off from the psychological and cultural unconscious, even as abjection now can be understood too as fundamental to gothic monster-making.

By this point, it is fairly easy to establish with students that the vampire is a near-perfect fit for such a scheme, even though out-and-out vampires first appeared in gothic fiction decades after Walpole's *Otranto*. Though the vampire is, in fact, a floating signifier that looks back as far as ancestor-ghosts in Chinese legend who drain the substance of their ungrateful descendants, it acquired, by the eighteenth century, the status in western Catholicism of a threatening dark opposite of Jesus Christ: the taker of blood out of its victims, as opposed to the giver of his blood to worshippers, who is resurrected by Satan as undead, cursed with a physical immortality sustained by endlessly chasing after blood, instead of by God as humanity's redeemer offering believers eternal life within the Holy Spirit (R. Stuart 13–20). This religious grounding, however, which Stoker's Dracula dimly retains (in being stymied by the cross of Christ and the wafer of the Eucharist), can be shown to students as waning by the middle of the eighteenth century, like the Catholic grounds of belief fading from Walpole's hollowed-out specters. By 1741, it turns out, *vampire* had become a traveling metaphor, as in an attack that year on government tax collectors as "vampires of the publick, and riflers of the kingdom" ("Vampire"). Consequently, again like Walpole's gothic ghosts, "vampire" for my students becomes a Janus-faced entity looking back to a Christian definition now receding from dominance while also looking forward toward a secular, mercantile, preindustrial context, in which the same figure is now free to be a metaphor for much more recent conflicts, such as the one between tax collection and free enterprise. In Polidori's *The Vampyre* of 1819, therefore, the cadaverous Lord Ruthven (pronounced *riven*), based partly by then on Polidori's anger at Byron, is implicitly linked to old traditions of undead bloodsuckers who have survived for centuries (Polidori xix–xxv, 41–43). But he is more explicitly connected with arousing unbridled sexual desire among women and young men and tempting the latter to gamble obsessively by investing in risky ventures and combining the ongoing luster of aristocrats with the "deadly hue" of their decaying social dominance (see Polidori 27–31 and Hogle, "Gothic Image" 17). Students thus see clearly that the first aristocratic vampire in fiction is a site for abjecting deep-seated quandaries of its time over constrained versus liberated sexuality (linking sex to vampirism long before *Dracula*), the expression versus the suppression of homosexuality, the possibilities versus the dangers of nascent

Jerrold E. Hogle   49

capitalism, and the celebration versus the denigration of the aristocracy itself. In addition, the Polidori *Vampyre* plainly shows students how all psychological and culturally based intimations visible in its title character are, like Aubrey's imagining him a "hero of romance" (Polidori 29–31), projections by his onlookers, including readers of *The Vampyre* and Byron, into his alluring "form and outline," which are actually (like Walpole's supernatural elements) becoming as barely connected to their inner meanings in old romance as the "dead grey eye" of Lord Ruthven's aristocratic face (27–28).

It is at this point that readings, class sessions, or both should address the similar and additional psychological and social factors that are abjected onto the aristocratic vampire in the many plays, operas, novels, penny dreadfuls, and even satires that adopt forms of Lord Ruthven, and by the 1870s include female vampire-aristocrats, across the nineteenth century (see Senf, *Vampire* 41–158; R. Stuart 41–178; Auerbach 21–60; Hogle, "Mutations" 75–81). This way Stoker's Count can be seen by students as what that character really is: partly derivative, thoroughly intertextual, and layered with many abjected contradictions just in what his precursors provide. These include the key augmentation in the penny-dreadful London serial *Varney the Vampire* that lets the aristocratic blood-sucker (attired here for the first time in a long, black cloak) sire new vampires of all classes, as some were said to do in very old folklore, by penetrating its living victims in a perversion of insemination (Rymer 76; see also Auerbach 29). As a result, these victims are killed and resurrected almost simultaneously—and so completely that no one can tell the difference between their living and vampiric forms—in a grotesque distortion of human childbirth (as in *Frankenstein*) and of Christ's self-sacrifice in giving up his blood to be the source of eternal life. From the late 1840s on, this addition calls up in readers their half-conscious fears of sexually transmitted diseases, of the inability to tell "normal" people from "queer" vampires by sight, and (again as in *Frankenstein*) of dehumanized, even mechanical reproduction without real sexual intercourse (see Sha). Additionally, students should be asked to recognize Stoker's extensions of the vampire tradition because of his own further reading, including his immersion in books on Transylvanian superstitions, particularly the writings of Emily Gerard, helpfully excerpted in the Norton Critical Edition of *Dracula* (347–54).

Even so, the teaching of this novel should ask students to keep linking Stoker with Polidori, since the class should start its close analysis of the former by tracking the abjected anomalies carried over from the latter before proceeding to the differences in *Dracula* itself. Once the foregoing steps have been completed, I therefore start my students' deep dive into Stoker's text by requesting that each of them, as members of the whole class group, articulate in their own words, first, the Janus-faced psychological and cultural quandaries that they see abjected in both Polidori's Ruthven and Stoker's vampire—pointing out exactly where they see each one in the text of *Dracula*—and, second, with just as much textual evidence, the further tugs-of-war between retrogressive and progressive beliefs or feelings that Dracula, his victims, or both abject because of monstrous

50   GOTHIC ABJECTION

figures since Polidori's that have added underlying features and meanings to the vampire tradition. I recommend asking students to submit their observations as chat-room messages that the class website then collates, with the instructor's help, so as to transmit a full composite list, with duplications eliminated, back to all the students. With all of them participating quite actively, the students thereby come to know a great deal about what the text of *Dracula* symbolizes, and they further understand the nature and process of abjection and how it has been enabled particularly well by specifically gothic symbol-making and the figure of the vampire.

From here, students can then be led to see that the text of the original *Dracula* both half suggests and half conceals, by gothically abjecting (see Hogle, "Stoker's Counterfeit" 206–07), further vexing psychological and cultural tugs-of-war, or complications of earlier ones, that existed as deep-seated undercurrents particularly in the 1890s with continuing implications today. To this end, I ask the students to divide into groups of four or five, each with a rotating spokesperson for conveying what each group has decided when they all come back together (as they do more than once). I then ask each group, over a week or so (both in class session breakouts and in online chats), to examine several portions of Stoker's text that emphasize a particular recurring image or theme and to consider those portions in the context of specified secondary readings. These images or themes, with their secondary contexts, include, for example:

> Dracula's visage, including its shifts and disguises, as Stoker (unlike any of his adapters) describes it, starting with the Count's "aquiline" face (Stoker, *Dracula* 27) and placing it in the context of Stephen D. Arata's essay excerpted in the Norton (499–507) and H. L. Malchow on "the vampire as racial other" (148–66);

> Dracula's vast range of shape-shifting in conjunction with the description of him as having a "child-brain" (Stoker, *Dracula* 294) and his symbiosis with the "zoophagous" asylum patient, Renfield (117–19), all in the light of Henrik Otterberg's article on "(d)evolutionary theory" in *Dracula*;

> Dracula's different effects on different women considering the novel's direct references to the conflicts of the 1890s over "the New Woman" (Stoker, *Dracula* 93–94), given what is argued by Phyllis A. Roth ("Suddenly Sexual Women") and Carol A. Senf ("*Dracula*") in their articles reprinted in the Norton; and

> The sexual ambiguity and amorphousness of Stoker's Dracula, beginning with his attraction to Jonathan Harker (47) and extending to his quasi-maternal "feeding" of Mina (261–62, a scene narrated twice) in connection with what Christopher Craft and Talia Schaffer reveal in the excerpts from them in the Norton.

If students already understand abjection as a gothic process and the unsettled conflicts between ideologies and feelings that abjection conceals—yet reveals by concealing—in vampire figures, such discussion groups can lead them to their own rich understanding of *Dracula*, the novel and the character, as metaphorizing and symbolizing-by-abjecting some of the most complex additional quandaries at the end of the nineteenth century: the tension between welcoming and demonizing the non-British races or populations (Jews, "Orientals," the Irish, Americans) pouring into England from the East and the West; the excitement and the horror aroused by Charles Darwin's theory of evolution, potentially a sign of civilization's progress yet just as much a threat to the stability of human identity, especially if evolution can be reversed into devolution; the striving of the fin de siècle toward greater women's rights and opportunities counteracted by inflammatory images of the widely feared threats that strong women were thought to pose to the norms of masculinity and family life; and the turn-of-the-century questioning, even blurring, of gender boundaries and sexual orientations that faced, and still face, strict containment by heterosexual, patriarchal, "respectable" family standards. Through this learning process that I have employed to considerable student enthusiasm, *Dracula*, the gothic, and history of the vampire can come to be illuminated together in all these powerful ways (and more). Those revelations can then be carried over into greater understandings of what is abjected in the later adaptations, variations, and haunting reappearances of Stoker's original novel.

Dracula and Irish Gothic Fiction

Richard Haslam

What is literary criticism? For the novelist Christine Smallwood, it constitutes "an ethical project to attempt the impossible task of allowing a text to speak on its own terms, from its own time, while never losing sight of the fact that whatever you find in it is colored by who you are and what you bring to it." Smallwood also maintains that comprehending literature "on a technical level" is indivisible "from reading for meaning" because "[l]iterary works signify through their style how they are put together, and so understanding how a given novel works is necessary to understanding what it means." Smallwood's definitions point to three important dimensions of literary criticism: rhetoric (the art of communication), wherein the author's work "speak[s] on its own terms"; hermeneutics (the art of interpretation), wherein readers' interpretations of the work are "colored by who you are and what you bring"; and poetics (the art of categorization), wherein readers seek to understand how the work *works*, through its style, structure, and shared characteristics.[1] In addition, Smallwood's observation that literary criticism comprises both an "impossible task" and an "ethical project" wryly acknowledges the abiding temptation to make texts say what we want them to say—to engage in eisegesis rather than exegesis.[2] Given this temptation, and our present situation on a globe aflame with hot takes, the need to cool our reading jets has never been more urgent.

That is why teaching *Dracula*—one of the world's most interpreted, even overinterpreted, novels—is so appropriate right now. This essay seeks to show how studying *Dracula* in an Irish gothic fiction course can encourage students to engage productively with crucial questions about rhetoric, hermeneutics, poetics, and ethics. Which themes, devices, tones, and rhetorical techniques prompt us to categorize fiction as gothic and Irish gothic? How might we validate ethically our interpretations and categorizations of Irish gothic fiction, especially with works like *Dracula*, which contain no explicit Irish references? Which rhetorical techniques do critics themselves employ to advance their arguments about Irish gothic poetics and hermeneutics? Chronicling how students grapple with these questions, the essay takes readers through the course, focusing on *Dracula* and on Neil Jordan's *Mistaken*, which is simultaneously an Irish gothic novel and an investigation of *Dracula* and the Irish gothic category.

Defining and Interpreting Gothic and Irish Gothic Fiction

We begin with an exercise in poetics. To identify which components prompt us to categorize fiction as gothic, I ask students to locate prominent devices, themes, and techniques in movie trailers for Guillermo del Toro's *Crimson Peak* and Jordan Peele's *Get Out*. After listing the students' observations on a whiteboard, I take a photograph so we can revisit and revise the suggested components across the semester. Even though *Crimson Peak* is set (mainly) in the English past and *Get Out* is set in the American present, students notice that in both trailers a vulnerable newcomer is welcomed into a large, strange house and subsequently threatened by its inhabitants and by supernatural (or preternatural) forces. Other shared components include thwarted romances, bizarre warnings, family secrets, a descent into subterranean regions, and an aesthetic goal of shocking and thrilling audiences in a pleasing way. As I subsequently mention to students, the writer-directors have acknowledged the influence on their movies of gothic novels like Joseph Sheridan Le Fanu's *Uncle Silas* (Del Toro) and Ira Levin's *Rosemary's Baby* and *The Stepford Wives* (Peele).

Next, we begin defining gothic fiction theoretically and historically by reading Ernst Jentsch's essay "On the Psychology of the Uncanny," Sigmund Freud's essay "The Uncanny," E. T. A. Hoffman's short story "The Sandman" (which both Jentsch and Freud discuss), and extracts from Horace Walpole's *The Castle of Otranto*. David Livingstone Smith's essay helpfully updates the concept of the uncanny, showing why Jentsch's approach is more accurate than Freud's and arguing that "creepy" is a more appropriate English-language term than "uncanny." Then, to understand why Edmund Burke's account of the sublime remains relevant to defining *gothic*, we utilize materials on the *Aeon* website (Warburton and Park; Shapsay). We also draw upon the British Library's resources, especially John Bowen's listing of key gothic components in his video "The Gothic" and his accompanying essay "Gothic Motifs." Bowen's video identifies seven components central to gothic atmospherics: "place and time" (involving themes of spatial incarceration and temporal incursion from the past into the present), "power," "sexual power," "the uncanny," "the sublime," "crisis" (involving religious and political turmoil), and "the supernatural and the real" (involving the question of whether the story ultimately endorses the supernatural, explains it away, or leaves readers in doubt). In his essay, Bowen adds another element: the distinction between terror and horror techniques. We then compare these characteristics with Frederick Frank's extensively researched list: "claustrophobic containment"; "subterranean pursuit"; "supernatural encroachment"; "aliveness of architecture and objects of art"; "'extraordinary positions' [Walpole 10] and lethal predicaments"; "abeyance of rationality"; "possible victory of evil"; "supernatural gadgetry, contraptions, machinery, and demonic appliances"; and "'a constant vicissitude of interesting passions' [Walpole 6]" (436–37; interpolations from Haslam, "Negotiating" 42). Finally, to encapsulate gothic fiction's traits and rhetorical goals, we combine definitions by Frank and Eve Kosofsky Sedgwick: "a tale of terror or horror with the action restricted or enclosed by a haunted [or apparently haunted] and partially ruined building" (Frank 435), expressed through "an aesthetic based on pleasurable fear" (Sedgwick, *Coherence* 11).[3] Our bracketed addition acknowledges explained-gothic

54   IRISH GOTHIC FICTION

narratives, which ultimately reveal that supposedly supernatural occurrences are actually natural (Haslam, "Investigating" 42).

Next, we seek to identify key elements of an *Irish* gothic aesthetic through reading stories by two Irish Protestant authors: Charles Maturin's "Leixlip Castle" and Le Fanu's "The Fortunes of Sir Robert Ardagh" and "Ultor de Lacy." Set in Ireland's eighteenth-century past, each story plays variations on the *Otranto* prototype of cursed families inhabiting haunted castles. Each narrative also alludes to or explicitly mentions Irish historical events and religious divisions; in addition, "Leixlip" and "Ultor" include references to Irish folkloric rituals and traditions, and "Robert Ardagh" incorporates two versions of its Faustian tale to explore contrasts and connections between the "lore" (or folklore) of "the distorting medium of tradition" and the (still "marvelous") "reality" (Le Fanu, "Robert Ardagh" 314, 317). Rather than serving as forced formulae, these stories about Irish families blighted by past misdeeds and suffering supernatural torment in an isolated dwelling offer "paradigm cases" for the Irish gothic mode (Haslam, "Negotiating" 46). If they do not embody—in the fullest sense—Irish gothic fiction, then what does?

The stories' explicitly Irish historical, political, sociological, and confessional dimensions prime us for the opening chapters of Maturin's *Melmoth the Wanderer. Melmoth* begins and ends in Ireland, but in between, it wanders the world. Nevertheless, even its middle section sporadically mentions Irish historical incidents in footnotes. In addition, like Maturin's and Le Fanu's stories, *Melmoth*'s opening chapters overtly reference Irish history, religion, and folklore. At the same time, the work's geographic scope challenges readers to connect its non-Irish-set narratives to Ireland without resorting to allegoresis, the millennia-old hermeneutic maneuver (frequently employed for salvaging purposes) of "explaining a work, or a figure in myth, or any created entity, as if there were another sense to which it referred, that is, presuming the work or figure to be encoded with meaning intended by the author or a higher spiritual authority" (Copeland and Struck 2).[4] The challenge of avoiding allegoresis returns with four out of the five works in Le Fanu's *In a Glass Darkly*, since they are not set in Ireland. Especially relevant is *Carmilla*, whose tale of vampiric seduction is one source for *Dracula* (Luckhurst, Introduction [Stoker, *Dracula* (Luckhurst)] xviii). A similar interpretive challenge occurs with Oscar Wilde's *The Picture of Dorian Gray*, whose English setting has not deterred critics from allegorizing it into a detailed political critique of England's colonial abuse of Ireland.[5]

Dracula *and the Lure of Wishful Linking*

Equipped with hermeneutic caveats from studying Maturin, Le Fanu, and Wilde, we turn to Stoker, exploring first how *Dracula* invokes older gothic conventions and invents new ones. With respect to older traits, even though *Dracula* was published a century after peak gothic (1780–1820), it exhibits all eight of Bowen's characteristics and eight out of nine of Frank's (excluding "aliveness of architecture and objects of art"). With respect to innovation, Stoker amps up and vamps up his monsters' attributes and strikingly contrasts "nineteenth century up-to-date" with the unkillable "powers" of "the old centuries" (*Dracula* 40–41). Having established the novel's older and newer gothic features, we then examine what is at stake (as it were) in terms of poetics, hermeneutics, rhetoric, and ethics in treating *Dracula* as Irish gothic. Like Maturin's *Melmoth* and "Leixlip Castle" and Le Fanu's "Robert Ardagh" and "Ultor de Lacy," *Dracula* exhibits an ambivalent fascination with superstition, Roman Catholicism, and the frightening return of the past; but, like *Dorian Gray* and much of *In a Glass Darkly* and *Melmoth*, it is not set in Ireland and lacks explicit references to Irish matters. Nevertheless, many critics—especially during the 1990s—claimed to have detected in *Dracula* a coherent, intentional allegory about Irish-English relations. This led Roger Luckhurst (editor of our class edition of *Dracula*) to ask, "Can we read an allegory of Ireland in Dracula's desperate attempt to escape his cursed lands and establish a new foothold in the imperial centre, his chance blown by his own limited racial inheritance?" (Introduction [Stoker, *Dracula* (Luckhurst)] xxv). Luckhurst answers his own question obliquely: "Yet perhaps Transylvania and the 'whirlpool' of south-eastern Europe are not merely allegorical conveniences, but are meant to be taken literally" (xxvi). Although reluctant at that point to reject allegorizing interpretations completely, six years later Luckhurst could not find space in his *Cambridge Companion to* Dracula for a chapter on Irish readings (Luckhurst, Introduction [*Cambridge Companion*] 8).

Luckhurst's question generates an in-class exercise: students receive a hand-out containing extracts from several allegorizing critics' essays and chapters and are asked to determine how these critics go about interpreting *Dracula* "as an allegory of Ireland," which kinds of evidence they supply to support their claims, and how well substantiated their evidence is. With respect to the first task, students note that Gregory Castle, Seamus Deane (*Strange Country*), Terry Eagleton (*Heathcliff*), and Declan Kiberd claim that Dracula allegorically represents an oppressive Anglo-Irish landlord, whereas (in a radically opposing manner) Stephen Arata, Joseph Spence, Michael Valdez Moses, and Bruce Stewart claim that Dracula allegorically represents a nationalist leader or group (Charles Stewart Parnell or the Land League).[6] With respect to the second task, students note that although the critics declare the novel to be an allegory, they advance no compelling evidence that Stoker intended it to be read as one. The typical technique of the allegorizing critics is to link observations about the novel to observations about nineteenth-century Ireland, but this wishful linking is substantiated rhetorically rather than empirically, through simile and analogy: "could be read as" (Arata 634); "consort well enough with" (Deane, *Strange Country* 90); "[l]ike many an Ascendancy aristocrat," "like the Ascendancy," and "[t]he Ascendancy, too" (Eagleton, *Heathcliff* 215); "like Parnell, Dracula" (Moses 69); "striking analogies" (Kiberd 386).[7] With respect to the

56   IRISH GOTHIC FICTION

third task, many students find the overall evidence underwhelming. They agree that *Dracula*, as published in 1897, was a gothic novel written by an Irish author and therefore—in the broadest sense—an Irish gothic novel, but they are often surprised to find that the critics offer no evidence other than strained similitudes for the claim that *Dracula* intentionally allegorizes Irish-English politics. To be clear, the pedagogical goal of this exercise is not to shut down inquiring minds but to open them up to the effects of cognitive and ideological biases and informal logical fallacies. The activity provides a vivid opportunity for students to learn that what we descry in *Dracula* can be (in Smallwood's terms) "colored by" our personalities and priorities.[8]

We follow this in-class exercise with an out-of-class one, analyzing later investigations of *Dracula*'s Irish political and cultural dimensions. After listening to two BBC radio documentaries, Patrick McCabe's "Was Dracula Irish?" and Eamonn Hughes's "Dracula's Irish Blood," students determine whether the arguments offered in these programs prove more persuasive than those advanced by the 1990s critics and, if so, why. As noted by students in the next class session, when interviewed by McCabe in "Was Dracula Irish?," Bob Curran employs a simile-linking technique in order to claim Stoker drew upon Irish folklore in creating Dracula's character. In another class handout, extracts from Stoker's "Working Papers" and "Research Papers" (Frayling, *Vampyres* 303–47) reveal the absence of corroborating evidence for Curran's hypothesis. The handout also contains extracts from Curran's related essay "Was Dracula an Irishman?" that engage in etymological speculation: "In Irish, droch-fhoula (pronounced droc'ola) means 'bad' or 'tainted blood' and whilst it is now taken to refer to 'blood feuds' between persons or families, it may have a far older connotation" (15). However, as Christopher Frayling notes, one source that we know Stoker consulted traces the name Dracula to the Wallachian language (*Vampyres* 319). As Jarlath Killeen rightly observes, despite its popularity this pseudo-etymology has never established a "convincing connection between Ireland and Stoker" ("Remembering" 34).[9]

Students can choose to pursue their explorations further in a research paper, examining the arguments of more recent critics, like Nicholas Daly (*Modernism*), Sarah Goss, Raphaël Ingelbien, Calvin Keogh, Robert Smart and Michael Hutcheson, Cannon Schmitt, and Joseph Valente (*Dracula's Crypt*).[10] Building upon earlier discussions about the hermeneutics of reading Maturin, Le Fanu, and Wilde, the class sessions, assignments, and papers on *Dracula* seek, overall, to highlight for students the necessity (and difficulty) of following Mina Harker's goal: to "think without prejudice on the facts before me" (Stoker, *Dracula* 304).

How Mistaken *Boosts* Dracula's *Irish Gothic Status*

In the semester's second half, we turn to novels by three twentieth-century Irish Catholic authors, Flann O'Brien, Deane, and Jordan. As we read O'Brien's *The Third Policeman*, I ask students to explore whether the many overlaps between the novel's themes, devices, tones, and techniques and the ever-evolving gothic repertoire are coincidental or deliberate, and which internal and external evidence they can find for either possibility. Students sometimes point to the extensive use of humor in *The Third Policeman* as a potentially disqualifying factor for its gothic status, since the gothic mode is rooted in "an aesthetic based on pleasurable fear" (Sedgwick, *Coherence* 11). However, I ask them to recall the episodes of mordant humor in *Melmoth* and *In a Glass Darkly*, the frequent badinage in *Dorian Gray*, and the "King Laugh" section in *Dracula* (156–59), reminding them that the gothic mode's rhetorical goal of "pleasurable fear" does not exclude phases of raillery and macabre wit.

There is no coincidence about the presence of the gothic mode in our next course text: Deane's auto-fictional novel *Reading in the Dark*. Wearing his scholar's hat, Deane wrote about Irish gothic in the 1980s (*Short History*) and, as general editor of the three-volume *Field Day Anthology of Irish Writing*, commissioned W. J. McCormack to edit the section "Irish Gothic and After (1820–1945)."[11] A few years later, wearing his novelist's hat, Deane wove into *Reading in the Dark* many of the motifs and techniques that scholars like Bowen, Frank, and Sedgwick have identified as distinctively gothic. Thus, in reading *Reading*, we explore exactly which gothic traits and themes it incorporates and renovates and why. Deane's account of growing up in the North of Ireland from the mid-1940s to the early 1970s under oppressive political and clerical regimes conjures up Maturin and Le Fanu's Irish gothic paradigms of persecution, incarceration, sectarianism, threatened damnation, cursed families, toxic secrets, ghostly visitations, and folkloric reverberations, all within an Irish setting. When asked to juxtapose the novel with *Dracula*, students also point to the swarms of rats in both works (Stoker, *Dracula* 219–22, 244–45; Deane, *Reading* 77–80) and to the protagonist's memory-haunted mother, who (like Lucy Westenra in *Dracula*) engages in "a kind of sleepwalking" and one half of whose split psyche lies in a "crypt behind" the other half (Deane, *Reading* 144, 152). However, one significant zone of difference between the two novels is that *Reading*'s readers can resist the siren call of allegoresis, since Deane's novel is set in Ireland and deliberately and explicitly employs the gothic mode to explore intersecting political and familial crises of the Irish past and present.

A similar explicitness and deliberateness mark our final course text, Jordan's *Mistaken*, which (like *Reading*) is a gothic bildungsroman. Once again, I ask students to investigate which gothic motifs the novel employs and why. Kevin Thunder, the novel's first-person narrator and protagonist, grows up in 1950s Dublin, next door to a house in which (a century earlier) Bram Stoker lived, so it is not surprising that *Dracula* haunts *Mistaken* in multiple ways.[12] As Kevin grows, so does his understanding of the vampire: from celluloid phantom to sinister local pedophile to emblem of institutional callousness and clerical sexual abuse to manifestation of his own guilty conscience. In addition, the novel

58   IRISH GOTHIC FICTION

repeatedly reflects on the puzzling relationships among Stoker, *Dracula*, and Ireland:

> I imagined Abraham Stoker there [in a Dublin church] with his wife Charlotte and his young son Bram, in this dowdy outpost of the empire upon which the sun will never set. How could this figure who would haunt my childhood come from such stolid, empirical particulars? Their hats were dark and hard, their suits were tweed, their voices tuneless, and their imaginations limited. Even the *Dracula* that he would come to write was an overwritten book, stolid and florid at the same time. And yet the Count existed. He would spread his seed. He would transform, like a Celtic shape-shifter or a manufactured virus, have as many lives as he needed to prolong himself.   (290)

Tormented by guilt over his role in a woman's death, Kevin also hypothesizes his own theory of Irish gothic: "The pattern finds a way of replicating without the knowledge of the participants. Like a curse. Stoker knew that. Le Fanu. Maturin. All the Protestant ones" (233).[13]

As students gradually recognize, *Mistaken* retrospectively strengthens *Dracula*'s Irish gothic validity. When published in 1897, *Dracula* possessed many gothic characteristics but few Irish ones other than its author's birthplace and its depiction of some rural Catholic beliefs and superstitions. However, by revamping *Dracula*'s Irish Protestant gothic tropes and techniques for a new country and century, Jordan supplies a blood transfusion for the novel's formerly anemic Irish gothic status.

The final exam gives students one more opportunity to explain which "pattern[s]" in poetics, hermeneutics, rhetoric, and ethics they have discovered over the semester and how *Dracula* and *Mistaken* might fit into them; it also gives them a chance to demonstrate an improved ability to build their arguments on solid evidence and "empirical particulars" (Jordan 233, 290).

Teaching Dracula *on a Paranoid Planet*

The recently released movie *Renfield* indicates that vampires remain box-office draws. They also remain ready metaphors, as seen in references to "vampiric chatbots" (Klein) and the "vampirical" nature of "[g]enerative AI art . . . feasting on past generations of artwork even as it sucks the lifeblood from living artists" (Crabapple et al.). The status of *Dracula* remains high, too, in Irish gothic studies, as shown in recent journal special issues and scholarly companions (Fox; Killeen, "Bram Stoker").

So it has never been more timely to teach this novel. As I hope to have shown, approaching *Dracula* from an Irish gothic fiction perspective can offer students valuable insights into rhetoric, hermeneutics, poetics, and ethics, insights that possess both literary critical and existential relevance. On our increasingly paranoid planet, students can learn about the risks—and not just the rewards—of "paranoid reading" (Sedgwick, *Touching* 123–51).

NOTES

For their enthusiasm and insights, I want to thank those students at the University of Liverpool and Saint Joseph's University who have taken the course (in its various titles and formats). I am also very grateful to Dr. William McBride and the outside reviewers for their revision suggestions.

1. On the centrality of rhetoric, hermeneutics, and poetics to literary criticism, see Culler, chapters 4 and 5 (56–69, 70–82).

2. For an explanation of the difference, see Killeen, "Irish Gothic Revisited."

3. Mirabile dictu, some analysts of Irish gothic find it "next to impossible" to define gothic fiction (Killeen, *Emergence* 16) or resist defining it at all (Morin, *Gothic Novel* 19–20 and "*Adventures*" 239–41).

4. For debates about allegoresis, *Melmoth*, and the Irish gothic category, see Haslam, "Irish Gothic: A Rhetorical Hermeneutics Approach" and "Irish Gothic"; Killeen, "Irish Gothic: A Theoretical Introduction" and "Irish Gothic Revisited"; Morin, *Charles Robert Maturin* 129–53. As Northrop Frye explains, "Genuine allegory is a structural element in literature: it has to be there, and cannot be added by critical interpretation alone" (54). On art and intention, see also Paisley Livingston 142–43, 168–69. On the history of allegoresis (known previously as *hyponoia*, or "under-meaning") as an interpretive practice (predating allegory as an expressive practice), see Jean Grondin 17–44. For a discussion of how debates about allegoresis relate to debates about "the intentional fallacy" (Wimsatt and Beardsley), see Haslam ("Investigating" 54).

5. See Haslam, "Hermeneutic Hazards," "Revisiting," "Seeking"; Killeen, "Greening."

6. The fourth episode of the series *The Story of Ireland* ("The Age of Union") provides an accessible source for understanding nineteenth-century Ireland, including the role of Parnell, and the third episode of *The Art of Gothic* ("Blood for Sale") seeks to situate *Dracula* in an Irish context (albeit by engaging in a little allegoresis). Students writing research papers exploring overlaps between *Dracula* and the Irish Literary Revival have benefited from the *Handbook of the Irish Revival* (Kiberd and Matthews).

7. The locus classicus of using simile for historicizing allegoresis is Henry Littlefield's "*The Wizard of Oz*: Parable on Populism." See also Haslam, "Investigating" 45–59.

8. For an example of an empirically rigorous reading of *Dracula*, see Frayling, "Mr. Stoker's Holiday."

9. For further examples of such pseudo-etymology, see Belford, *Bram Stoker: A Biography of the Author of* Dracula 264; Lloyd 119; McIntyre 25; Titley 345–46.

10. For an examination of Valente's methodology, see Haslam, "Irish Gothic" 88–89. Ingelbien and Keogh usefully survey the 1990s critical debate about *Dracula*'s supposed Irish dimensions, but neither critic highlights the hermeneutic problems caused by confusing allegoresis with allegory, and both endorse the allegorizing approach (as do Goss and Smart and Hutcheson). Frayling is skeptical about allegorizing tendencies and refreshingly advocates for "radical empiricism" and "post-post-modernism" ("Mr. Stoker's Holiday" 183, 186).

60   IRISH GOTHIC FICTION

11. Unlike many other analysts of *Dracula*'s Irish dimensions, McCormack resists the temptation to allegorize (842–46, 889–90).

12. Given Jordan's fascination with doubles and doppelgängers, it is unsurprising that *Mistaken* mentions Edgar Allan Poe's "William Wilson" and Robert Louis Stevenson's *The Strange Case of Dr Jekyll and Mr. Hyde* (151, 212). Jordan also stages a double act between his own depictions of north and south Dublin and those of James Joyce.

13. For some reason, Kevin omits Oscar Wilde from this list, despite the doppelgänger themes of *Dorian Gray* and many other overlaps with *Mistaken*.

ETHNIC STUDIES

Dracula in a Latinx Context

Lisa Nevárez

Bram Stoker's *Dracula* opens with the iconic scene of Count Dracula welcoming Jonathan Harker to his castle with these words: "Welcome to my house! Enter freely and of your own will!" (25). In many ways, this setting provides the tone for the novel, which is heavily grounded in European folklore and Western society, as the action shifts between Transylvania and England. These European characters and their cultures form the very fabric of the novel and provide a richness that enhances the mystery and horror of the sequence of events, culminating, of course, in Dracula's demise and Mina Harker's redemption. For many college students who read *Dracula*, a cast of Western characters, featuring European aristocrats, is entirely in keeping with the evolution of the character Dracula and, more broadly, vampires, although in the twenty-first century this image is giving way increasingly to other types of vampires with differing backgrounds. The challenge in a college classroom is addressing the strength of the novel while simultaneously making it relevant to the college learner and, as is the focus of this essay, to the Latinx student learner. Ultimately this novel is entirely malleable and can speak under its umbrella of monster studies to all student learners. In this essay I offer some suggestions for positioning *Dracula* toward the Latinx student learner by offering analogies, discussion prompts, and activity suggestions.

Perhaps the most natural starting point is to acknowledge where in the novel Stoker includes non-European references. These references emerge in particular after Lucy's demise. In chapter 28, in his explanation to his vampire-fighting comrades, Dr. Abraham Van Helsing informs them about the origins of the vampire. Dr. Van Helsing observes that "he is known everywhere that men have been. In old Greece, in old Rome; he flourish in Germany all over, in France, in India, even in the Chersonese; and in China, so far from us in all ways, there even is he, and the people fear him at this day" (223). Further, while there are no Latinx characters in *Dracula*, there are references to Latin America. The Texan Quincey Morris has traveled to South America with Arthur

62   LATINX CONTEXT

Holmwood, Lord Godalming, and makes reference to their time at Lake Titicaca on the border between Bolivia and Peru (68). In chapter 27, Morris recalls being forced to shoot his horse after a vampire bat attack: "I have not seen anything pulled down so quick since I was on the Pampas and had a mare that I was fond of go to grass all in a night. One of those big bats that they call vampires had got at her in the night, and what with his gorge and the vein left open, there wasn't enough blood in her to let her stand up, and I had to put a bullet in her as she lay" (148). Despite its acknowledgment of the vampire's broad cross-cultural manifestations, in some ways the novel appears to hit a dead end when speaking to Latinx students. My approach to unpacking the novel for these students encompasses two key elements. One is acknowledging the work done to date on race and ethnicity in *Dracula*, and the other is understanding the Latinx student learner. Both are necessary steps to incorporating a significant analogy and possible classroom activities.

An engaging and fruitful direction is to focus on race and ethnicity in the novel, especially considering Dracula as an other, as scholars such as Stephen D. Arata, Matthew Gibson, and Thomas McLean have done. In the contemporary classroom, this conversation can be a multidimensional one paired with sociohistorical looks at Victorian culture and literature and at Stoker's biography. Contemporary adaptations of *Dracula* can play a vital role in reflecting upon race. Other pedagogical volumes on teaching with vampires that may provide further classroom strategies for discussing otherness include *The Vampire Goes to College* (Nevárez), *Race in the Vampire Narrative* (Anyiwo), *Gender in the Vampire Narrative* (Hobson and Anyiwo), and *Buffy in the Classroom* (Kreider and Winchell). In addition, situating the novel within monster studies more broadly allows a further point of access to otherness by introducing the student learner to more general concepts of monsters in various texts and time periods. Background texts such as *Monster Theory* (Cohen), *Classic Readings on Monster Theory* (Mittman and Hensel), and *Monsters in the Classroom* (Golub and Hayton) may prove useful for the instructor.

However, while this approach by way of race, culture, ethnicity, and otherness provides wonderful material for classroom conversations, we also need to look at who is having these conversations. Crucial to making *Dracula* and its issues more transparently pertinent and accessible to BIPOC students broadly and, here, Latinx students specifically is understanding the current demographics of the Latinx student learner.

It is well established that the Latinx population in the United States is growing rapidly. In 2020, 62.1 million people in the United States—19% of the population—self-identified as Latinx (or as "Latino/a" or "Hispanic" when surveys used those terms). This number is up from 50.5 million in 2010. Over the past two decades, Latinx college enrollment has tripled, and in 2016, the population of Latinx college student learners reached 1.7 million students (Bauman). From 2000 to 2015, the rate of Latinx high school students identified as college-bound grew from 22 to 37 percent, and three million Latinx students enrolled in undergraduate programs in 2015 (Field). Most of these students can be found in two-year and publicly funded colleges and universities ("Hispanics"). Latinx students are overrepresented in public two-year associate's degree programs and underrepresented in bachelor's degree programs. For instance, in fall 2020, 21.8% of students enrolled in public four-year bachelor's programs were Latinx, 56% were white, 8% were Asian, and 12% were African American ("Latino Students").

So, in which classes can we find these Latinx college students? The Georgetown Center on Education and the Work Force determined international business to be the most popular major among Latinx students, followed by multidisciplinary and interdisciplinary studies, engineering, foreign languages, and international relations ("Hispanics"). Although Latinx students are increasing in number and are enrolled in a range of majors, the cost of college tuition remains a stumbling block for many and can negatively affect retention, as can responsibilities as caregivers or parents (Ray). Another part of the retention challenge lies in the fact that Latinx students do not see faculty members that share their backgrounds. For instance, in fall 2017, in postsecondary institutions the percentage of part-time faculty members who identified as Latinx stood at 5.3%, whereas 71% identified as white; full-time faculty percentages were 4.8% Latinx and 72.6% white ("Postsecondary Faculty and Staff"). The trajectory of Latinx students in higher education is continuing to evolve given the pandemic, along with that of their peers in other racial and ethnic groups. As instructors we must continue to be mindful of where this data is trending (see *State*).

Below, I offer two windows into reading and teaching *Dracula* for Latinx student learners, recognizing that these approaches to diversity can be adapted for inclusivity and expanded to include other BIPOC identities.

First, as acknowledged earlier, there exists excellent scholarship on *Dracula* and race. By his amorphous, shape-shifting nature and his national and ethnic makeup, Dracula is situated as especially pertinent to a Latinx racial demographic, which is itself fluid. Dracula is a central European who is himself made up of difference, marked as he is by his homeland. He expounds to Jonathan Harker, "[W]e Szekelys have a right to be proud, for in our veins flows the blood of many brave races who fought as the lion fights, for lordship" (33). With regard to a Latinx individual, this "blood of many brave races" is significant. Tellingly, most twenty-first-century survey forms separate ethnicity from race in a nod to the colonizing histories that are the lineage of Latinx people. Regarding ethnicity, respondents are asked to select "yes" or "no" for the descriptor "Hispanic/Latino" (in some cases, "Latinx" or "Latine" may be offered as an option). Then the individual is asked to select from multiple descriptors of race and is typically invited to mark "all that apply." This structure acknowledges that Latinx people are from a plethora of racial backgrounds. There is not "one" Latinx person. In this way, the Latinx physical body is as elusive as the shape-shifting Dracula, whose own physiognomy transcends the idea of racial characteristics.

64   LATINX CONTEXT

Another pivotal analogy pertinent to the Latinx student is the theme of borders. *Dracula* begins with Jonathan Harker's journey across Europe as he travels to Dracula's castle. And there is quite a lot of border crossing in the novel, from Dracula's voyage to England to the return journey to Transylvania. The idea of a widely traveled vampire has been expanded upon in multiple texts and predates *Dracula*. The Grand Tour undertaken by the human Aubrey and vampire Lord Ruthven in John Polidori's *The Vampyre*, or the vampire hunters' journey through central Europe in *Dracula*, may not be the most attainable for many college learners; however, the theme of border crossing is a significant access point for enabling Latinx learners to gain further insight into the novel.

It is of course no surprise that the United States has been experiencing a twentieth- and twenty-first-century border crisis. The issue is multifaceted and quickly evolving, but suffice it to say that contemporary readers of *Dracula* are likely aware of the contested border. For the Latinx student, this theme will perhaps resonate more keenly, as many migrants into the United States are of Latinx background. Some statistics reveal the sheer numbers. In 2018, legal immigrants from Latin American or Spanish-speaking Caribbean points of origin accounted for 36.1% of the total US immigrant population ("US Immigration Trends"). And, of the 10.5 million unauthorized immigrants in 2017, 4.9 million were Mexican, 1.9 million were Central American, and 775,000 were South American (Passel and Cohn). In looking at *Dracula* as a novel of migration and border crossing, taking into account Latinx family histories may help build connections with students. Of course, the modes of transport of the vampire (a coffin filled with dirt) and of the privileged English voyagers (train, boat, carriage, horseback) are not of the same nature as the crossing of migrants across US borders.

While some may immediately think of the Mexico-US border and its vast miles of desert, especially the Devil's Highway area, located in Arizona, there are other equally porous borders. For instance, the US-Canada border is a site of crossings by Latinx individuals who have flown into Canada and wish to enter the United States. Other Latinx migrants travel by boat or raft, such as from Cuba to the United States. The issue of migration and borders is fundamentally crucial to the Latinx student, and this allows us a fresh way of looking at Count Dracula, a migrant who smuggles himself into England, albeit with significant differences from a present-day Latinx migrant. It is important to clarify that the terms *immigrant, migrant, refugee*, and *asylum seeker*, all used to identify a person looking to enter a different country, are all distinct from one another. I use the term *migrant* here for consistency, but the distinctions between the terms and experiences are undoubtedly worth unpacking in the classroom.

Arguably, Dracula's voyage to Whitby Harbor as cargo is enabled by his undead status, whereby he is not a person. Without a passport or ticket documenting himself as human, he smuggles himself in a box aboard the *Demeter*, where he picks off the crew one by one. In the historical time frame of the novel and of its publication, restrictions on immigration such as are common today did not exist. It was not until Parliament's Aliens Act of 1905 that immigration and registration controls were implemented in the United Kingdom for the first time. In other words, Dracula's traveling as a human without a passport or other documents would not have necessarily raised suspicion. Important to acknowledge is that Dracula has the wealth and means to travel, even in this manner as cargo, and as the reader of the novel knows, he has already purchased English accommodations. Dracula, then, even without a potentially anachronistic passport, is a privileged Victorian traveler, with the freedom to cross borders as he chooses, even in a box.

Despite the fact that Dracula has the means to travel as a person with a first-class ticket, he deliberately chooses—which in itself is admittedly a privilege—to circumvent borders as best he can. He situates himself as an object, the better to avoid detection. A vivid analogy is the migrant crossing through a checkpoint while hidden inside a vehicle, such as in the engine compartment, in the trunk, or in a similarly camouflaged space, with the intention of disguising themselves. That comparison is certainly apt for looking at this novel in a Latinx context; there is plenty of news footage of crossings in such a way to share in the classroom. Like a migrant navigating the open desert of the American Southwest, such as the Devil's Highway, Dracula crosses the vastness of the waters leading him from Transylvania to England and Whitby. He too leaps—under cover of a false identity—onto land, much as a border crosser from a Latin American nation may themselves take on a false persona or otherwise engage in other measures to enter the United States.

However, key to emphasize here is Dracula's end goal of preying upon London. In this respect a comparison with a present-day migrant stops cold. A stark comparison that further highlights this discrepancy is the life story of Henry Brown, later named Henry Box Brown. The enslaved Brown shipped himself from Richmond, Virginia, to Philadelphia, Pennsylvania, where he arrived as planned at the door of a noted abolitionist in 1849. Brown sent himself as cargo, secreting himself in a box marked "dry goods" and outfitted with an air hole. The journey took approximately twenty-four hours. Brown survived this mailing and authored a memoir of his experience, *Narrative of Henry Box Brown*. Neither of these disenfranchised individuals—the present-day migrant and the nineteenth-century fugitive from slavery—looks to embed themselves in a new city and conquer it by consuming its inhabitants; that is specifically the vampire's purview. Rather, a migrant or a fugitive from slavery is looking for independence in all senses: physical, legal, moral, financial, and more. Concealing oneself in an engine or a box is not a choice to be made lightly. This comparison then enables us to further understand Dracula as a monster. He is not persecuted or enslaved, or economically or socially disenfranchised; rather, he desires a new life in a new place and has the resources to act upon that wish. Dracula could be seen as the migrant in search of a "better" life, although the analogy should perhaps end there, as a vampire and a migrant are quite distinct from each other.

66   LATINX CONTEXT

I find in my undergraduate classroom that careful unpacking of anti-immigrant rhetoric—past and present—is essential. In a Latinx context, as discussed here, I have found that in-class reflective writing to address perhaps unconscious biases is useful, followed by think-pair-share, where students can respond to their peers. The instructor can incorporate current events by sharing recent media coverage or dedicating class time to a news search by small groups. These various strategies seek to first identify preconceptions and experiences outside of class and then scaffold with peer engagement followed by a whole-class conversation. This approach guides students in navigating any tension between monster and migrant and seeks to provide a nuanced discussion.

Of course, Dracula is a male character, and gender matters as we look at intersectionality. Dracula as a man has access to legal and financial resources in a way a female traveler of his era, let alone a present-day migrant, does not. It was only in 1870 and 1882 that the Married Women's Property Acts were passed in England, increasing some women's financial and legal autonomy. Given the extensive scholarly discussion of the New Woman embodied by Mina and arguably by Lucy, this awareness of gender roles in society is important to cultivate in readers. Ultimately, looking at the Count himself as a migrant who crosses borders may resonate with a Latinx student differently and thus provide opportunities to further nuance terminology and motivations.

One can pair *Dracula* with Latinx vampire works and characters keeping this parallel in mind. Such works provide evidence of how literature and contemporary culture have embraced the diversity of *Dracula* and vampires. Perhaps the most prominent example is the film *From Dusk till Dawn*. Memorably, the vampires at the Titty Twister bar, led by Santánico Pandemonium (Salma Hayek), have originated from an Aztec temple, which appears in the closing shots of the film. Building on the success of the film, the television series *From Dusk till Dawn* appeared on El Rey Network for three seasons, from 2014 to 2016. Two other recent examples are the film *Vampires vs. the Bronx* and the FX television series *What We Do in the Shadows*, which features the Latinx character Guillermo (Harvey Guillén). Literature offers the *Casa Dracula* novels, by Marta Acosta; the Felix Gomez vampire-detective series, by Mario Acevedo; and Raymond Villareal's *A People's History of the Vampire Uprising*. Important to add to that list are the graphic novels *Bite Club*, by Howard Chaykin, David Tischman, and David Hahn, and *Life Sucks*, by Jessica Abel, Gabe Soria, and Warren Pleece. These references are not exhaustive but provide a starting point for the educator seeking to incorporate more Latinx vampire authors and texts into their teaching.

These avenues can make the novel from 1897 pertinent to a contemporary Latinx student. The following are suggestions for class activities or guided reflections intended to connect this novel with the Latinx student and to enhance themes in the novel that all students, regardless of background, would benefit from understanding.

First, engage in a reflective activity, paired with student research, on border crossings. As mentioned earlier, these are not just overland in the Southwest but can be in California, at the US-Canada border, and over water. Some migrants have traveled great distances, such as on trains riding through Mexico, before even reaching a US border. Digging further, a student can research the perilous conditions on the Devil's Highway, a well-documented entry point into the US from Mexico. Suggested nonvampire texts that depict migrant experiences include *The Devil's Highway* (Urrea), *The Line Becomes a River* (Cantú), *The Death of Josseline* (Regan), *Enrique's Journey* (Nazario), *Solito* (Zamora), and *Tell Me How It Ends* (Luiselli). One can also look at contemporary Latinx fiction about borders, of which there is a plethora, or poetry such as Javier Zamora's collection, *Unaccompanied.*

Consider Latinx vampire texts such as those named above in the light of the questions, Where and how does the Dracula or vampire figure prove itself to be adaptable? What stands out in this update? *From Dusk till Dawn,* acknowledged as a crucial Latinx vampire film, pairs nicely with the more recent *Vampires vs. the Bronx.* One could also look at vampires in Latin American literature, such as Carlos Fuentes's *Vlad.*

Cultivate connections to other BIPOC student learners. African American or Black, Asian, and Native American vampires certainly appear in literature, television, and film. Examining texts that have such a focus provides a nice point of contrast and discussion prompt for European-centered vampire texts and a complement to Latinx texts. For a connection to a Black or African American vampire, both Octavia E. Butler's novel *Fledgling* and the *Blade* film franchise, not to mention *Blacula*, provide rich material for discussions on race and hybridity. One recommended text featuring a Native American vampire is Drew Hayden Taylor's *The Night Wanderer.* Asian cinema and television offer numerous examples. For discussions of the myriad of such texts, one can look at two edited collections: *The Global Vampire* (Coker et al.) and *Vampire Films around the World* (Aubrey).

A suggested student research project is uncovering the points of intersection with vampires in folklore. The text of *Dracula* itself and Van Helsing's list, quoted above, may be supplemented with early work by Paul Barber and by Radu Florescu and Raymond T. McNally. Turning to the Americas, northern Mexico and the Southwest have numerous shape-shifting legends and mysterious animals, such as the *chupacabra* (literally, "goat sucker"). This is an opportunity to examine Indigenous Aztec, Mayan, and Incan tales as well. James E. Doan's essay "The Vampire in Native American and Mesoamerican Lore" offers a good starting point.

These activities can help make *Dracula* even more relevant to a Latinx student learner, which is especially important given the rise in enrollment of Latinx college students. While *Dracula* may open with an invitation to a British traveler, it also welcomes the Latinx student learner.

The Absence and Fear of Black People:
Dracula in a Course on
African American Vampire Fiction

Jerry Rafiki Jenkins

When I decided to teach an upper-division course on African American vampire fiction at San Diego State University, I felt it was necessary to include a discussion of Bram Stoker's *Dracula*. I usually assign *Dracula* when vampires are the theme of Critical Thinking and Composition through Literature, a course I teach at Palomar College. Although the critical thinking course focuses on the "new" vampire, who emerged in the United States during the 1970s and is most associated with the vampires of Anne Rice's *Interview with the Vampire*, we also read Stoker's *Dracula*, since the novel's Transylvanian Count represents the "old" vampire (see Zanger 17; Carter, "Vampire" 27). While including *Dracula* in a course that examines the differences between the old and the new vampires and what those differences can tell us about late-twentieth-century American culture makes sense, including Stoker's novel in a course on African American vampire fiction might seem unnecessary and contradictory, since I have argued elsewhere that "to use Dracula as the starting and ending points on what constitutes a vampire is to racialize the vampire as a white figure" (*Paradox* 12). While *Dracula* may appear to be out of place in a course on African American vampire fiction, I propose in this essay that Stoker's novel can be useful for such a course because it will allow students to think critically about why Dracula's vampirism was dominant in American culture until the 1970s and why that vampirism rarely appears in African American vampire fiction.

The introduction to my African American vampire fiction course takes place over three classes and focuses on what I call the vampire's Blackness, a brief history of vampire myths from Africa and the African diaspora. I begin with an overview of the vampires of precolonial Africa (e.g., the *adze, asasabonsam, obayifo,* and *witch wives*), colonial Africa (e.g., the *wazimamoto, banyama,* and *batumbula*), and the Black Caribbean (e.g., the *loogaroo, asema,* and *sukuyan/soucouyant*) to show that "although African American vampire fiction is a late-twentieth-century development, vampire myths are not foreign to Africa or the African diaspora" (Jenkins, *Paradox* 2). I also use that overview to point out that Stoker's *Dracula* is a latecomer to vampire mythology. I explain that the vampire, using Christopher Frayling's words, is "as old as the world" (qtd. in Beresford 8), and its widespread presence throughout the ancient era indicates that the vampire has a history that "predates the word 'vampire' and the biological notion of race" (Jenkins, *Paradox* 5). Thus, the fears and desires that vampires evoke are "deeply rooted in the human psyche, not just in the white psyche" (2).

Despite *Dracula*'s latecomer status, I maintain that an examination of Dracula is important because he defined the vampire in the twentieth-century American imagination until the rise of the new vampire, who, unlike Dracula, is "secularized," "socialized," and "humanized" (Zanger 22). Moreover, the rise of the new vampire is linked to the release of *Blacula*, which is not only the first Hollywood-produced film to feature a Black vampire but also the film that "initiated America's departure from the vampirism of Stoker's Dracula" (Jenkins, *Paradox* 15). Through its creation of a vampire who is more human than monster, *Blacula* not only engendered the blaxploitation horror genre and helped shape the cinematic adaptations of *Dracula* by John Badham (*Dracula*) and Francis Ford Coppola (*Bram Stoker's* Dracula) but also led to the release of Bill Gunn's *Ganja and Hess*, the Black vampire film whose philosophical considerations would become the foundation of Rice's *Interview* (Benshoff 32, 37–38, 45). Thus, before discussing the Black vampire films of the 1970s and ending the discussion of the vampire's Blackness, I examine Stoker's iconic novel to give a sense of the deeply rooted fears and desires that helped make Dracula the foundation of America's archetypal vampire, whom Kendra R. Parker describes as "a tall, slender, seductive, and economically privileged white male who blends in with society until humans expose his vampire origins" (xiii).

The deeply rooted fear and desire that I use as the primary framework for textual analyses is the fear of death and the desire for immortality. According to Mary Hallab, all vampires, despite their diversity, "address issues and attitudes about death and immortality that are meaningful in all times and places" (*Vampire God* 5). However, I inform students that while all vampires address questions regarding death and immortality, they do not address these questions in the same ways, represent the same responses to such questions, or even focus on the same questions. Indeed, among the notable differences between Dracula and the Black literary vampires I cover in this course are the immortality narratives that they embody. According to Stephen Cave, humanity has created four immortality narratives—"staying alive," "resurrection," "soul," and "legacy"—that contain all attempts that have been and will ever be made at achieving everlasting life and solving the "mortality paradox," the notion that death in the human mind is "both inevitable and impossible" (16). While Cave believes that these narratives will never makes us immortal, he acknowledges that they do show that our desire for immortality is "embedded in our very nature" and, not surprisingly, in the foundations of our religions, philosophies, myths, arts, and civilizations (2–3). I note that one trait that Dracula, Blacula, and some of the new literary vampires (e.g., Lestat of *Interview* and Edward Cullen of Stephenie Meyer's *Twilight*) share is the resurrection narrative, which posits that although we must die, we can one day "rise to live again" in the same bodies (Cave 89). Given our focus on the vampire's Blackness, we read Stoker's novel with the following question in mind: Is there any relationship between Dracula's resurrection vampirism and the absence of Black vampires, as well as Black people, in *Dracula*?

70   AFRICAN AMERICAN VAMPIRE FICTION

Using Lisa Lampert-Weissig's approach, I introduce Stoker's novel as representing "the 'pulse' of his time"—that is, as a collection of the anxieties that haunted late-nineteenth-century London (32). I also reference Christopher Herbert's "Vampire Religion," which argues that a critical reading of *Dracula* must acknowledge that Stoker's text might be the "most religiously saturated popular novel of its time" and that Stoker's vampire is "an emanation of the world of superstition and an image of a terrible menace posed by the superstitious mentality to decent Christian existence" (101). Considering the insights by Parker, Cave, Lampert-Weissig and Herbert, I ask students to consider the following question: What can the forces that facilitated Dracula's resurrection tell us about the social anxieties surrounding race that haunted late-nineteenth-century England and twentieth-century America? I point out that while Van Helsing identifies Dracula as a revenant, one who has returned, in this case, from the dead, he is unclear about the process of Dracula's transformation from man to "man-that-was" (225). What makes Van Helsing's ignorance about Dracula's resurrection process noteworthy, I argue, is that it suggests that resurrection itself is not an issuing source of horror for Van Helsing and his crew of vampire hunters, but the forces that facilitate resurrections and those being resurrected are.

Given that "Dracula, for Stoker and Stoker's readers, is the Anti-Christ" (Zanger 18), the forces responsible for Dracula's resurrection are considered by turn-of-the-century Londoners as not Christian. Indeed, although Van Helsing is aware that the pre-vampire Dracula studied alchemy, which was "the highest development of the science-knowledge of [Dracula's] time" (Stoker, *Dracula* 278), he also makes it clear that Dracula's resurrection is due to his and his ancestors' studies at the Scholomance, a school of the occult, "where the devil claims the tenth scholar as his due" (225). I also note that Harker's identification as an "English Churchman" is stated in contrast to the Carpathians, whose religious beliefs and practices are referred to as "idolatrous" and "ridiculous" (15), and the "gipsies," who are described as a "fearless" people "without religion, save superstition" (49). Moreover, these superstitious forces are imagined as a threat not only to England's Christians but also to America's, as symbolized by Quincey Morris, the Texan who dies in the fight to kill Dracula and whose name is passed on to Harker and Mina's son in remembrance of his contribution to that fight (344). While the examples above indicate that non-Christian faiths and Christian denominations that do not follow the tenets of the Protestant Church of England (e.g., Romanian Christianity and Roman Catholicism) represent the superstition mentality that threatens Christian existence in *Dracula* (Stoker, *Dracula* [Hindle] 440n10), they also allude to the novel's distinctions between whiteness and nonwhiteness.

To discuss race in *Dracula*, I begin with Maurice Hindle's introduction to the Penguin Classics edition of *Dracula*, where he notes that the anxieties that haunted the British bourgeois population in the late nineteenth century were largely due to the "fundamental shift" that the British economy was experiencing when Stoker's novel was published. "As the beginnings of economic decline set in" Hindle writes, "competition from abroad mounted, particularly from nations like America and Germany. In literature, the appearance of 'foreign' (particularly Semitic) scapegoats became more apparent" (xx). According to Jack Halberstam, "Jews in England at the turn of the century were the objects of an internal colonization" because the anti-Semitism of their time marked Jews as threats to capital, masculinity, and nationhood (*Skin Shows* 14). I suggest that an example of the novel's anti-Semitic tendencies is the description of what Harker refers to as Dracula's "very marked physiognomy" (Stoker, *Dracula* 27). For example, Dracula's nose, regardless of the human form the character takes, is depicted as a difference that cannot be concealed and a marker of monstrosity. Indeed, it is described by various characters as "'ook[ed]" (136), "beaky" (165–66), or "thin" with a "high bridge" and "peculiarly arched nostrils" (27). As Halberstam demonstrates, Dracula's appearance "resembles the Jew of anti-Semitic discourse," in which the face and body of the fictional Jew represent nineteenth-century notions of criminality and degeneration (*Skin Shows* 92–93). Thus, the "explicit" link between the monster and Jew in *Dracula* indicates that both were viewed as "the antithesis of 'Englishness'" (14).

I also propose to students that what makes the Jew of anti-Semitic discourse even more monstrous for Stoker's intended audience, as implied by Dracula's desire for Mina and by Mina's description of Dracula having sex with Lucy as an act akin to bestiality (Stoker, *Dracula* 95), is the threat of interracial sex between white women and nonwhite men. John Allen Stevenson argues that *Dracula* can be read "in terms of inter*racial* sexual competition" in which Dracula's "crime" is "excessive exogamy" (139). The fear of sex between white women and nonwhite men (as well as sex between folks of the same sex) is captured by Harker as he explains why his "terrible desire" to kill Dracula emerged after seeing the Count resting "like a filthy leech" in his coffin: "This was the being I was helping to transfer to London, where, perhaps, for centuries to come he might, amongst its teeming millions, satiate his lust for blood, and create a new and ever-widening circle of semi-demons to batten on the helpless" (Stoker, *Dracula* 59). Harker's fear that Dracula intends to father "semi-demons" manifests when Dracula brags to Van Helsing and his crew of white Christian men, whom Dracula calls "pale faces," that "[y]our girls that you all love are mine already; and through them you and others shall be mine" (282). Thus, as Stevenson argues, Dracula's "real horror" is that he is "the ultimate social adulterer, whose purpose is nothing if it is not to turn good Englishwomen like Lucy and Mina away from their own kind and customs" (140). If such a "horror" is not prevented, as represented by Dracula's declaration to the "pale faces," he and his vampire race could weaken "the stock of Englishness by passing on degeneracy and the disease of blood lust" (Halberstam, *Skin Shows* 95).

While the Jew in *Dracula* is racialized as the nonwhite threat inside late-nineteenth-century England, I ask students what they make of the fact that

72   AFRICAN AMERICAN VAMPIRE FICTION

there are no Black characters in *Dracula*. Does this absence mean that Black people played no role in the novel's understanding of nonwhiteness? According to Halberstam, "While the black African became the threatening other abroad, it was closer to home that people focused their real fears about the collapse of nation through a desire for racial homogeneity" (*Skin Shows* 14). If Halberstam is correct, then the absence of Black people in *Dracula* can be attributed to the fact that Jews, not Black people, were the "monsters at home" who posed the most immediate threat to everyday life in the nation and to the realization of white racial homogeneity. For Parker, however, "to understand more deeply the sociopolitical contexts of *Dracula*," we must keep in mind that the American Revolution, the Haitian Revolution, the French Revolution, and the abolition of the slave trade and slavery itself are all "markers of a destabilization of social norms from within." According to Parker, "While such history may not seem relevant, the rhetoric of anti-Semitism toward the end of the nineteenth century is similar to the rhetoric used at the end of the French Revolution—a revolution that completely reshaped the way the British understood national identity" (xxix). From Parker's perspective, there should be signs of how the Black threat from abroad shaped late-nineteenth-century Englishness in *Dracula*, since other threats from abroad shaped and were shaped by social norms from within. As Patricia McKee puts it, "While Stoker details an historically localized racialization of white identity, he also clarifies that the power accruing to whiteness depends on its universal claims" (49).

Using Halberstam's and Parker's remarks as a starting point, I begin our discussion on how to read Black people's absence in *Dracula* by examining one of Lucy's letters to Mina, where she discusses the happiness and misery of entertaining three marriage proposals in one day. That experience, Lucy writes, allows her to "sympathize with poor Desdemona when she had such a dangerous stream poured in her ear, even by a black man" (64). Lucy's reference to *Othello* is noteworthy because it reminds us that anti-Blackness in England is much older than Stoker's novel and that the racialized threat from abroad that Black people represented in late-nineteenth-century England was the threat at home for white America. Indeed, if we consider that *Dracula* was published one year after the United States Supreme Court decided *Plessy v. Ferguson*, which legalized racial segregation in America, and a little more than thirty years after the term *miscegenation* was coined in an 1863 pamphlet (Kaplan 277), Quincey's role as a man vying for Lucy's hand in marriage and as a member of the "pale faces" can be read as an attempt to highlight the threat that sex between white women and Black men posed for white racial homogeneity in the United States. This helps explain why Dr. Seward believes that key to the nation's becoming a twentieth-century power is the reproduction of white men like Quincey: "I believe in my heart of hearts that [Quincey] suffered as much about Lucy's death as any of us; but he bore himself through it like a moral Viking. If America can go on breeding men like that, she will be a power in the world indeed" (Stoker, *Dracula* 167). Such breeding, Seward implies, cannot take place if Black and other nonwhite men can claim, just as Dracula does, that white women and men at home or abroad are theirs.

Using the arguments and examples above as well as Alexandra Warwick's claim that "[t]he monstrosity of blackness is one of the final contributions of the nineteenth century to the modern myth of the vampire" (216), I propose that while Black people and Black vampires are absent in *Dracula*, the fear of Black people is not, and that fear helps to explain why Lucy scoffs at the thought of a Black man asking her to marry him as well as Quincey's presence in the novel. Some students ask, almost immediately, if my take on the absence of Black vampires in *Dracula* applies to the absence of Black vampires in twentieth-century American culture. To address that question, I reference the work of Kathy Davis Patterson, who argues in "Echoes of *Dracula*: Racial Politics and the Failure of Segregated Spaces in Richard Matheson's *I Am Legend*" that "[t]hanks largely to the lasting impact of slavery and its attendant prejudices, the black African in [the twentieth-century American] context is constructed as a monstrous Other that threatens the dominant society just as the Jew was perceived to threaten England: *from within*" (19). Regarding the absence of Black vampires, Patterson contends that even though the vampires in Matheson's novel "have no obvious racial attributes per se," in the mind of Robert Neville, the novel's white, male protagonist, these vampires are "consistently referred to in connection with blackness," creating a "subtext within the novel that makes racial difference and vampirism synonymous" (20). Considering Patterson's argument, I suggest that one could put forth the claim that the Black vampire threat operated in the twentieth-century American vampire narrative as it did in *Dracula*—though it is physically absent, its threat is felt through the thoughts and actions of white characters. Indeed, Neville's metaphorical "condemnation of interracial sex," especially between Black men and white women, as well as his "desperate desire to restore homogeneity" (Patterson 23), which echoes the fears and desires symbolized by Quincey and the "pale faces," imply that the threat of sex between Black men and white women shaped the horror of the vampire myth in American culture until the release of *Blacula*.

The link between interracial sex and vampirism in *Blacula* is noteworthy because the release of the film and the subsequent rise of the new vampire occurred less than a decade after the Supreme Court's ruling in *Loving v. Virginia* (1967), when a state's authority to prohibit marriages on racial grounds was nullified (Kennedy 105). In fact, one of the ways that *Blacula* distinguishes itself from Stoker's *Dracula* is its approach to the question of interracial sex. I note that, on the one hand, Blacula's desire to be in a monogamous relationship with a Black woman can be read as a critique of Dracula's sexual obsession with whiteness as well as a denunciation of the rationale that white Americans gave for lynching Black men during Jim Crow—the Black male's supposed hypersexuality and obsession with white women. On the other hand, Blacula's pursuit of a heteronormative relationship can be read as reiterating a Black nationalist understanding of Blackness in which his murder of an interracial gay couple

74   AFRICAN AMERICAN VAMPIRE FICTION

is a sign of his racial authenticity.[1] My goal in pointing out the various ways of reading Black male desire and interracial sex in *Blacula* is to show that even though the film shares Dracula's resurrection vampirism, its secularization of Blacula's resurrection as the product of slavery instead of the God-Satan conflict, its socialization of his Blackness through the question of racial authenticity, and its humanization of Black male desire provided the narrative conditions for America's departure from Dracula's vampirism, as evidenced by the release of *Ganja and Hess* and the rise of the new vampire.

Having identified African American vampire fiction as both a rejection of Dracula's vampirism and a "corrective" to the new vampire (Jenkins, *Paradox* 15), I conclude our discussion of *Dracula* with questions intended to get students to start thinking about the differences between the vampirisms of Dracula and the new vampire and that of the Black literary vampires we will examine. How, I ask, does the Blackness of the Black literary vampire differ from the treatment of Blackness in *Dracula*? That question, I note, becomes more intriguing if we consider that some of the Black vampires whom we will read about are not native-born African Americans. Indeed, since Dracula eventually settles in London and represents the xenophobe's image of the immigrant, do the Black immigrant vampires who settle in twentieth-century Black America represent the same threat as Dracula did for nineteenth-century white Londoners and twentieth-century white Americans? Moreover, since the protagonist of the first African American–authored Black vampire novel, Jewelle Gomez's *The Gilda Stories*, is lesbian, what can the Black literary vampire tell us about the racialization of gender and sexuality in the United States that Dracula's vampirism cannot? Finally, since Black upward mobility in the United States has historically been viewed as leading to white poverty, how do we understand the differences between the economic privilege associated with Dracula and that associated with the Black literary vampire? As suggested by these questions, reading *Dracula* in a course on African American vampire fiction can shed light on how the fear and absence of Black people in Stoker's novel inspired the rise of this fledgling genre of Black speculative fiction.

NOTE

1. I have argued elsewhere that Blacula's murder of the Black-white gay couple is a sign of his racial inauthenticity, since he upholds the view that Black gay men are inauthentically Black, a view that functions in the film as an example of Black "internalization" of white supremacist ideology (Jenkins, "*Blacula*" 71).

Why Fear Endures:
Dracula in a Postmillennial Indian Classroom

Srirupa Chatterjee

When I introduce Bram Stoker's *Dracula* to undergraduate engineering students at a prestigious institute of technology in India for an elective course entitled Genre Fiction, I am not surprised to encounter both curiosity and skepticism. My students' questions and observations on the rationale for teaching Stoker's classic in the present millennium are completely understandable. Why should an epistolary Victorian novel named after its famous undead protagonist engage young minds trained to deal with cutting-edge issues in science and technology? Why should young millennials willingly suspend disbelief to yield to the gothic narrative of a mythical demon far removed from their geographic as well as cultural terrain? What relevance does a fiend from old European folklore have to issues of nationality and identity for Indian readers? And, last but not least, how does a Victorian vampiric figure facilitate compelling discussions on patriarchy, sexuality, gender politics, and postcolonial sentiments in contemporary India? While such questions inevitably arise during introductory classes on *Dracula*, they also implicitly set the stage for a compelling analysis of a text that has globally immortalized the concept of the undead.

Informed by my experiences of teaching *Dracula* to postmillennial Indian students, this essay discusses Stoker's novel keeping in mind themes and topics that make it both relevant and engaging for readers spatiotemporally far removed from the notorious Romanian Count. After a brief discussion on the significance and prevalence of horror fiction in India, I address the psychology of fear to demonstrate how this elementary emotion persists even within scientifically informed postmillennial minds. I subsequently turn attention to the forceful emergence of colonial and postcolonial politics in Stoker's *Dracula* and then to the Victorian notions of sexuality, power, and patriarchy inherent in the novel that continue to be some of the most compelling issues that engage contemporary readers. Readers will grasp not only how Stoker's classic tale continues to generate numerous critical debates in classrooms across the world but also how *Dracula* testifies to the fact that fear, humanity's most visceral response to life itself, endures.

The Demonic in Literature and Popular Culture

For the purposes of both historicizing and contextualizing *Dracula* before students, I largely draw upon works such as Noël Carroll's *The Philosophy of Horror*, which is extensively informed by genre theorists and experts on gothic

76   POSTMILLENNIAL INDIAN CLASSROOM

horror such as H. P. Lovecraft, Montague Summers, J. M. S. Tomkins, and Tzvetan Todorov, among others. Carroll claims that "horror is, first and foremost, a modern genre" and that "[t]he immediate source of the horror genre was the English Gothic novel, the German *Schauer-roman*, and French *roman noir*" (4). For Carroll, the first gothic novel is Horace Walpole's *The Castle of Otranto*, which emerged in 1765 from "the preceding generation of graveyard poets" and was followed by "Matthew Lewis's *The Monk*," which "is the real harbinger of the horror genre" (4). "Other major achievements" of the gothic in this period according to Carroll are Mary Shelley's *Frankenstein*, John Polidori's *The Vampyre*, and Charles Robert Maturin's *Melmoth the Wanderer* (5). Furthering this chronology up to Stoker's novel, Carroll mentions works such as Robert Louis Stevenson's *The Strange Case of Dr. Jekyll and Mr. Hyde*, Oscar Wilde's *The Picture of Dorian Gray*, and Stoker's *Dracula* (6). Evidently, then, the history of horror writing is deeply connected to the development of supernatural and gothic fiction and has to do with the undead or ghosts who return to the human world to fulfill something left undone, thereby displaying a secret motive (98). Further, horror stories rely on the "discovery plot" and rouse the reader's interest through "variations," often compounded with the presence of an "overreacher," such as "the mad scientist or the necromancer" (Carroll 118). These tropes ultimately lead to a successful paradox—that of attracting readers through repulsion. This background is useful not only in situating *Dracula* within a literary tradition but also in initiating classroom discussions on the psychology and politics of horror.

While the basic underpinnings of fear as an emotion are universal, they carry different connotations in Indian aesthetics than in European traditions. Classical Indian aesthetics, based on the *rasa* theory from the *Nāṭyaśāstra* (meaning "compendium on dramaturgy"), defines nine *rasas*, literally meaning "'taste' or 'flavor'" (Tieken 119), that are evoked by a work of art. The *Nāṭyaśāstra* discusses fear as an outcome of the *bībhatsa rasa*, or "dislike," which invokes *bhaya*, or "fear," and "belongs to the *bhayanaka* or fearful *rasa*" (123). The *rasa* theory indicates that the flavor a work of art finally invokes is a combination of *rasas*, and so fear is very often an outcome of a mixture of other emotions, such as *raudra*, or anger, and *karunya*, or the "pathetic" (Tieken 117). Fear aroused by mythical *asuras*, or demons, in epics such as the *Ramayana* and the *Mahabharata* attests to *bībhatsa rasa*. In my classroom discussions I explain how, although such classical concepts persist, horror literature in India has also changed considerably under colonial and other global influences. Particularly in the twentieth century, noted writers like Rabindranath Tagore (in "Manihara" ["The Lost Jewels"] and "Konkaal" ["The Skeleton"]), Tarashankar Bandopdhyay (in "Daini" ["Witch"]), Ruskin Bond (in "A Face in the Dark"), O. J. Vijayan (in "The Little Ones"), and Satyajit Ray (in "Anath Babu's Terror") have developed the horror story in ways that not only retain an Indian cultural ethos but also incorporate several elements of gothic horror to critique society's failings.

Where connections between Stoker's novel and India are concerned, historians such as Aditi Sen and Alok Sharma mention that "Stoker's family had served in India and he became fascinated with Indian occult" and that "[h]e knew Sir Richard Burton . . . who translated the Sanskrit collection of stories, *Baital Pachisi*, that featured Vetala the vampire," adding that "Burton often spoke of how he had discussed Hindu myths with Stoker, and Stoker studied *Baital Pachisi* thoroughly before writing *Dracula*." Approaching the question from a different direction, Marcin Ciemniewski argues that contemporary Indian horror writing draws heavily upon Western forms. Ciemniewski outlines horror's presence in popular Indian imagination by examining comic books, whose advent is concomitant with "American comics publishing companies," which "around 1950" began attracting adult readers to their "horror and thriller stories." The Indian market "quickly adapted this trend, launching a very popular comic book series in Hindi of thrill, horror and suspense," which was entirely missing from "Indian literature and popular culture," claims Ciemniewski (161). In the tradition of Western superheroes who fought "vampires, zombies and other spooks," Indian popular culture, especially in Hindi-speaking regions, became "awash with Indian spooks haunting" the nation's "cities and villages," who needed to be exorcised by heroic saviors (165). Further, Ciemniewski describes how Count Dracula "visits India for the first time in *bhūtmahal* (*The Haunted Mansion*), a comic book from the Ram-Rahim series by Manoj Comics." Here, Dracula is a "villain character" who "[plots] a dastardly revenge on teenage secret agents," and in the course of the series he "keeps growing stronger, and evolves from a rather harmless, childish monster to a savage villain from outer space" who is unstoppable (167). Other popular series, such as *Khooni Dracula*, by Diamond Comics, also make a compelling example of Dracula's characterization in India. Within Indian horror cinema, too, the Count has had a powerful presence in films ranging from *Bandh Darwaaza* to *Dracula Sir*. Hence, if Stoker's nefarious Count perhaps shares an Indian ancestry, he is also palpably different from his Indian avatar. Naturally, such complicated ontologies of Stoker's Count engender stimulating classroom conversations.

The Psychology of Horror

Lovecraft famously remarked that "[t]he oldest and the strongest emotion of mankind is fear" (12). Responding to the disdain that "didactic literature" bears toward horror, Lovecraft claimed that "in spite of all this opposition the weird tale has survived, developed, and attained remarkable heights" (12), a telling statement on the universality of fear as an emotion. Later, Todorov posited that "the fantastic [or the horrific] is based essentially on the hesitation of a reader—a reader who identifies with the chief character—as to the nature of an uncanny event" (157). Such interpretations of fear as an emotion are integral to my classroom discussions, where young minds devoted to the study of science and technology are uneasy with the prospect of granting supernatural horror—which often lacks a rational explanation—credibility. I therefore draw upon psychological theories that define fear as an evolutionary concept that helps humanity cope with the ultimate threat or the death threat.

Humanity's greatest fear, according to Dennis L. White, is largely associated with a need for safety or an "integrity" that when "violated" becomes "a threat to our ego's ability to protect itself" (9). More recently, Carrol L. Fry tells us that "the adaptive behaviors that enabled survival of our primal ancestors—such as territoriality, tribalism, mating, fear of the predator, assimilation and distrust or hatred of the Other—remain in *Homo sapiens'* genetic inheritance and whisper to us today, influencing our response to timeless narratives [of fear and horror] embedded in film and fiction" (9). Representing everything that is uncanny, evil, and threatens our well-being, Count Dracula thus remains undead in our imagination. Since the Count is one who, according to Dr. Abraham Van Helsing (the Dutch physician turned vampire slayer), "cannot die by mere passing of time" (Stoker, *Dracula* 224), he outlives death and is all-powerful. In fact, we know that the Count is omnipresent, since "[i]n old Greece, in old Rome; he flourish in Germany all over, in France, in India, even in the Chersonese; and in China, so far from us in all ways, there even is he . . ." (223). He therefore becomes a symbol of the ultimate threat that stupefies mere mortals. And in trying to save both Great Britain and its women from the Count, Van Helsing, Jonathan Harker, and their troupe attest to the Jungian understanding of the "heroic element," whose purpose is to safeguard itself from the "world of the living dead, or unconscious" (Perlman 104–05). Arguably, then, Count Dracula, with his need to kill and control along with his immortality, his immense wealth, and his ability to threaten Victorian masculinity and to promote gender fluidity, stokes the deepest unconscious fears of human civilization. It is for this reason that while *Dracula* makes a "Christian allegory of the fight between the Good and the Anti-Christ" (91), the Count also embodies human powers and failings that resonate deeply with humanity's lived experiences. And it is for transcending the binaries of good and evil that *Dracula* continues to be one of the greatest symbols in imaginative art's response to human limitations as well as human fear.

Colonial Anxieties

While teaching *Dracula* I often find students willing to explore how this classic relates to their own identity and cultural history. Since postmillennial Indian identities are deeply rooted in a period of colonial rule stretching from the eighteenth to the twentieth centuries, a discussion on colonial politics and race in *Dracula* finds enormous relevance in classrooms. For this, I draw attention to how horror relates to colonial discourses and hence to postcolonial subjects. I begin by outlining how in *Dracula* an Englishman outwits "Dracula's stronghold of terrors" to finally defeat "the dead fiend's plot for domination" (Lovecraft 78) and progress to issues of "reverse colonization" or "responses to cultural guilt" (Arata, "Occidental Tourist" 623). Here, I also refer to the novel's imperialist Victorian project, which itself was in a process of decay when Stoker crafted his magnum opus. I bolster such claims with the help of the fact that much of "[l]ate-Victorian fiction," including *Dracula*, reveals an anxiety of "irretrievable decline" (622) where British culture and its global political hegemony were concerned. I further the analogy between the Count's and Victorian England's devastating imperialistic missions by underscoring the fact that, like the decaying Carpathians over which the Count reigns, colonies such as India and Africa lay in ruins and suffered enormous decay and displacement, over which Queen Victoria reigned. In addition, I suggest that since the Count is recursively represented as a warrior and a bloodsucking monster, his depiction implicitly forges deep connections between race and the aggressive practices of the colonial masters.

Discussions on colonial anxieties and their manifestation through the vampire myth find greater relevance when we scrutinize how the Count embodies several mental and physical attributes that were hailed by the imperialist Englishmen themselves. Since Count Dracula is not only well read, dexterous, and clairvoyant but also healthy and virile, he exemplifies the kind of robustness that was viewed as an elemental trait of the imperial master. Ironically, however, Stoker demonstrates that if the Count's powers "invigorate [his] victim[s]" (Arata 631), they ultimately enslave and destroy them, much like the forces of colonialism. Clearly, this helps us view the Count as "the most 'Western' character in the novel" (636), whose powers and charisma mimic those of the white imperialists who held the colonized in thrall while also deeply exploiting them. At this juncture, we also discuss how the Count becomes Jonathan Harker's gothic double and turns concepts of white rationality and morality on their head. We therefore conclude that by investing the monstrous figure of the Count with all the qualities the British used to establish their racial supremacy, and by attributing to him plans and motives akin to those of the colonialists, Stoker deftly deconstructs the racial pride that lay at the heart of the imperialist mission.

Similar interpretations of *Dracula* that powerfully undercut the supremacy of the colonial enterprise emerge in discussions on colonial anxieties and the concept of the grotesque as represented in the novel. Since Count Dracula confounds with his "striking Englishness and modernity," his similarities to the British imperialists are redolent of "Homi Bhabha's notion of mimicry" (Yu 163). In fact, we note how in Count Dracula, Stoker creates an uncanny sameness between the colonizer and his colonized subject, or what Robert Young describes as "[t]he mimic man," a double in whom "the colonizer sees a grotesquely displaced image of himself" (qtd. in Yu 163). *Dracula*, I therefore argue, makes possible a subversive narrative in which monstrosity in all its grotesqueness is associated with the racial pride of the white master. Such readings of *Dracula* find enormous relevance in contemporary postcolonial classrooms, which are keenly perceptive of globally dominant Eurocentric beliefs that continue to treat the oriental other as a lesser or even a disgusting being. Since

80   POSTMILLENNIAL INDIAN CLASSROOM

endless instances of racial hatred across Europe and North America continue, rereading *Dracula* through a postcolonial lens helps unearth the monstrosity inherent in the white world's racist tendencies, prevalent even to this day.

Postcolonial interpretations of *Dracula* are further instantiated by discussing how if the Count disgusts Victorians as "an anti-British, occultly communicative, and Oriental villain" (Galvan 436), he in many ways resembles the Indian Revolt of 1857–58, which, Jill Galvan claims, was similarly loathed by the British. History tells us that it was the Revolt of 1857 that more than any other event exposed the fragility of Britain's imperialistic powers both at home and abroad. Discourses on both racial hatred and political unrest during Britain's colonial rule therefore find manifestation in the oriental dwelling and the persona of the Count. This discussion is carried forward when we examine how Stoker's narrative refers to a white male project to save the unguarded and the vulnerable feminine, Mina Harker, which in reality may be compared with the imperialist project of purportedly saving India from the natives in the Revolt of 1857. While such arguments effectively locate *Dracula* within a postcolonial debate, they also make it a compelling narrative for Indians, whose nation is still fighting hard to find its rightful place within a globalized yet Eurocentric world. Like Joseph Conrad, who in *Heart of Darkness*, published just two years before *Dracula*, facilitates an understanding of the deep and malicious ambivalences at the heart of the colonial project with Kurtz's famous line "The horror! The horror!" (123), Stoker, too, either by design or even inadvertently, exposes the terrible exploits of white imperialists by reversing the colonial gaze and granting his nefarious monster traits and powers that are synonymous with the grand narrative of the colonial mission.

Victorian Oppressions and Horrors of the Body

Once the Orient-Occident debate in *Dracula* surfaces, the masculine-feminine and sexuality-spirituality binaries cannot be far behind. Naturally, the discursive paradigms manifested by the horrors of colonization provide an appropriate platform to initiate an analysis of gender, class, and sexuality in Stoker's novel. My classroom conversations on *Dracula* therefore examine how when a wealthy Transylvanian patriarch seduces his "chaste" English female victims with an aim to take control of their land, he exposes the fear of unbridled sexuality that lurked behind veneers of civility in a deeply gendered Victorian world. One of the most significant interpretations of this can be observed in the fact that "only relations with vampires are sexualized in the novel" and that all other romantic heterosexual relationships "are spiritualized beyond credibility" (Roth, "Suddenly Sexual Women" 545). In fact, Stoker's novel subverts the facade of civility that governed Victorian customs, including the repression of sexuality for its connotations of original sin.

Since Victorian imperialism carried forward its message of sexual taboos and prudery to all its colonies, the problem of repressed sexuality in *Dracula* becomes an especially significant thematic for Indian students, who are aware that theirs was a profoundly liberal and sexually permissive culture before the arrival of the Islamic and the British rulers. Hence, in my discussions on repressed sexuality in *Dracula* I point out not only the "Oedipal rivalry" (Roth, "Suddenly Sexual Women" 546) between the Count and Dr. Van Helsing's men in the fight over Mina but also the threat to Victorian patriarchy posed by women such as Lucy and Mina—who are enamored of the Count. Not surprisingly, a sexualized Lucy is decimated, and Mina, once "corrupted," must be made "chaste" again. Stoker's novel ends with "the 'salvation' of Mina" to prove that women's sexuality uncontrolled by Victorian men and morals needed to be exorcised because it "threaten[ed]" all Englishmen (Roth, "Suddenly Sexual Women" 552). Such discussions prove that frank sexuality, especially when it was female sexuality, was viewed as a monstrous concept by Victorians, who abhorred it just as they abhorred the racial other.

We further note how in the Carpathians, the Count's is a sexually permissive world that challenges and undermines Victorian culture, where sexuality in all its natural frankness is grotesque; it is a threat. Hence, only the vampire women in Dracula's castle can afford sexual hunger, which among Englishwomen is unacceptable. Such sexual appetite was often associated with uncivilized natives, reprimanding and cleansing whom was often the moral duty of the white imperialist. Since to the Victorians, "only fallen . . . women enjoyed sex," and since the three women in Dracula's palace appear as "'ladies by their dress and manner'" (Demetrakopoulos 106), they craft the concept of a sexualized white lady who deeply destabilizes all notions of Victorian piety. Naturally, it is only by overcoming them that Jonathan Harker proves himself to be a true knight, whom Dr. Van Helsing sets on a mission. Sexuality is thus attributed to the realm of the grotesque, and the Count's fluid sexuality or his desire to seduce "pious" white women becomes an extreme form of perversion to prudish Victorians. Hence, in killing Dracula's "unchaste" brides and later Lucy, Van Helsing and his troupe are curiously suggestive of the "knights of the Round Table," who "by driving a stake through [the] heart[s]" (Demetrakopoulos 108) of "impure" women fulfil their sacred phallic and nationalistic duties. Not surprisingly, Jonathan Harker, before embarking upon exorcising the "corrupting" Count, claims in a patronizing tone that he is very "glad that [Mina] consented to hold back and let [the] men do the work" despite the fact that "it is due to her energy and brains and foresight that the whole story is put together" (231). And once this is accomplished, the white men are made secure by regaining control of their land along with the minds and bodies of "their" women. *Dracula*, then, above all profoundly critiques the maladjusted Victorian world corrupted by racist and sexist practices. Remarkably, one finds that in its imperialist mission, Great Britain often unapologetically laid claim to women from colonized territories much like Stoker's predatory Count. Ironically, however, decimating sexual predatoriness is a mission that white men in Stoker's novel appropriate as their sacred duty. *Dracula* therefore exposes how the Victorians perpetuated a

82 POSTMILLENNIAL INDIAN CLASSROOM

duplicitous culture of political annexation and sexual repression not only within Britain's domestic confines but also across its colonies. Such insights resonate deeply with contemporary readers, especially postcolonial readers, and provide new meanings and contexts to their political, ethnic, and gendered identities.

Humanity continues to be fascinated by horror. The popularity of recent films (from *The Conjuring* and *The Invisible Man* to Indian films such as *Bhoot* [*Ghost*]), television shows, web series (from *American Horror Story* and *Castle Rock* to Indian series such as *Tumbbad* and *Ghoul*), video games (from *Resident Evil* to *Visage*), and the like across the world testifies to this fact. This is because figures of horror speak to our most intimate selves and mirror our deepest fears, reminding us of dormant unconscious passions and desires, repressed by civilizational constraints. In transgressing the boundaries that hegemonic culture so powerfully erects, horrific figures simultaneously represent for us anarchy and liberty, which is why horror repulses us as much at it attracts. Hence, stories of Baital or Dracula, ghosts and goblins, or *bhoots* and *chudails* ("evil female spirits") make us willingly suspend disbelief to attain a vicarious pleasure in reading or viewing that is as shocking as it is enticing.

Teaching Stoker's *Dracula* to postmillennial Indian students is a profoundly thought-provoking experience. As my class's skepticism gradually but surely gives way to passionate engagement with Stoker's classic, I experience the satisfaction of awakening their curiosity and interest. I find that students use this tale to examine normative customs and explore how horror and horrific characters facilitate subversive interpretations of our cultural constructs—interpretations they can employ to make meaning of their postcolonial identities and power divisions across the world. *Dracula* thus helps me reiterate to my students that fear and horror, perhaps the most poignant of human emotions, are not meant merely to thrill but are also potent springboards for questioning and subverting the very conditions that engender them.

MEDICINE

Nervous Systems: *Dracula* and Fin-de-Siècle Gender Trouble

Elizabeth Way

> Why can't they let a girl marry three men, or as many as
> want her, and save all this trouble?
>> —*Bram Stoker,* Dracula

"A brave man's blood is the best thing on this earth when a woman is in trouble. You're a man, and no mistake. . . . God sends us men when we want them" affirms Professor Van Helsing, relieved that the very stalwart Quincey Morris appears just in time to offer Lucy Westenra her fourth blood transfusion in ten days (Stoker, *Dracula* 146). Perhaps the professor doth protest too much? Van Helsing's absolute confirmation of Quincey Morris's manhood is a validation that gets repeated numerous times—indeed obsessively—throughout the novel and applied to all members of the "Crew of Light" (Craft, "Kiss Me" 109). Why do Bram Stoker's male characters continually fixate on their manhood in a novel where Dracula, the undead, bloodsucking predator, is clearly the main source of horror? Or is he? These questions and more often trouble discussions in the undergraduate courses in which I teach *Dracula*, including my first-year seminar on the science of nineteenth-century gothic fiction, my introduction to British studies course, and a gothic course for Wake Forest University's Lifelong Learning Program. Indeed, Stoker's novel deftly shape-shifts for all levels of academic instruction. As Nina Auerbach incisively reminds us in *Our Vampires, Ourselves*, "Because [vampires] are always changing, their appeal is dramatically generational" (5).

At the time of Stoker's publication of *Dracula*, fin-de-siècle England was experiencing a crisis of masculinity and femininity. Many events contributed to this matrix of nervousness: the women's rights movement, the emergence of the New Woman figure along with the rise of the male dandy, the homosexual panic connected with the 1885 Labouchère Amendment defining homosexual men as deviant, and the 1895 trials of Oscar Wilde. A rise in professionalism

84   FIN-DE-SIÈCLE GENDER TROUBLE

among men as well as new scientific studies of the mind and male and female criminality presented new arenas for measuring the quality and quantity of one's sex and gender. Can a lawyer be as masculine as a soldier? Is it possible for a medical doctor to possess as much brawn as a butcher? And what about the New Woman's appetites? How do sex and gender inflect criminality? Enter into such a perfect storm of gender trouble Stoker's *Dracula* as a significant source of nightmarish horror on the fragility of sex and gender in fin-de-siècle England.

My main aim in this essay is to suggest some strategies by which students can connect gender anxieties in fin-de-siècle England to several familiar gothic trappings and identify them as major bases of fear in the most famous vampire story of them all. By examining the role of gender norms of the time in the context of contemporary medical discourse and procedures and sexual mores, I strive to show students how to recognize and appreciate threats of gender inversion portrayed as central causes of dread in *Dracula*. My approach is primarily historical. Understanding the context in which *Dracula* was written is key to solid, nuanced literary analyses. We therefore read selections from works by eighteenth- and nineteenth-century scientists, physicians, psychologists, psychiatrists, and others. But, while my entry point is to think about how contemporary science inflects these works in very direct and pervasive ways, I also stress studying other epistemological sources in gothic fiction, like narrative form, technology, religion, imperialism, and gender and sexuality. In doing so, I hope to show how *Dracula* presents readers with the gender troubles of fin-de-siècle England as important expressions of angst in this novel. For the purposes and scope of this essay, I focus on science, sexuality, and gender norms in late-nineteenth-century England.

In the undergraduate courses I describe above, students have read and discussed Mary Shelley's *Frankenstein* and Robert Louis Stevenson's *Strange Case of Dr. Jekyll and Mr. Hyde* by the time we get to *Dracula*. So they are familiar with some key gothic features, including the mad scientist, doppelgängers, haunted dwellings, the epistolary novel form, monstrous or spectral others, and modern, urban settings replacing the "long ago and far away" scenes of earlier gothic novels. I usually convey this information through lectures, slides, and handouts. We read *Dracula* after four to five weeks of lectures, discussions, blog posts, and informal oral presentations on the gothic and nineteenth-century science. Therefore, students have a solid foundation with which to approach these topics in *Dracula*. I group these three gothic novels by Shelley, Stevenson, and Stoker under the subheading "The Science of Nineteenth-Century Gothic Fiction." In an introductory lecture on vampires through the ages, we trace the undead from the *strigoi* of early Romanian mythology and Vlad Ţepeş through the rise of the British vampire stories of the nineteenth century to Bela Lugosi's iconic debut as Dracula in Tod Browning's 1931 film, which set the standard for almost all vampire portrayals thenceforth, and different incarnations of the vampire in TV, books, and film into the twenty-first century. When I ask students, at the end of this lecture, if vampires are real, after a few moments of nervous smiles and shuffling about in chairs, they seem fairly relieved to hear the definitive "no" from me on this topic. But their hesitancy to confirm or deny the existence of vampires leads into a discussion of how science has sought to explain seeming vampiric activity. Some instances of such activity have been attributed to cases of premature burial or to the effects of human decomposition or of diseases such as tuberculosis, the bubonic plague, porphyria, and rabies, which can give the appearance of signs of vampirism. And yet my students' uncertainty persists. This discussion prepares students for considering how challenging it was for the Crew of Light—especially Dr. John Seward—to find hard evidence either way. As Van Helsing asserts, "Ah, it is the fault of our science that it wants to explain all; and if it explain it not, then it says there is nothing to explain" (Stoker, *Dracula* 182). In order to tie the gender trouble of fin-de-siècle England as portrayed in *Dracula* to the science of its day, I organize our classes into sessions using the trope of nervous systems. First, we consider English society's nervous systems about sex and gender and how we see those appearing in the novel. Next, we move into readings about male and female nervous systems, how blood transfusions are nervously tied to gender in the novel, and how deviant behavior is classified by sex by some key scientists of the period.

Dracula provides a wealth of examples of social anxieties regarding masculinity and femininity—a kind of nervous system of sex and gender haunting the novel. Students first notice this in the opening chapters of Jonathan Harker's travel diary, which are written in Transylvania. The first near-vamping scene involving Harker and the three female vampires exhibits "a displacement typical both of this text and the gender-anxious culture from which it arose" (Craft, "Kiss Me" 110). More horrific, however, is Dracula's declared intention to vamp Harker at some unspecified future time. Ultimately, Harker fears being unsexed by such an encounter, whether it be by a male or female vampire. Before attempting to escape Castle Dracula, then, Harker cries, "At least God's mercy is better than that of these monsters, and the precipice is steep and high. At its foot a man may sleep—as a man" (Stoker, *Dracula* 60). Harker's avowal that he would prefer death to being vamped because it would preserve his manhood inaugurates similar proclamations from other men in the novel when faced with the specter of emasculation from Dracula's vamping. Later in the novel, the captain of the cryptically named ship transporting Dracula in his boxes of earth, *Demeter*, exclaims, "[I]n the dimness of the night I saw It—Him! God forgive me, but the mate was right to jump overboard. It is better to die like a man; to die like a sailor in blue water no man can object" (90). From here, students begin to find, because they are now looking for them, many instances in *Dracula* of men crying, fainting, feeling weak, turning pale, and being emotional. These moments, however, are kept in check by the repeated affirmations that these characters' manhood is overwhelmingly apparent. Fire in the eyes, flaring nostrils, stalwart corporeality, and an iron nerve—all these images and more saturate the text. So much repetition of descriptors like these

86   FIN-DE-SIÈCLE GENDER TROUBLE

throughout the novel reveals one of the main roots of anxiety in *Dracula*: the shadowy menace of gender trouble that at times seems more sinister than the threat of the undead.

Students also notice the men's fears of overly sexual and intelligent women in the novel. Mina has a "man's brain—a brain that a man should have were he much gifted—and woman's heart" (220). Van Helsing's compliment pushes the boundary of separate spheres for Victorian men and women but ultimately reaffirms Mina's femininity by concluding with an assessment of her heart. This makes clear what Mina's most important quality is: her nurturing, caring heart. Mina seems to most resemble John Ruskin's queen from his "Of Queens' Gardens": "her intellect is not for invention or creation, but for sweet ordering, arrangement and decision. . . . She must be enduringly, incorruptibly good; instinctively, infallibly wise—wise, not for self-development, but for self-renunciation: wise not that she may set herself above her husband, but that she may never fail from his side" (Ruskin 77, 159). With such impossible standards, could any woman other than Wilhelmina Murray Harker succeed? It seems unlikely. This contemporary concept of the ideal woman parallels the excessive pronouncements of manhood in the novel. *Dracula* appears in the heyday of the New Woman figure, and though Mina scoffs at the phenomenon (Stoker, *Dracula* 93, 94), she displays many of the New Woman's characteristics, being intelligent, autonomous, industrious, and composed. But Stoker limits her to these less threatening traits and aligns her capabilities as supporting her husband rather than seeking to be superior to him. On the other end of the spectrum from Ruskin's queen, Lucy blatantly asserts her sexual desire. After three marriage proposals in the same day, Lucy Westenra muses, "Why can't they let a girl marry three men, or as many as want her, and save all this trouble? But this is heresy and I must not say it" (65). This unabashed confession of her desire to be wife and sexual partner for three or more men at once crosses a line of what the chaste Victorian woman is expected to express, much less actually feel. She reins in her statement, however, as "heresy," thus defusing its power. My students almost immediately ask what Lucy could possibly have been doing leading up to this moment to convince three men to propose marriage to her. Curiously, Lucy's expressions of desire for each man do not appear in the text; unspeakable and threatening to status quo gender norms, such scenes contradict expectations for women to be docile, weak, obedient, and sexually repressed. Ultimately, Lucy seems more like Cesare Lombroso and William Ferrero's female criminal—more on that in the next section.

The term *New Woman*, potentially suggesting an "evolutionary mutation" (Skal, Preface xi) in a Darwinian world, was coined by the Irish writer Sarah Grand in an 1894 article for the *North American Review* entitled "The New Aspect of the Woman Question." I assign her article as well as Ouida's response, "The New Woman," from a later issue of the same journal. Students are surprised to find that these two articles have as much or more to say about the failure of the man in the domestic sphere and his diminishing masculinity as about the New Woman's characteristics. In the *Punch* cartoon "The Sterner Sex!," two women debate the attractiveness of male attire. On the right, a woman holding a tennis racket is dressed in a traditional female hat, blouse, and skirt. When the woman on the left, in a man's hat and jacket, asks her friend if she likes her outfit, the friend responds, "It makes you look like a Young Man, you know, and that's so effeminate!" *Punch*'s cartoon prompts the question of which woman represents the sterner sex: the woman on the left, in her male garments, or her friend, offering the gender critique with tennis racquet in hand? Lively discussion among my students ensues and usually ends with no clear winner. Spotlighting tennis as one of the common sports women played at this time, the cartoon prompts students to recall that Lucy plays tennis with Arthur (Stoker, *Dracula* 109) as part of their courtship. Tennis was a fashionable recreation for the upper class in which it was nevertheless important for women not to seem too athletic, too competitive, too male. This is gender trouble indeed.

Moving on to actual human nervous systems inaugurates our discussions on medicine and gender anxieties in the novel. To begin, students read selections from Thomas Laycock's *Mind and Brain* that affirm differences in nervous systems based on sex: "Woman, as compared with man, is of the nervous temperament. Her nervous system is therefore more easily acted upon by all impressions, and more liable to all diseases of excitement" (317). Essentializing and pathologizing the female body, Laycock asserts that this susceptibility is related to women's "natural sensibility" (317)—that is, to sexual differences that appear naturally in women. Imputing sex-related inferiorities to women's blood raises issues of health but also degeneration once Van Helsing starts Lucy's several blood transfusions. Victorian social mores influence the blood transfusions performed on Lucy. In the nineteenth century, an exchange of bodily fluids was seen as a sexualized act; therefore, a spouse, or, as in Arthur's case, a fiancé, was usually chosen as the blood donor. To give my students perspective, I inform them that James Blundell, an obstetrician at the United Hospitals of Saint Thomas and Guy, performed the first human-to-human blood transfusion in 1818, using a syringe to transfer blood from husband to wife to treat a post-labor hemorrhage (Blundell, "Successful Case" 431–32). The sketch of a blood transfusion procedure using Blundell's Gravitator in "Observations on the Transfusion of Blood, with a Description of His Gravitator" in *The Lancet* portrays the scene Stoker's readers would most likely have imagined when reading about transfusions in the novel (321). The man stands at the woman's bedside with his muscular arm extended confidently outward at shoulder level, his fist clenched, and the Gravitator's needle inserted in the crook of his arm. He watches as his blood flows down through a tube into an intravenous line in the woman's arm resting on the bed; she, however, turns her head away from the procedure. Believing that men's blood was richer and flowed more freely than women's and that men were less likely to faint, physicians preferred men as donors, thus further

88   FIN-DE-SIÈCLE GENDER TROUBLE

pathologizing the female body according to assumptions of sexual difference (McLoughlin 506). Given a lack of knowledge about blood types in 1895 when *Dracula* was published—Karl Landsteiner would not discover different blood types until 1900—who is to say that the mixing of blood from the many men who tried to save Lucy—an act that could be construed as promiscuous given the sexual connotations of transfusion—might not have inadvertently contributed to her decline? With regard to the sexual implications of transfusions from multiple donors, we consider whether this medical practice guided by gender norms would have seemed more or less horrifying than Dracula's terrors in the light of the gender anxieties and sexual mores of Stoker's time. The concealment from Arthur of the fact that four different men give their blood to Lucy is evidence of the transgression suggested by the procedure (Stoker, *Dracula* 128). Students articulate the further disgust of the sexual double standard involved: the men are allowed to feel pleasure from donating blood to Lucy, while the condemning portrayal and brutal treatment of Lucy once she is undead are justified as her "purification" from such pleasurable sexuality. Finally, it can be suggested that Dracula, in receiving all the men's blood from Lucy, in this way has vamped them as well.

In order to contextualize Victorian ideas of gender and criminality, I assign selections from Lombroso and Ferrero's *The Female Offender* to consider the ways that Lucy, an unwitting victim of Dracula's vamping, resembles their description of blameworthy female criminals and "lunatics":

> We see, then, that another characteristic of the female lunatic, and consequently of the criminal lunatic, is an exaggeration of the sexual instincts. These which in male lunatics are almost always in abeyance, lead in women, even in very old women as in quite young girls, to the most disgusting and unnatural excesses. . . . Nymphomania transforms the most timid girl into a shameless bacchante. She tries to attract every man she sees, displaying sometimes violence, and sometimes the most refined coquetry. She often suffers from intense thirst, a dry mouth, a fetid breath, and a tendency to bite everybody she meets . . .
>
> (Lombroso and Ferrero 295–96)

This description mirrors the depiction of Lucy in the graveyard once she has become a vampire. *The Female Offender* remained the primary source on female criminals well into the twentieth century. While the female criminal's wantonness is the most damning of Lucy's traits in the eyes of the Crew of Light, her dark hair is another common characteristic of female criminals in Lombroso and Ferrero's study (70). Many students ask why Mina does not turn out the same way after Dracula vamps her. Moreover, if Lucy is the "bad" girl in the text, why does Mina have to get vamped? It becomes clear at this point that Stoker presents Mina undeniably as a sympathetic figure—Jonathan even says he would follow her into vampirism if it comes to that (Stoker, *Dracula* 274), which is not at all Arthur's reaction when Lucy morphs into a vampire—far from it.

In terms of the men, we discuss the uncanny resemblances between the Crew of Light and Dracula: intense hatred, criminal activity (breaking and entering and bribery, for starters), savage delight at the prospect of murder, and more. For this, we turn to Gina Lombroso-Ferrero's *Criminal Man, according to the Classification of Cesare Lombroso* (Stoker read Cesare Lombroso's original text in the French translation, *L'homme criminel*, in 1895) and Max Nordau's *Degeneration*, key texts of the era. Nordau defines degeneration as *"a morbid deviation from an original type"* (16). Van Helsing and Mina reference Lombroso and Nordau in their appraisal of Dracula as fitting these descriptions of criminals (Stoker, *Dracula* 312–14). After reading some excerpts from these two texts (Lombroso-Ferrero xiv–xv, 135–36; Nordau 5–19), students quickly point out the similarities between the criminals discussed therein and the Crew of Light. Does fighting against the deadliest vampire of them all exonerate the Crew of Light of their own criminal actions? Students hold lively debates on this issue, and having Nordau's and Lombroso's texts on hand offers yet another way of connecting *Dracula*'s pervasive motif of dread to sex, gender, and science of the fin de siècle.

Dracula is a novel of horrors. The immense amount of blood lost, shed, given, and circulated stands out as one of its ghastlier features. Even Jonathan and Mina's son, whose "bundle of names links all [their] little band of men together" (Stoker, *Dracula* 344), hypothetically possesses the blood of all members of the Crew of Light circulating within him since Mina was forced to drink Dracula's blood, which contained that of all the men who gave their blood to Lucy. Our class discussions conclude that by the end, obtaining proofs of identifiable, conventional masculinity and femininity in Stoker's novel rivals the quest for obtaining proof that vampires exist and guaranteed means of killing them. Like so many other gothic novels, Dracula reflects the pulse of the times—both then and now, Auerbach would say. By considering the ways that the nervous systems of fin-de-siècle England pose their own villainy in *Dracula*, we are reminded that many times the real person next door can evoke more dread than the imagined monster hiding under the bed. *Dracula* thus invites us to reconsider what is most horrifying in the most famous vampire story of them all—the undead, Victorian science and medicine, or gender norms? The academic classroom provides a vital space for considering such questions. Ultimately, *Dracula* becomes a text in which gender is clearly and at times devastatingly created by "the political and cultural intersections in which it is invariably produced and maintained" (Butler 4–5).

Contagion and Otherness:
Dracula in the Age of COVID-19

Ess Pokornowski

Well before COVID-19, I found *Dracula* a helpful book in teaching lower-division literature and first-year writing courses; however, the book has a reinvigorated relevance in the context of the pandemic. The novel lends itself to lower-division writing and literature courses: it invites readings from a variety of critical perspectives, and the key themes and topics parallel major contemporary issues. In the first section of this essay, I explain my approach to teaching *Dracula* in relation to contagion and otherness. In the second part, I outline pedagogical changes I made in response to pandemic remote teaching and my approach to an equity-minded pedagogy of care. The third section provides a brief overview of some of the interdisciplinary lenses I use to frame the text, and the final section provides assignment suggestions.

Over the last decade, I've taught *Dracula* at four institutions with widely varying demographics: the University of California, Santa Barbara; Rio Hondo College; Whittier College; and, most recently, two differently diverse programs at the University of Michigan, Ann Arbor. These represent major research institutions, a majority Latinx community college, and a Hispanic-Serving / Asian American and Native American Pacific Islander–Serving Institution.

In all these contexts, approaches to *Dracula* that addressed the way contagion intersected with social injustice were well received, but students came with unevenly equipped vocabularies to discuss issues of race, sex, gender, and justice. To remedy this, the first activities of the course are designed to help students contextualize personal experiences within broader social phenomena, which allows us to build a critical vocabulary together. By the time students engage directly with critical race theory and postcolonial theory, for example, many are invested in expanding their critical vocabularies and eager to think about structural and systemic issues.

Dracula *and the Contagion of Pervasive Otherness*

Before the pandemic, it was easy to overlook just how relevant *Dracula* is to the contemporary moment. The novel takes place at the knife's edge of modernity. Published in 1897, the text foregrounds then-cutting-edge technologies—wax cylinder phonography, blood transfusions, long-distance telegraphy—as essential to the heroes' triumph over the Count. At first, this treatment contributes to a sense of the book as ancient, what with all the journal entries, letters, telegrams, and Seward's antiquated recordings. The novelty with which the book handles mundane, and downright dated, concepts stands out to students: blood transfusion is new and risky, modern psychology is a fledgling discipline, and the verbiage of debates over the "New Woman" and those with "sexual inversion" seems laughable and offensive to many contemporary readers. If we juxtapose that historical setting with our own, though, it becomes uncomfortably ripe. Consider the parallels: the rise of modern telecommunications and digital culture, the emergence of genetic medicine, and the recurring cultural conflicts over issues of sex, gender, and sexuality. It can be striking to read those journal entries, letters, telegrams, and recordings in dialogue with our own blogs, vlogs, emails, instas, TikToks, tweets, DMs, and texts. While the technologies and ideas in *Dracula* themselves may seem dated and require translation, the anxieties of the text are even more familiar: the criminological, the eugenic, the xenophobic, the sexual. As I teach it, the heart of the text is less a story of "good versus evil" and more a study in how hegemonic sociocultural values spur othering and mark difference as deviance.

This reading of the novel is inspired by four key texts. The first are two extremely influential articles from the 1990s: Stephen D. Arata's "The Occidental Tourist: *Dracula* and the Anxiety of Reverse Colonization" and Jack Halberstam's "Technologies of Monstrosity." These studies emphasize, respectively, *Dracula* as a narrative focused on late Victorian fears of reverse colonization and the Count's embodiment of a racial, sexual, and gendered alterity that threatens Victorian norms. Along those lines, I see *Dracula* as a novel that blends two popular late-nineteenth-century narratives: the outbreak and invasion (or reverse colonization). I bring these readings of *Dracula* into dialogue with two books from the 2010s to deepen our understanding of the connections between race, xenophobia, the history of coloniality, and contemporary biopolitics and biosecurity: Mel Y. Chen's *Animacies* and Neel Ahuja's *Bioinsecurities*.

Chen chronicles how affective hierarchies of animacy—"described variously as a quality of agency, awareness, mobility, and liveness"—are at play in recent major cultural debates about sexuality, race, and affect (2). Furthermore, Chen explains that examining animacy thusly "helps us theorize current anxieties around the production of humanness" (3). For Chen, then, a critical examination of affective hierarchies reveals the ways in which sexuality, race, affect, and disability are entangled with the ways that we imagine, define, and produce humanness.

Ahuja focuses on the connection between disease intervention and imperial politics, and the preface is particularly useful in thinking about *Dracula*. There, Ahuja explains that the titular play of "bioinsecurities" captures how "imperial states extend tentacles of intervention into varied domains of life in order to displace the crises of reproduction and legitimacy they inevitably generate" (vii). Put more simply, the "book is about how disease outbreaks, medical technologies, and the relations between humans, animals, bacteria, and viruses galvanized racialized fears and hopes that determined the geopolitical form of US empire" (ix). As Chen demonstrates how ideas of humanness are shaped by

92   CONTAGION AND OTHERNESS

sexuality, race, and disability through affective hierarchies of liveliness, Ahuja demonstrates how structural relations related to adaptability, risk, and medicine shaped the racialized anxieties and hopes that drove empire. What is *Dracula* about if not the limits of the human and the racialized, sexualized, gendered, and abled anxieties of empire?

Taken together, Arata, Halberstam, Chen, and Ahuja ground a reading of the novel that dramatizes a threat that is at once biological or biomedical (Dracula carries the plague of vampirism) and imperial and political (he is vaguely angling to overthrow English power). And we might add to these four foundational texts Kirsten Ostherr's *Cinematic Prophylaxis* and Priscilla Wald's *Contagious: Cultures, Carriers, and the Outbreak Narrative*, which both foreground the roles of outbreak narratives and othering in policing and producing the social and political imaginary.

In other words, along with contemporaneous texts like H. G. Wells's short story "The Stolen Bacillus," Stoker's novel explores an emergent regime of bioinsecurities. Bioinsecurity serves as a core concept for my approach to teaching *Dracula*: the Count represents a threat to Western, white supremacist cisheteropatriarchal hegemony that is at once biomedical, social, and political. The international coalition of actors that clandestinely travels abroad to assassinate him therefore acts in the interest of the spiritual, medical, and social health of the world. Surely, the Count is no innocent victim, but the classic readings of "good and evil" become muddied when one reads his early monologue about Wallachia, race, blood, and war as an anti-imperial rebuke. This framing establishes a unifying set of themes woven through the novel about empire, hegemony, otherness, and disease intervention and maps how social, political, and medical discourses intertwine to defend the norm and sanction violent intervention against contaminating deviance.

Equity-Minded Pedagogies of Radical Care

Once we have a salient reading of the inextricable connection between alterity and contagion in *Dracula* and a dynamic way to frame the text for students, how can we practice this reading protocol ethically in the midst of a global pandemic? The connections to contemporary debates about racial justice, police reform, disaster and pandemic preparedness, genetic editing and disabilities, gender and social norms, and xenophobic conspiracy theories that have plagued us throughout the pandemic are obvious to students. I've found that the challenge is not getting students to connect these with *Dracula* but rather doing so in ways that do not simply reproduce or entrench trauma.

With that in mind, I approached teaching *Dracula* during the pandemic with three new goals: to find ways to embrace the visual aspects of remote instruction, to emphasize and embrace the narrative's own "remote" technologies and media in the midst of a pandemic, and to make the experience accessible, manageable, and meaningful. The last of these proved conceptually challenging. To develop a remote pedagogy of care, I drew inspiration from (and incorporated into the course) readings that might first appear incongruous: essays from both Audrey Watters and Mai'a Williams.

Drawing on Watters's blog post and keynote "The Ed-Tech Imaginary," I thought about how my class might engage with technologies of surveillance and the ed-tech imaginary: how would "remote" instruction look, and how would I make sure it was student-driven and equity-minded? I wanted my class to operate on a "carrier bag theory" of remote education (Watters). That is, I wanted to offer a set of narratives or histories of the ways we conceive of "health" that was neither triumphal nor tragic but instead offered tools to build and sustain communities. In discussing the social construction of health, I often ask students to grapple with histories of medicine that critique white supremacist and patriarchal legacies. So, for example, in the unit before *Dracula*, we examine the "rest cure" as gendered medicine (Stiles), as racialized medicine (Briggs), and as a cultural phenomenon entangled with the policing of sex, gender, and sexuality (Gilman). The idea that legacies of social oppression have affected the way we understand and practice health and health care then runs throughout the course and serves as a neat preface for our reading of *Dracula*.

My courses rely heavily on intersectional histories and criticism. In my experience, this material initially shocks and outrages students, which can drive engagement. By semester's end, though, some students have reported feeling disheartened at the accumulation of historical oppressions. I reasoned that the pandemic would intensify these feelings, so, at the recommendation of a colleague, Anne Cong-Huyen, I turned to Black feminist theories of radical mothering to help my class envision liberatory histories and futures. I found Mai'a Williams's "Radical Mothering as Pathway to Liberation" especially helpful. It provided a hopeful counterpoint to the historical critiques of white supremacist, cisheteropatriarchal medicine that framed the course. It also inspired me to think about my own pedagogy in this pandemic as an opportunity to provide radical care: we were going to critique, but we were also going to build community and resilience through interdependence as discussants, learners, and colleagues.

As much as I value theory, I realize it is unactionable without concrete examples, so here are some of the ways I moved toward an equity-minded pedagogy of care:

> Deadlines became flexible as long as students communicated why more time was needed. This policy led to frequent extension requests; however, it also increased student dialogue and made it easier to identify distressed students.

> Each class began with organized opportunities for students to discuss their feelings. When these revealed the majority of the class to be tired or stressed, we course-corrected. These moments allowed students to see that stress and anxiety were shared experiences and respond communally.

94   CONTAGION AND OTHERNESS

> Students were organized into semester-long workshop groups and assigned weekly group workshop assignments. I converted one of our scheduled weekly meetings into an optional synchronous or asynchronous workshop, where students engaged in structured activities and discussions with their peers. I flipped this section of the class by providing framing content in advance. This allowed students in different time zones, students with demanding work schedules, and students with technological limitations more flexibility in collaborating with classmates and completing work.
>
> Students had regular check-ins with me by videoconference to discuss course progress and plan major assignments.
>
> In lieu of traditional lectures, to make content more digestible and entertaining in the remote context, I provided lecture content in five-to-fifteen-minute, podcast-style mini-lectures (with an accompanying script for accessibility purposes). This made content more accessible to students with visual or auditory impairments, attention deficit issues, or limited Internet access. Students frequently said they found this format engaging and entertaining.

This was, indeed, an extraordinary semester, but it made *Dracula* seem more relevant, more personal, and perhaps more troubling than ever before. The cultural saturation with contagion and the prevalence of medical professionals in public discourse sharpened student observations and highlighted the text's focus on discourses tied to medicine, monstrosity, and social norms. In the midst of all of this, our own focus on community, care, and interdependence stood in stark contrast.

Interdisciplinary Approaches to Dracula: *Overlapping Critical Lenses*

Above, I outlined how I use a focus on contagion, contamination, and otherness in reading *Dracula*; below, I explain how I focalize the text through a series of overlapping critical lenses. This method introduces students to interdisciplinary approaches to criticism; offers them opportunities to bring their own knowledge, interests, and expertise into the classroom; and subverts totalizing or generalizing readings of the text. While contagion, contamination, and otherness cut across the different critical perspectives and ground our analysis, how those terms are defined and what they look like shift as our critical lenses change. This creates a metacritical teaching opportunity to discuss how academic disciplines also discipline us. The way that otherness is defined or presented, the sociocultural boundaries it transgresses, and the hallmarks of its transmission appear differently from each of the different critical perspectives; however, all these ways of seeing help us understand how sociocultural values and prejudices are in coproduction with representations of fantastic monstrosity. In other words, we see how the characteristics that make the Count so monstrous are defined by his transgression of social and cultural norms. This parallax view offers glimpses of intersectionality without being prescriptive or heavy-handed; instead, students see for themselves how fantastic monstrosity, hegemonic social values, and representational violence are connected.

The critical lenses through which I teach *Dracula* are developed out of my own academic education and research, so this approach is a provocation rather than a prescription. I draw on texts from history of medicine, science and technology studies, postcolonial theory, critical race theory, queer theory, disability studies, and feminist and gender studies, to inform topical or thematic approaches to thinking about the text. Most recently, I focalized the text through four rough topics: social construction and the history of medicine, reverse colonization and bioinsecurities, theories of social contamination and degeneration, and technology, surveillance, and media. Below, I frame each critical lens in a brief paragraph. After that, I offer assignment suggestions.

Social Construction and the History of Medicine

This lens explores the social construction of health and the role of social values and norms in the history of defining, diagnosing, and treating illness. We draw on feminist histories of medicine and on disability studies to examine how our ideas about what constitutes health or illness are shaped by social norms and values. We also bring in information about how this influences medical care. Some relevant histories to explore include the history of "hysteria" and the racializing and gendering of mood disorders (Koerber, Briggs); "the rest cure" and inequitable, gendered, and racialized treatments at the turn of the twentieth century (Stiles; Briggs; Levine-Clark); the history of the doctor-patient relationship and the regendering of medicine through the history of its professionalization; shifting historical definitions and diagnoses regarding gender and sexual nonconformity (De Block and Adriaens); and the idea of the norm and the invention of disability (L. Davis). In *Dracula*, this approach deepens discussions of the Count's gender and class nonconformity; the hypersexualization of the vampire women; the social deviance of Lucy as the "bloofer lady" (Stoker, *Dracula* 170); the fraught complexity of Mina's role from a feminist perspective; and contemporary medical inequities tied to race, class, sex, gender, sexuality, and ability.

Reverse Colonization and Bioinsecurities

Drawing on postcolonial and decolonial readings of *Dracula* and contemporary scholarship on biopolitics and biosecurity, this lens recontextualizes the xenophobic play between East and West that occurs at the start of the novel (Arata). It also offers a more complex view of the Count's remarks about the pride of his race and his anti-imperialist motivations. Taken together alongside

96 CONTAGION AND OTHERNESS

contemporary biopolitical theory and discourse on biosecurity (Ahuja; Masco), this approach gives students language to discuss how lives are managed and valued differently by social grouping and how this connects to histories of empire, coloniality, and state racism and ableism.

Theories of Social Contamination and Degeneration

This lens is shaped by placing social theories from the late nineteenth and early twentieth centuries in dialogue with contemporary cultural criticism on disability, illness, and othering. In terms of historical social theory, we briefly engage with social Darwinism, phrenology, criminology, eugenics, and crowd theory, and we examine how these ideas codeveloped with social anxieties about the contamination of the national body with undesirable stock (Lombroso; Nordau; Le Bon; Harris; Kevles; Glover, "*Dracula*" and "*Vampires*"; Tomaszewska). This scaffolding supports our discussion of othering and the outbreak narrative (Ostherr; Wald) and the historical ties between eugenics, genetics, race, and ability (Kevles; Wailoo et al.). As a result, a different weight is added to the novel's physical descriptions of vampires—especially Jonathan Harker's early descriptions of Dracula and Van Helsing's explicit claim that "Nordau and Lombroso" would classify the Count as criminal, degenerate, and "of an imperfectly formed mind" (Stoker, *Dracula* 313). Dracula's assault on Mina and her self-described "corruption" can also be seen as triggering and traumatic. Queer theory and a historical look at the sociocultural stigmas around HIV can provoke compelling readings centered on sexuality, disease, and stigma.

Technology, Surveillance, and Media

Given the controversies surrounding privacy, surveillance, and user rights in relation to proctoring and videoconference technologies used in remote teaching (Hope; Harvard), this lens might most easily focus the book for students. It opens up an opportunity to engage with the history of technology and discuss wax cylinder home recording and phonography (Seward's dictation method), wireless telegraphy, and the multimodal textuality of the novel itself. From there, one might consider how technologies of transportation and communication allow the Count to infiltrate England but also enable the heroes to track the Count and coordinate to thwart him. Meanwhile, Mina's role as a medium or conduit to Dracula—and the attempts by both sides to manipulate that as a channel of surveillance—open up our discussions about media, technology, and surveillance and neatly combine with our considerations regarding transmission and contagion.

Assignment Suggestions

Below, I offer loose conceptual sketches for possible assignments. Like the heroes of Stoker's novel, I try to be flexible and adaptive and to take a multimodal, multimedia approach to assignment design. Critically exploring bioinsecurities and histories of oppression can be exhausting and depressing, so these assignments endeavor to empower students and to collaboratively build consensus and community.

Critical Juxtaposition

This assignment asks students to analyze a character or representation across texts by comparing and contrasting. Students critically analyze two different but related representations, one from the novel and one of their choosing; instructors can be as prescriptive, suggestive, or open-ended as they wish about what representations are fair game. The challenge, though, is that students cannot simply list evidence or compare and contrast features; rather, they have to devise a cohesive argument that addresses both representations. This gives students the freedom to explore representations across time and media but requires that they think analytically, argumentatively, and synthetically. So, for example, they might choose to look at the Count in *Dracula* and in the new *Netflix* series, or they might look at Mina from Stoker's novel and the Mina in *League of Extraordinary Gentlemen*.

Historicizing Ideas

This assignment involves students in the work of historicizing the text. First, it provides students with a list of technologies, theories, individuals, or concepts that are referenced in the novel—such as criminology, degeneration, miasma, telegraphy, blood transfusion, and *nosferatu*—then asks students to research, define, and historicize these terms. Such an approach works well as a group research and discussion exercise. It can also be an ongoing assignment that builds a collaborative set of keywords for understanding the text and can be adapted so the focus falls more on the practice of research or critical reading skills.

Scene Adaptation

This assignment uses creative writing strategies to help students connect with the text on a more individual and inventive level. It asks students to adapt a scene from Stoker's novel that they find particularly important by setting it in the present and then reflecting on what they've scripted. At minimum, students will make connections regarding technology and social norms. Many students will ask deeper questions about plot and character: What would happen, for example, if Seward ran a weekly psychology podcast or if Lucy were an *Instagram* influencer? The prompt should specify that students adapt a finite portion of the text and follow that with a critical reflection explaining what changes were made, why, and how those alter the tone, the themes, and even the plot arc.

Dracula and the Medical Humanities

William Hughes

Dracula is a novel preoccupied with learning. The titular Count—who is described as possessing a "child-brain," albeit one with both the time and the mental capacity to absorb knowledge (Stoker, *Dracula* 278)—invites Jonathan Harker to Transylvania as much to instruct his host in English manners and customs as to formally complete the legal transfer of a London property. Harker, crossing Europe by rail and stagecoach, struggles with languages imperfectly learned and demotic gestures hardly understood before comprehending that, in distant Romania, the past is not dead and its living conventions and causalities substantially shape and define the present. Harker's associates in England—a congeries of professional gentlemen-adventurers, supplemented by a token independent woman—must likewise come to contemplate that *their* ostensibly confident understanding of the modern world remains incomplete without a grasp of those discarded knowledges which have preceded current Western epistemology. A true polymath, whose qualifications embrace medicine, letters, and law, Van Helsing is the pedagogue who will instruct these earnest students regarding the threat that impinges upon their comfortable world. That threat is not unprecedented, for the professor corrects their ignorance through recourse to ancient and contemporary medical authorities as well as the ephemera of folklore and legend. Moreover, though, he integrates the group's preexistent experience and understanding—the individual skills they have learned in the surgery, the classroom, the solicitor's chambers, and the wilderness—into an intellectual process whereby each may, as an independent learner, apply that knowledge in his absence. Van Helsing holds the balance between past and present, theory and practice, and ignorance and enlightenment. He is a worthy model for twenty-first-century teachers of Stoker's intriguingly polymath novel, redolent as it is with concepts and issues now faded from living memory, to follow in their own attempts to convey its historical content to the incredulous student.

Dracula, as its often-overlooked foreword pointedly states, is a collection of archival documents duly edited and arranged for the convenience of the reader of 1897. That reader's successor in the twenty-first century must emulate those fictional characters who, under Van Helsing's guidance, have engaged with the dimly perceived concepts of an occluded past. Accessing that past has, however, become a somewhat easier process in recent years with the rise of the digital humanities, where archival information hitherto available only to readers at a specific locality is now widely disseminated online. This is not to suggest that online resources are yet at such a stage of development that printed works have been rendered wholly redundant. Much of the cultural archive of the nineteenth century—most notably those ephemeral books, pamphlets, and popular newspapers less likely to have been carefully curated by Victorian librarians—remains unavailable to the digital reader and is likely to continue as such for some years to come. A systematic approach, though, where online research is imbricated with traditional archival study, and where these two crucial research activities exist in reciprocal relationship, is best calculated to produce innovative conclusions and new resources.

Many of the allusions and nuances within *Dracula*, though familiar—if not obvious—to the Victorian reader, will be obscure to those approaching the novel in the twenty-first century. *Dracula* is, for example, punctuated by allusions to fox hunting, the British legal system, the theater, and imperial adventure. Stoker, though a former civil servant, a trained lawyer, and a theatrical manager, does not appear to have hunted to hounds or indeed to have traveled far outside of the urban centers of Europe and the United States, though he most likely encountered many who had. Effectively, the linguistic traces of activities such as these were incorporated into the everyday speech even of those not actually active in them—much as, indeed, phrases from computing or finance frequently appear in nonspecialist discourse today. *Dracula* is thus a tissue of keywords, quotations, and allusions, some now obscure, others still familiar, all taunting the modern reader with the restricted understanding that comes with partial knowledge, the need as it were to engage more fully with those specifically Victorian concepts that are indexed through fin-de-siècle phraseology.

Dracula, however, is overwhelmingly freighted with the language and conceptuality of Victorian medicine, a specialist discipline whose comprehension may present potentially acute challenges to the nonclinical reader. For general readers in the twenty-first century, medicine may prove a problematic discourse for a number of reasons. In its twentieth- and twenty-first-century incarnations, medicine exists for many nonspecialist perceivers as a seemingly opaque practice that locates the nonclinician very much on the outside of both debate and understanding. Heavily inflected with chemical and physiological terminology in modernity, professional medicine is a discipline that characteristically renders the patient as a passive recipient of information rather than an active participant in its formulation. Tacitly, self-diagnosis is discouraged by institutional medicine other than in its capacity to lead the patient to the doctor. Arguably, it is only in locations characterized by extreme poverty or else geographical isolation that demotic—self or amateur—medical practice persists in the modern age.

Such was not the case in the nineteenth century, however, and this is one reason why the coherent medical script within Stoker's novel was accessible to the general public rather than merely to clinicians. Stoker's grounding in contemporary medical knowledge was in part derived from encounters with clinicians: his elder brother, William Thornley Stoker, was president of the Royal College of Surgeons in Ireland between 1894 and 1896, and his younger brother George served with distinction as a military surgeon in Europe and South Africa. Stoker, by his own admission, was a sickly child who—it has been speculated— may have been treated for an extended period by doctors of various clinical persuasions (Murray 25–26; Senf, Dracula 74; Shuster). The literal ministration

100 MEDICAL HUMANITIES

of medical professionals in all stations of social life, from the proletarian to the bourgeois, was supplemented further by a vast literature of popular diagnostic volumes, colloquially termed "Home Doctors" or "Home Physicians," which instructed their possessors, for example, how to recognize the symptoms of cholera, mix an emetic, or stitch an open wound (Medical Man 641, 740, 725–26). These cheap publications were written in accessible language, with symptoms and their projected outcomes tabulated systematically and often graphically. Though short-lived, and in many cases anonymous or pseudonymous, these volumes functioned as a major conduit of practical knowledge and evocative terminology from clinician to lay reader. In essence, by widely disseminating symptomatologies and nosologies, such works made pathological states, be they associated with transmissible disease or the morbid consequences of sexual or alcoholic excess, available to the moralizing author of fiction as well as to the interpreting reader. In doing so, such works established a complicity in which depictions of physical or mental disorder carried within them additional cultural and moral values and judgments. The ephemeral Home Doctor is thus an index not merely of symptoms but of the moral and social associations that accompanied them. Though such volumes are now rarely encountered in thrift shops and may be prohibitively expensive when sourced through antiquarian booksellers, a significant number may be freely accessed online by way of digital repositories including *Google Books* as well as specialist clinical archives such as the Wellcome Trust (see, for example, Thomson; Mackenzie). The dictionary-like structure of many of these works, which often includes a separate index of symptoms, should be regarded as an invaluable aid to the pathologizing and diagnosis of fictional characters generally and to popular understandings of disease specifically.

The medical plot of *Dracula* revolves around a central complex of diagnosis and prognosis in which both the individual and their surrounding culture are equally implicated. This complex provides an ideal thematic center through which to encourage student understanding not merely of a wide range of contemporary pathologies but also of the moral implications associated with them, of the respective values accorded to professional and amateur diagnosis, and of the intimacy between physiology, psychology, and sexology in certain gendered complaints represented in Stoker's novel. *Dracula* represents medical crises with unusual intensity; in this respect, its exemplar status will empower the student seeking morbid pathology elsewhere in nineteenth-century fiction, particularly where gender and race are perceived as significant cultural contexts in the representation of dis-ease and its amelioration or eradication.

Readings of *Dracula* by way of gender studies have quite rightly noted how the vampire condition, which is persistently condemned by the God-fearing men of the novel, specifically liberates women from repression, the undead hunger for blood eliding quite easily into a culturally inexpressible desire for another richly emblematic saline secretion produced by the male body (Senf, Dracula 52; Roth, "Suddenly Sexual Women" 544). Taking this well-known theoretical interpretation of *Dracula* as a starting point, students might profitably be encouraged to condition its implications by way of Michel Foucault's discursive interpretation of blood as "a reality with a symbolic function" (147) where the conscious cultural meanings encoded in the fluid are modified by the literal processes of secretion, circulation, depletion, dilution, and transfer. The interpretations provided by both of these twentieth-century schools of thought can be brought together through a contemplation of the evocative Victorian medical concept of the spermatic economy. Accepted by some accredited practitioners, and by many more amateurs in medical diagnosis, the spermatic economy considered semen to be a direct by-product of blood, albeit one obtained at the cost of a significant depletion of the sanguine circulation (Barker-Benfield). This now discredited assumption within physiological medicine has immense implications for the novel and its frequent descriptions of pallid lassitude or florid repletion. The pallid man may be a habitual masturbator, depleting his personal economy and debilitating in consequence the integrity of his racial heritage (Mason 103). The pale but voluptuous woman's desire for semen will likewise weaken both her lover and the nationalistic virility his blood metaphorically represents (Mason 40, 43). The Count, it should be specifically noted, openly exhibits not merely the pallor, lassitude, and solitariness of the habitual onanist but also the hairy palms of a once popular sexual mythology.

It should be clear from the novel's protracted interweaving of pallor and sexual deviancy that medicine is a discourse ready to apply moral judgment and condemnation to any perceived deviancy whose symptoms are written on the body. The student might profitably consider the way in which Lucy Westenra's symptoms are considered from the point at which her fiancé unknowingly invites one of her former suitors, the alienist John Seward, to investigate her increasing lassitude. Seward is reluctant to diagnose, however, and it is not so much the case that he does not suspect a likely cause for her condition as that he fears the moral implications of voicing that diagnosis himself. To summon Van Helsing as a specialist in "obscure diseases" (Stoker, *Dracula* 114) is thus to pass the burden of judgment to one not directly connected to the patient. Lucy's complaint, it might be deduced, is one whose presence is likely to compromise her ostensible purity of mind as much as of body. Its focus is, again, sexual desire and the immodest need to engage in coitus. This much is already known to the reader following Lucy's privately expressed, and possibly lighthearted, desire to "marry three men" (65). Its textual presence, though, while affirming twentieth-century assumptions with regard to the repressed nature of Victorian sexual culture, points symptomatically toward a contextual clinical diagnosis of hysteria. A reading of the symptoms displayed by the Count's first victim on English soil might be undertaken by the student and these symptoms juxtaposed with those depicted in the most influential clinical texts on the complaint—most notably *On the Pathology and Treatment of Hysteria*, by Robert Brudenell Carter—as well as the more frenetic images of fainting, prostrated collapse, and sexually wayward expressiveness in popular medical works.

102   MEDICAL HUMANITIES

The "cure" for hysteria, in respectable terms, was marriage: Lucy's postmortem approach to her lover, carefully worded as it is to entice him to a version of the marriage bed, might be seen as the culmination of her own attempt to alleviate the carnal hunger that prompts her symptoms. A comparison of Lucy's prostration with the apparently hysterical crises experienced by both Harker and Van Helsing would also greatly assist the student in comprehending the gendered nature of Victorian medicine.

To read the ostensible sexuality of *Dracula* is, of course, to necessarily implicate the self within the twentieth and twenty-first centuries' preoccupation with that topic, possibly to the exclusion of other compelling interpretations available to scholars of the medical humanities. To facilitate both breadth and an awareness of criticism as a discipline, it is thus important that students of *Dracula* be introduced to the nonsexual medical content of the novel. *Dracula* embodies, in particular, an extensive and accessible encounter with the physiological model of mental development popular at the fin de siècle, this being a context referenced explicitly in the novel through the pointed phrase "unconscious cerebration" (Stoker, *Dracula* 76, 251). This cerebral process, whereby the mind is assumed to be able to unconsciously develop a complex idea or reach a conclusion while otherwise consciously occupied (W. Carpenter 515–43), was popularized by the British physician William Benjamin Carpenter. The theoretical assumption that the logical processes of the mind might be trained by conscious repetition—in a manner somewhat similar to that in which the muscles "learn" to move without conscious direction in the act of walking—is signaled implicitly in *Dracula* by way of Lucy's somnambulism and Seward's unconscious but safe handling of a sharp surgical instrument (W. Hughes, *Beyond* Dracula 141–51). Outside of the novel, the curative possibilities of this process led to its deployment in contemporary "lunatic asylums," where patients were habituated into approved (rather than deviant) mental processes and beliefs.

Though the student of *Dracula* might here be invited to contrast this wholly Victorian version of the unconscious mind with the model proposed by Sigmund Freud in the early twentieth century, the ethics of its application might well form another topic for discussion. Seward, who manages a private asylum in the novel, is perceptibly influenced by Carpenter's model of mental physiology, though the latter is not explicitly referenced in *Dracula*. Two other doctors—David Ferrier and John Burdon-Sanderson—are, however, mentioned (Stoker, *Dracula* 77), and their respective ethics might be said to inform *Dracula* as much as Carpenter's theory. Ferrier and Burdon-Sanderson were controversial vivisectionists, experimenting upon the brains and bodies of conscious animals in the pursuit of surgical techniques that might be applied curatively to human subjects. Seward's fictional practice represents an extension of vivisection from the animal to the human subject and from the physiological to the psychological. His selection of the obsessive patient R. M. Renfield as an experimental subject is both legally and ethically questionable, for no consent is sought from the concerned friends who have legally consigned Renfield to the doctor's care.

Seward, as a "humanitarian and medico-jurist" (Stoker, *Dracula* 229) whose professional career embraces law as well as medicine, would—of course—know this. Further, Seward openly admits that, rather than guiding Renfield's mind away from his idée fixe—as he ought to do if deploying unconscious cerebration as a curative tool—he deliberately schemes "to keep him to the point of his madness" (Stoker, *Dracula* 67): Seward's practice, in other words, is anything other than curative. The student might thus be led to place this aspect of *Dracula* in the context of the Victorian debate on vivisection, noting not merely the polemical writings of anti-vivisection campaigners such as Frances Power Cobbe but also evocative fictions such as Robert Browning's sardonic poem of 1870, "Tray" (Hamilton; R. Browning), and the more protracted accounts of experimentation on the human subject in Wilkie Collins's anti-vivisection novel, *Heart and Science*. An earlier novel by Collins, *The Woman in White*, also contains a discernible curative application of Carpenter's mental theory within an asylum context. Both novels present excellent—and detailed—foils to *Dracula*.

Though evidently informed by contemporary British practice, *Dracula* is also punctuated by allusions to Continental medical thought. The novel's explicit references to the ideas of Jean-Martin Charcot, Cesare Lombroso, and Max Nordau facilitate reader access to a somewhat fluid intellectual field in which ostensibly orthodox medicine successfully coexists with a range of concepts and ideologies now dismissed as pseudosciences. As Van Helsing suggests, in a discipline whose principles must remain under active development, it is purblind to reject any radical hypothesis that has some logical relationship to accepted thought; hence, if a physician embraces the then-fashionable medical hypnotism of Charcot, why is it not also logical to accept mind reading, materialization, or the existence of astral as well as corporeal bodies? Stoker's depiction of hypnotism, though it acknowledges the Victorian Charcot, might profitably be compared by the student to the essentially eighteenth-century system of fluid-based animal magnetism proposed by Franz-Anton Mesmer, particularly in those scenes where a channel of communication is established through the ingestion of blood (W. Hughes, *That Devil's Trick* 21–40). Stoker's vision of hypnotism appears oddly anachronistic in the novel, given his employment of contemporary practice not merely in the fictional asylum but also in the practical surgery of blood transfusion and trephining (O'Connor and Dunbar; Eighteen-Bisang and Miller, *Bram Stoker's Notes* 178–83). The possible motivations for this departure are themselves worthy of consideration by the student, their implications perhaps exceeding the mere demands of plot and pointing toward a critique of materialistic attitudes within contemporary science.

Beyond hypnotism, and by way of Lombroso and Nordau, *Dracula* also engages with the pseudosciences of physiognomy and (racialized) degeneration; these in turn are associated with the perceived decadence of the Victorian fin de siècle. This situation poses a number of questions with regard to the novel's complex relationship to late Victorian culture. Given its explicit antipathy to such contemporary developments as the progressive New Woman, its more pervasive

104   MEDICAL HUMANITIES

disdain for European Jewry, and its dismissal of the working classes as alcoholic and eminently purchasable by the invading Count, the cultural conservatism of *Dracula* sits rather oddly against its production out of the cultural milieu of London decadence. Stoker was familiar with the decadent *Yellow Book* (*Catalogue* 238), and the first edition of *Dracula* itself appeared between emblematic yellow covers (Constable). He was a college associate, also, of the aesthetic and decadent writer Oscar Wilde and owned fiction by Wilde's sometime lover, Richard Le Gallienne; further, his management of the Lyceum Theatre would have brought Stoker into contact with fashionable and artistic London. The medicalizing of uranism—a Victorian euphemism for homosexuality, a sexual identity itself supposedly characteristic of the decadent lifestyle—is a further context that might profitably be explored by the student. *Dracula* appears highly conscious of the coded languages, both medical and subcultural, by which such ostensibly repressed sexual identities are communicated, though it will most likely never be proved with certainty that the author of the novel was a closet homosexual or, indeed, whether his death was a consequence of syphilis contracted in heterosexual coitus (Schaffer, "Wilde Desire"; Farson 233–35). The medical humanities, again, will provide an opening for considerations that may further engage students with the ongoing work undertaken in queer studies, psychobiography, and cultural history.

In *Dracula*, the symptoms of vampiric predation are comprehended first in their individual physiological stigmata and only latterly in a visible compromising of personal moral, racial, or gendered characteristics prior to death. As Van Helsing observes, though, death is not the end, for the compromised corpse persists as a localized contaminant, having the potential to infect others within what Harker terms "an ever-widening circle" (Stoker, *Dracula* 59). The epidemic potential of the vampire is, to be sure, a theme that is as pertinent to the twenty-first century as it was to the Victorian fin de siècle. At that time, cultural infection was perceived to come, like Count Dracula, from an eastern Europe fractured by pogroms and populated by debilitated or degenerate peasants (Pick). On trade routes from farther east also came the cholera witnessed by Stoker's mother (Farson 13–15), and a variety of further epidemic infections, it has been argued, may have underwritten a significant proportion of deaths in Britain across the nineteenth century (Mooney). More recently, the image of *Dracula* has been deployed extensively in AIDS-awareness campaigns (Bak xi–xv). The onset of COVID-19, however, arguably revives much of the ambience of Victorian cultural epidemiology, particularly the deployment of pseudomedical rhetoric in anti-immigrant polemic, the association of the geographical East with unhygienic or primitive practices, and the fear that unknown vectors of disease are circulating within the uninfected population. Though coronavirus may not yet have been depicted in fiction as a vampire, the student of *Dracula* may still temper a reading of contemporary crisis culture through a knowledge of the occluded medical past.

SEXUALITY AND GENDER

Dracula's Fluidity:
Beyond Queering the Vampire

Jolene Zigarovich

With the rise of third-wave feminism and sexuality studies, the late 1990s and 2000s marked the queering of gothic studies. In the light of this, William Hughes and Andrew Smith recognize in their introduction to *Queering the Gothic* that the gothic has "always been 'queer'" (1). Previous to this, George E. Haggerty, Eve Kosofsky Sedgwick, Ellis Hanson, and others have suggested that a wide range of late-eighteenth- and nineteenth-century writers used *gothic* to evoke a "queer" world that attempts to transgress the binaries of sexual decorum. Assertive women (the New Woman) and gay men, and the conscious and unconscious sexualities of Bram Stoker's *Dracula*, have thereby been consistently explored in studies of the novel. While critics such as Talia Schaffer and Christopher Craft have examined *Dracula* and the vampire in terms of the homosocial and homosexual, and the ambivalent sexual morality of the vampire hunters has been examined by Alan Johnson, Carol Senf (*"Dracula"*), and others, today's student will benefit from not only a literary review of these main concepts and concerns but also an updating in terms of gender and sexuality studies. In "Letting Dracula out of the Closet," Ariane de Waal reads the novel in terms of Judith Butler's conceptions of "gender trouble," invoking Butler's theories of gender performance as she interprets *Dracula* as "Drag-ula, a Trans-sylvanian drag show in five acts" (177). De Waal's essay is helpful in terms of seeing the vampire as a figure that troubles normative genders and sexualities. This essay discusses *Dracula* beyond conceptions of gender performance and instabilities. Specifically, it introduces students to the queer, transgender, and genderqueer/nonbinary possibilities of the figure of the vampire as well the vampire's fluid sexuality. In a broader sense, it shows that contagious and contaminating, vampiric sexuality stands in for more general Victorian anxieties about sexual health and threats to heterosexual and gender norms.

When teaching the novel, part of my aim is to introduce students to ways in which nonnormative, "monstrous" sexualities and genders can be a productive

106   BEYOND QUEERING THE VAMPIRE

force in interpreting not only the literary vampire but all monstrous others. "Monstrous" is both a construction (a figure who signifies a culture's unbearable, abject elements) and a narrative (the power of monstrous narratives to dismantle gender binaries and heteronormative social constructs). While in *Our Vampires, Ourselves* Nina Auerbach famously disavows the boundary-crossing instability of vampiric activity and argues that Count Dracula is obsessed with hierarchies and maintaining boundaries, I wish to counter this reading by expanding the lens with which we can assess the perpetual movement and fluidity of the vampire. When in 1984 Craft pronounced that the novel generates a "desire mobile enough to elude the boundaries of gender" and "releases a sexuality so mobile and polymorphic that Dracula may be best represented as bat or wolf or floating dust" (Excerpt 448), he was anticipating not only homosexual and queer readings of the novel but trans and genderqueer interpretations as well.

Historically, gothic studies have worked with a conservative, binary-based approach such as "female" versus "male" theories of the gothic. In fact, the classification "female gothic," a term famously coined in 1976 by Ellen Moers (90), has been abundantly helpful in interpreting a subgenre of eighteenth-century literature focused on women's anxieties about domesticity, sexuality, and childbirth (see also Hoeveler; Williams, *Art of Darkness*; Clery, *Women's Gothic*; Horner and Zlosnik; Smith and Wallace; Wallace and Smith). In the work of critics like Donna Heiland and Diane Long Hoeveler, feminist theory uncovered the masquerade of the professional female writer who "exploded the limited gender constructions" of her tightly demarcated social sphere (Hoeveler 31). Yet the gendered classifications relegated authors and texts to this binary system, according to the gender of the author and the content of the plot. In the wake of both poststructuralism and queer theory, a destabilization of this gendered binary proved inevitable and fruitful. As Sedgwick revealed in the groundbreaking *The Coherence of Gothic Conventions*, gothic literature challenges and questions heterosexual norms and subsequently inspires paranoia and homophobia. Transgressive expression emerges in the gothic as textual symptoms of the denial not only of female desire but also of same-sex desire; gothic literature necessarily depicts gender variance as violent, monstrous, and demonic.

With or without a theoretical background, students are aware that when it comes to choosing victims, Dracula doesn't discriminate. I often teach *Dracula* along with Joseph Sheridan Le Fanu's *Carmilla* in order to compare the female vampire's inclination for young, local, female victims with Dracula's more liberal democratic victim-philosophy: woman, man, beast, child, all representing a diversity of animal forms, classes, nationalities, and races. Approaching Carmilla as a lesbian vampire who offers a literary model for questioning patriarchal power and gender constructions, I ask students to consider how in their violent rejection of norms gothic monsters can provide not only potentials for transgressions but also new possibilities for sexual identities. Queer theory thus offers a frame with which students can recognize difference and otherness as positive and celebratory rather than as elements to be destroyed. I compound this queer line of inquiry with close readings of the intimate act of vampirism itself: the penetration, pleasure/pain, oral acts, and exchange of bodily fluids necessary for the vampire's survival and "infection" of others. I ask students to locate textual evidence for vampiric embodiment of victims, such as when Van Helsing recognizes that "Madam Mina, our poor, dear Madam Mina is changing. . . . I can see the characteristics of the vampire coming in her face. . . . Her teeth are some sharper, and at times her eyes are more hard" following contact with the Count (Stoker, *Dracula* 296). Her changing body symbolizes an acquiring of phallic and penetrative power such as that exhibited by Dracula's three vampire wives. Van Helsing's well-discussed description of Mina's brain power and acumen also speaks to her gender-bending characterization even before she is attacked: "Ah, that wonderful Madam Mina! She has man's brain, a brain that a man should have were he much gifted, and a woman's heart" (220). It is also important to note that with her female heart and "man's brain" Mina in ways defies stable gender categorization, perhaps making her more susceptible to the Count.

In the face of Dracula's monstrous sexuality and gender, the male vampire hunters also experience various forms of gender destabilization. For example, at the beginning of the novel, when Jonathan is attacked by Dracula, he is essentially unmanned (Craft remarks that when he is attacked by the three vampiric women he "enjoys a 'feminine' passivity" [Excerpt 445]). At Dracula's castle, he is physically imprisoned; in addition, Dracula takes his possessions and controls his correspondence. Harker records this transformation in his journal, where he describes himself as "sitting at a little old oak table where in old times possibly some fair lady sat to pen, with much thought and many blushes, her ill-spelt love-letter" (Stoker, *Dracula* 45). When he returns to England following his lengthy illness, he is languid and lethargic, needing Mina for physical and emotional support (he must hold her arm when he walks, and after he has had the shock of seeing the Count on the street, she takes him aside to a park, where, she recounts, "he went quietly asleep, with his head on my shoulder" [166]). This passive yielding to his captivity and identification with the feminine seem to compromise his masculine identification. As Lucy's health declines from Dracula's vampiric attacks, her fiancé, Arthur Holmwood, experiences an emotional collapse that is given a feminized description by Seward: "His very heart was bleeding, and it took all the manhood of him" (148). Following Mina's attack by and exchange of blood with Dracula, Van Helsing experiences his own attacks of hysteria. Dr. Seward records, "The moment we were alone in the carriage he gave way to a regular fit of hysterics. He has denied to me since that it was hysterics" (167–68). Seward continues:

> He laughed till he cried, and I had to draw down the blinds lest anyone should see us and misjudge; and then he cried till he laughed again; and laughed and cried together, just as a woman does. I tried to be stern with

108   BEYOND QUEERING THE VAMPIRE

> him, as one is to a woman under the circumstances; but it had no effect.
> Men and women are so different in manifestations of nervous strength or
> weakness!   (168)

Though not one of Dracula's victims, Van Helsing experiences a disruption to gender norms in the presence of the vampire. In fact, one of Dracula's main threats is that he unmans men and masculinizes women, genderqueering all in his vampiric wake.

The large amount of critical work on the Victorians, sexuality, and the vampire provides students and instructors with a range of frameworks to explore LGBTQIA+ interpretations of *Dracula*. To assist students in considering how the vampire symbolizes challenges to gender and sexual norms at the fin de siècle, I typically assign critical selections from Bram Dijkstra, Judith Walkowitz, Jack Halberstam (*Skin Shows*), and, in relation to *Dracula*, Craft, Schaffer, Dejan Kuzmanovic, and Xavier Aldana Reyes. Robert Azzarello provides a helpful queer-ecocritical interpretation in "Unnatural Predators: Queer Theory Meets Environmental Studies in Bram Stoker's *Dracula*." We also discuss the emergence of the dandy and the Oscar Wilde trials, the New Woman, and Victorian theories of sexual degeneration and inversion. Students thereby understand the same-sex implications of vampiric acts and the "disease" of homosexuality that the vampire potentially infects his victims with. Selections from the work of Victorian sexologists such as Richard von Krafft-Ebing and Havelock Ellis (Ellis and Symonds), and Edward Carpenter's *The Intermediate Sex*, which posit that a culture based on heterosexual norms does not guarantee a subject's sexual preferences, place nonnormative sexualities and theories of inversion in context. For Carpenter, masculine homosexuals and feminine male heterosexuals challenge the notion that gender identity and sexuality are ideologically linked. Degenerative theories of sexual deviancy (see Nordau; Lombroso) demonstrate how dominant masculine gender scripts are pathologized in the culture. This is seen in the characterization of Jonathan Harker, who is represented as a middle-class, passive professional, emasculated in the face of Count Dracula's manliness, which, ironically, is pathologized. In *Victorian Demons: Medicine, Masculinity, and the Gothic at the Fin-de-Siècle*, Andrew Smith recognizes that "Harker's gender instability aligns him with sexological debates while the Count's Lombrosian characteristics associate him with degeneration" (36).

Students have also found it helpful to read Stoker's essay "Women as Men," which seems to praise the New Woman but ultimately reinforces traditional female gender norms. Stoker pronounces, "One of the commonest forms of imposture—so common that it seems rooted in a phase of human nature—is that of women who disguise themselves as men" (*Famous Impostors* 314). He reasons that the "legal and economic disabilities of the gentler sex" forced some women of his time to cross-dress in order to give themselves more economic opportunities. Interestingly, he aligns the cross-dressing female with languid, vampiric ailments: "Her sedentary habits, and the less perfect condition of her blood when resident in towns" affect her nervous system, resulting in hysteria, he claims (317). With a trans lens, what Stoker describes would be associated with transgender phenomena, much like the phallic female vampire and the languid, feminized male victim. In contemporary literature, vampirism is often a metaphor for transitioning and symbolic of gender affirmation. In Victorian literature, the shape-shifting abilities of supernatural characters, such as Richard Marsh's Beetle, often signal the disruption of gender norms. Dracula is similar in that he shape-shifts (bat, wolf, mist) and has supernatural strength. These elements speak to his fluid embodiment; his biology and identity are in constant flux. We see this in his victims as well: Mina grows harder and more masculine; Harker grows more feminine and delicate but also acquires some of Dracula's physical skills, such as climbing walls; and Lucy's sexual desire is ravenous as she rejects monogamy and the maternal.

To supplement our reading of *Dracula* in my first-year seminar on monsters, I assign Schaffer's "'A Wilde Desire Took Me': The Homoerotic History of *Dracula*" to assist students in their understanding of the sociosexual threat Victorians feared in male homosexuality. Schaffer argues that in an effort to juxtapose Stoker's relation to Oscar Wilde, the novel depicts the intended homosexual relationship between Jonathan and the Count. Her brilliant reading of the novel's ending, which posits that the destruction of the Count and the birth of Mina's child are "the apotheosis of Stoker's attempt to transform homosexual 'infection' into heterosexual 'procreation'" (Excerpt 569–70), typically sparks debate in class. One of my students was so inspired by Schaffer's claims that in their research essay for our first-year seminar class on monsters they deconstructed her interpretation of the homosexuality of Jonathan, Quincey, and Dracula, which in her view produces Little Quincey. The student argued that Schaffer does not take into account Jonathan's numerous anti-homosexual acts and proclamations throughout *Dracula*. The student also claimed that Jonathan's execution of Dracula in the name of his beloved wife is a complete rejection of Schaffer's reading of his homosexual relationship. Instead, the student interpreted the ending as a rejection of any homoerotic implications, citing Stoker's endorsement of Victorian patriarchal values. Responses such as these often inspire further class discussion about Stoker's conservatism and the novel's upholding of heteronormativity in the face of monstrous "acts" and "infections."[1]

Equipped with this diverse contextual and theoretical background, many of today's students understand that binary gendered models fail to account for the diversity of gender and sexual expressions at the fin de siècle. I argue that trans studies help us push back on the gothic's normalization in literary studies to once again destabilize how it is approached.[2] While Moers's umbrella term spawned designations such as "women's gothic," "feminist gothic," "lesbian gothic," and others, we can agree with Smith and Diana Wallace that these are too essentializing, as are various forms of "queering the gothic." When I covered female and male gothic forms and tropes and queer gothic in my classes, students still questioned interpretations of gothic monsters and noted that the

110   BEYOND QUEERING THE VAMPIRE

umbrella term *queer* often couldn't fully account for gender-variant characters. Susan Stryker's groundbreaking trans scholarship and its intersection with the gothic offers students an additional perspective and theoretical approach. In "My Words to Victor Frankenstein above the Village of Chamounix: Performing Transgender Rage," Stryker claims a transsexual embodiment that does not aim to reaffirm gender binaries but rather attains a "monstrous" subjectivity. Stryker calls attention to the virulent speciotransphobia that has categorized her (and her body) in terms of a Frankensteinian monster. By declaring "I am a transsexual, and therefore I am a monster" (254), she is reclaiming the word *monster* in order to relieve it of its power. More important, she uses abjection as a tool with which to further challenge and problematize conventions of socially constructed gender categories (see Phillips; Koch-Rein). Diffracting Mary Shelley's gothic novel through her own personal experience, Stryker eventually "claims her own transsexual body as a monstrously powerful place" (Stryker and Whittle 244). Stryker's intersection of trans embodiment and gothic monstrosity helps students grasp the capaciousness of a trans approach to *Dracula*. With my coining of *transgothic* in the classroom, students understand how a trans approach works with—but also disrupts—a "comfortable" queer gothic. A transgothic approach acknowledges *trans-* as suggesting something unstable, transient, or in-between, but also offers *trans-* as connoting transformation, development, creativity, reorganization, and reconstruction (Zigarovich, "Transing" 4).

Transylvania, transcribing, transfusion: of the forty-seven instances of *trans-* words in *Dracula*, these three are the most prevalent, and they represent the vampire's mobility and migrations. As Stephen D. Arata deftly demonstrates, the exoticized descriptions of Transylvania align its locale as foreign and other. Upon Harker's arrival, Dracula explains that Transylvania will seem "strange" to someone from England: "We are in Transylvania; and Transylvania is not England. Our ways are not your ways, and there shall be to you many strange things. Nay, from what you have told me of your experiences already, you know something of what strange things there may be" (Stoker, *Dracula* 30).

With his mobility and "strangeness," Dracula threatens European, heteronormative culture (in a footnote, Auerbach reminds us in the first Norton Critical Edition that "The word *strange* in late Victorian England was often suffused with homoerotic undercurrents" [Stoker, *Dracula* (Auerbach and Skal) 30]). Violent reactions to his presence and ability to infect others with sexual and gender fluidity thereby reflect a form of speciotransphobia that Stryker's essay touches upon. The "hard" phallic teeth of the vampire combined with the "soft, shivering touch of the lips" mark the vampiric mouth as a sexual mixture (Stoker, *Dracula* 47). Thomas M. Stuart recognizes that "[t]his is a trans-figuration of the organ, on the border between phallic and vaginal" (220). And, uniquely, Dracula can penetrate as well as procreate and symbolically breastfeed.

Craft was one of the first critics to underscore the vampire's "dangerous mobility" as well as to read Lucy's blood transfusions as sexual. He states, "These transfusions represent the text's first anxious reassertion of the conventionally masculine prerogative of penetration; as Van Helsing tells Arthur before the first transfusion, 'You are a man and it is a man we want'" (Excerpt 454). Each of the male vampire-hunters' blood is the source of Lucy's transfusions and extensions of life, but the transfusions provide the Count with strength, weaken Lucy, and ultimately contribute to her death. If we read this with a trans lens, the transfusions signify her vampiric transformation but also her monstrous gender transformation and embodiment. Male blood empowers Lucy's trans afterlife, allowing her the sexual freedom Victorian society disavowed for women and punished. Van Helsing explicates how the existence of vampirism expands social thought. He says to Jonathan:

> Do you not think that there are things which you cannot understand, and yet which are; that some people see things that others cannot? . . . Ah, it is the fault of our science that it wants to explain all; and if it explain not, then it says there is nothing to explain. But yet we see around us every day the growth of new beliefs, which think themselves new; and which are yet but the old, which pretend to be young—like the fine ladies at the opera. I suppose now you do not believe in corporeal transference. No? Nor in materialisation. No? Nor in astral bodies. No? Nor in the reading of thought. No? Nor in hypnotism— (Stoker, *Dracula* 182)

This "corporeal transference" resembles transgender embodiment, and vampiric monstrosity, shape-shifting, and corporeal exchange speak to the malleable corporeality that vampirism engenders. We can thus correlate the unexplainable, "new yet old" beliefs with the expansion of sexual taxonomies and the gender spectrum in the period.

Yet this potential for transpositivity and empowerment must be eventually destroyed. Dracula's three wives, the admission that he "too can love," and his ownership of Harker ("This man belongs to me!" [Stoker, *Dracula* 47]) signal his fluid, unrestrained, mobile sexuality, which threatens to infect society. Recognizing Dracula's strengths—"He has the strength of many of his hand. . . . He can transform himself to wolf. . . . [H]e can be as bat. . . . He can come in mist. . . . He come on moonlight rays as elemental dust"—Van Helsing also describes the limits of Dracula's transformative powers: "He can do all these things, yet he is not free. Nay; he is even more prisoner than the slave of the galley, than the madman in his cell. He cannot go where he lists; he who is not of nature has yet to obey some of nature's laws—why we know not" (Stoker, *Dracula* 224). Stoker ensures that Van Helsing and the vampire hunters discover the limitations of the Count's trans-vampirism. The unnatural vampire—who defies "nature's laws" through his corporeal malleability, sexual mobility, and gender-shifting—is ultimately a prisoner of his culture. While Dracula serves as a galvanizing and destabilizing figure, with his destruction, relationships, sexualities, and genders are consolidated in the end.

BEYOND QUEERING THE VAMPIRE

Whereas the fragmented form of gothic narrative represents the breakdown of social order and status quo, gothic bodies also disrupt stable notions of the gender binary. The gothic body's tabooed sexual acts are played out in order for heteronormative sexuality to be restored in the end. With its portraits of monstrous sexuality, *Dracula* is no different in this. The polymorphous, transformative body of the vampire dramatizes the breakdown of Victorian norms. *Dracula* depicts fluid gender subjectivities—masculine women, feminine men, nonbinary vampires—offering a portrait of gender continuums and possibilities to mortal humanity. While difference is inevitably a reason for the destruction of the Victorian vampire, difference can also be celebrated, since the vampire's transitions and metamorphoses symbolize spectrums of modern sexualities and genders (spectrums with which he has infected his victims and which linger in the end). This approach is exciting to teach since it invites students to reassess the late Victorians and their cultural norms; question the motives behind the characters' actions; consider the monstrous in more complex, positive, and creative ways; and perhaps assess their own sexuality and gender identity.

NOTES

A portion of this essay was published in "Victorian Literature as Trans Literature," *The Routledge Handbook of Trans Literature*, edited by Douglas A. Vakoch and Sabine Sharp, Routledge, © 2024. Reproduced by permission of Taylor and Francis Group.

1. Subsequent critical work also approaches triangular love in the novel. Gregory Luke Chwala, for example, argues that the novel's triangular relationships both support and oppose homosocial bonding in a homophobic Victorian England.

2. Gothic has always been queer and is a repository for the transgressive, yet the term *queer* doesn't fully explain radical gothic texts such as William Beckford's *Vathek* and *Episodes* and Charlotte Dacre's *Zofloya*, which features a masculine villainess with an insatiable and sadomasochistic sexual appetite. Hughes and Smith recognize that the movement of the gothic from the margins to "the mainstream of academe" must be resisted by the reconsideration of the genre's queerness, which will critically push the genre "once more away from the comfortable center and back towards the uneasy margins of transgression and experimentation—a place where it undoubtedly belongs" (5). Numerous recent book-length studies such as those by Paulina Palmer, Max Fincher, and Ardel Haefele-Thomas illustrate how queering the gothic is a necessary and continual project.

Dracula and Masculinity

Andrew Smith

Masculinity is a key topic in *Dracula* because its study provides a way of engaging with wider social and political contexts, such as theories of degeneration and accounts of colonialism. An examination of masculinity thus produces an important way of thinking historically about the novel. The approach described in this essay reflects my teaching of *Dracula* on a final-year undergraduate module on the fin-de-siècle gothic at the University of Sheffield. The seminar introduces students to how theories of degeneration and accounts of colonialism (which address Anglo-American relations during the period) provide a critical context for evaluating the novel's representation of masculinity.

This approach to *Dracula* is typically delivered over two sessions after a fifty-minute lecture that outlines theories of degeneration. In the first seminar, we discuss contemporaneous theories of degeneration and how they can be applied to Jonathan Harker's opening journal. Students are presented with extracts from Edwin Lankester's *Degeneration: A Chapter in Darwinism* and Max Nordau's *Degeneration*. The extracts from Lankester (33, 58–61) demonstrate how he employs analogies to empire, class, and masculinity—key topics explored in Stoker's novel. In particular I draw attention to this passage: "Any new set of conditions occurring to an animal which render its food and safety easily attained, seem to lead as a rule to Degeneration; just as an active healthy man sometimes degenerates when he suddenly becomes possessed of a fortune; or as Rome degenerated when possessed of the riches of the ancient world" (33). Lankester asserts that modern civilization leads to a degenerate decline when the masculine subject (that once "active healthy man") becomes weak and emasculated. For Lankester, the absence of a Darwinian struggle for species ascendancy enfeebles the subject and by extension the nation (here represented by Rome), meaning that there is an elision between the body and the body politic. We also discuss how a specifically middle-class version of the subject is implicated in this, one that reflects Lankester's wider anxiety that the civilized man (and the nation that he represents) generates the very possibility of his overthrow. How these issues relate to class-bound models of degeneration is explored further in relation to Nordau (6–7). Nordau identifies a number of sources of degeneration, but it is in his critique of art that we find a clear position taken on emasculation. He notes of the degenerate that

> [h]e laughs until he sheds tears, or weeps copiously without adequate occasion; a commonplace line of poetry or of prose sends a shudder down his back; he falls into raptures before indifferent pictures or statues; and music especially, even the most insipid and least commendable, arouses in him the most vehement emotions. He is quite proud of being so vibrant

114   *DRACULA* AND MASCULINITY

> a musical instrument, and boasts that where the Philistine remains com-
> pletely cold, he feels his inner self confounded, the depths of his being
> broken up, and the bliss of the Beautiful possessing him to the tips of his
> fingers. (Nordau 19)

Here the subject is defined by an emotional overreaction to culture. As in Lankester, civilization, or a heightened overly elaborate response to it, initiates a
degenerate decline. We also explore more broadly how Nordau asserts a cultural symptomology in which a "sick" culture (for him represented by the texts of
Oscar Wilde, Henrik Ibsen, and Émile Zola, among others) indicates that society
has become infected by the disease of degeneration. Nordau thus applies a language of medical symptomology to a reading of culture as part of a denunciation
of fin-de-siècle decadence. Nordau concludes that some texts were unhealthy
to write and are also unhealthy to read. This provides a helpful framework for
thinking about readers and writers in *Dracula* that leads us to focus on the function of Jonathan Harker's opening journal.

Harker's journal registers an emotional journey from jaunty optimism to a
resigned pessimism when, at the end, he contemplates suicide as the only possible means of escaping the predations of the three female vampires at Castle
Dracula. We discuss this trajectory and relate it to ideas about middle-class
masculine identity and associated ideas of social respectability and economic
success (forms of "civilization"). Harker is proud of his recent promotion to
solicitor, and with a fiancée (Mina) who is skilled in providing him with professional support, he is middle-class and upwardly socially mobile. However,
in Lankester's terms, this is a potential cause for concern. The novel as a
whole will pose the question of how it will be possible to transform Harker
from a middle-class pen pusher into a man of action capable of dispatching
the Count at the end. The opening journal raises these issues by establishing
a clash between the different masculine identities of Harker and the Count.
The Count, as a feudal aristocrat, views the world in quite a different way to
that of a middle-class professional such as Harker. We discuss the lengthy
speech in which the Count dwells upon his aristocratic lineage and repeatedly emphasizes the importance of blood and its political significance. He
begins, "We Szekelys have a right to be proud, for in our veins flows the blood
of many brave races who fought as the lion fights for lordship" (Stoker, *Dracula* 37). He proceeds to outline a series of European conflicts in which this
heroic blood has demonstrated its mastery. His speech concludes with the
lament that "[t]he warlike days are over. Blood is too precious a thing in these
days of dishonourable peace; and the glories of the great races are as a tale
that is told" (39). We relate this speech to the model of degeneration outlined
by Lankester, which also suggests that "the glories of the great races are as a
tale that is told" (as witnessed in the decline of ancient Rome, for example).
The Count represents the type of struggle that Lankester casts in Darwinian
terms as necessary in order to maintain the strength of the individual and

thus a robust nation-state. In Lankester's treatise there is an implicit lament for a lost world of heroism that has been supplanted by a world of peace administratively presided over by middle-class professionals such as Jonathan Harker (to support this, I provide students with extracts from H. G. Wells's "Zoological Retrogression," in which Wells mocks Lankester's use of metaphors about middle-class authority [249–50]). The Count thus represents a world of lost heroism that needs to be reconnected to if, paradoxically, the Count is to be defeated. This takes us toward the conundrum concerning degeneration in the novel.

Harker notes in his description of the Count's appearance, "His face was a strong—a very strong—aquiline, with high bridge of the thin nose and peculiarly arched nostrils; with lofty domed forehead. . . ." He also records the Count's "peculiarly sharp white teeth" and his "extremely pointed" ears (Stoker, *Dracula* 27). As many critics have noted, the description is a paraphrase of the archetypal criminal identified by Cesare Lombroso in *Criminal Man*. Harker fails to make the connection, but Mina Harker is more adept at seeing the link when she concludes, "The Count is a criminal and of criminal type. Nordau and Lombroso would so classify him" (313). The novel suggests that in order to defeat the degenerate Count it is necessary for Harker to become more like him. It is, paradoxically, the Count's masculinity that provides the antidote to the progressive emasculation of Harker that we witness in his opening journal, and it is here that Nordau provides some additional context.

It will have already been noted that Nordau associated certain types of writing and cultural consumption with emasculation. In the seminar, we explore this context and how it relates to Harker as a writer whose text increasingly articulates a delirious loss of control. We discuss the passage where Harker notes the following about his record keeping: "Here I am, sitting at a little oak table where in old times possibly some fair lady sat to pen, with much thought and many blushes, her ill-spelt love-letter, and writing in my diary in shorthand all that has happened since I closed it last" (Stoker, *Dracula* 45). Harker's self-identification with a blushing female writer of love letters evokes the type of femininity that Nordau saw as symptomatic of a degenerate decline. Harker records his increasing passivity and his seduction by the female vampires, reporting having closed his "eyes in a languorous ecstasy and waited—waited with beating heart" (47) for the vampire's bite.

Harker is left behind at Castle Dracula and is aware that he has been abandoned to the female vampires to dispose of. He contemplates suicide as the only means to regain his masculinity. He notes of the steep terrain in which the castle is situated that he can jump and that "[a]t its foot man may sleep—as a man" (60). When he escapes, he takes his journal with him, which is given to Van Helsing to assess. For Harker, the journal seems to represent a degenerate decline that bears witness to his mental and moral frailties. For him, as for Nordau, an "ill" text represents the emasculation of the subject in that the writing

116   *DRACULA* AND MASCULINITY

demonstrates an overly emotional response and so illustrates the subject's lost grip on reality. For Nordau, as for Stoker, this leads to feminization unless a text provides a true reflection of objective events. Van Helsing's confirmation that,"[s]trange and terrible as it is, it is *true!*" has a restorative effect on Harker, who acknowledges that "[i]t seems to have made a new man of me" (178, 179). Without this confirmation, Harker "felt impotent" (179). The lost, emasculated subject regains his masculinity because his text is not "sick" after all but in fact full of useful clues about the Count's vampiric identity that the vampire hunters subject to a healthy, quasi-scientific scrutiny.

However, it is not enough that Harker's version of events be proved true. It is also necessary to emphasize that the vampire hunters need to become more like the Count if they are to become transformed into men of action who can defeat him. That the world of the vampire and that of the vampire hunters might echo each other is indicated in alternative articulations of vampirism that also implicate models of masculinity. In the seminar, we look at the scenes relating to Lucy's blood transfusions, which transform the vampire hunters into symbolic vampires as they look to replace her bad blood with their blood. We discuss a Freudian perspective, which suggests that blood and semen are symbolically linked (Freud, *Three Essays* 133–34) and helps establish the erotic context of the blood transfusions. All the vampire hunters are happy to donate their blood to Lucy, and most of them have a prior personal interest in her (Morris, Seward, and Holmwood have all proposed to her). Van Helsing oversees the blood transfusions, which begin with Holmwood because he is Lucy's fiancé. Seward, the second donor, is advised to conceal his donation from Arthur because it would "enjealous him" (128)—an acknowledgment of the personal nature of the procedure. At this point we discuss Stephen D. Arata's observation that the blood donations are sequenced in terms of their class and national importance (632). The sequence consisting of Holmwood, Seward, Van Helsing, and Morris traces a hierarchy of aristocratic, bourgeois, European, and American blood. This sequence emphasizes that the central theme of national revitalization is reflected in images of potent masculine blood, beginning with Holmwood, who is described by Van Helsing as "young and strong and of blood so pure" (123). We also note that Van Helsing and the Count can be construed as doubles, as both are associated with their mastery over particular forms of knowledge, which again suggests links between vampire and vampire hunter.

At this point we summarize our conclusions from this first meeting. We reflect on how theories of degeneration provide a context for the novel's representation of masculinity. We also acknowledge that the ostensibly degenerate Count possesses the type of heroic masculinity that is the antidote to middle-class formations of degenerate emasculation. We reflect on ideas about healthy writing (Harker's narrative is not, after all, reflecting a degenerate decline) and heathy reading (exemplified in Van Helsing's scientific confirmation of Harker's journal). We note the blurring of vampire with vampire hunter but also note that despite their symbolic ceremonial expression of authority, the blood transfusions fail. We also discuss their sequence and consider why it is that Quincey Morris, a brave and heroic frontiersman, goes last. This raises the issue of masculinity, nationalism, and colonialism, which are the themes explored in the following class.

In the second seminar I outline Franco Moretti's reading of *Dracula* in *Signs Taken for Wonders*. Moretti attributes Quincey Morris's odd behavior— including missing the Count with his gun when he is meant to be a crack marksman and losing sight of the Count in one of the early crucial pursuits—to the fact that Morris, by virtue of being an American, shares the Count's ambitions to imperially subjugate Britain. The Count has effectively invaded Britain to infect the "teeming millions" of London and so generate a colony of vampirized subordinate subjects. Moretti argues, "So long as things go well for Dracula, Morris acts like an accomplice. As soon as there is a reversal of fortunes, he turns into his staunchest enemy. Morris enters into competition with Dracula; he would like to replace him in the conquest of the Old World. He does not succeed in the novel but he will succeed, in "real" history, a few years afterwards" (95). This is a critical position that students tend to find counterintuitive because Morris seemingly plays such an important role on the team of vampire hunters, where he is the only real man of action that they have. Before delving further into this question, we consider the apparent moment of sanity in which Renfield addresses the vampire hunters and acknowledges their place in the modern world. Renfield refers to Morris's home state of Texas: "Its reception into the Union was a precedent which may have far-reaching effects hereafter, when the Pole and the Tropics may hold allegiance to the Stars and Stripes. The power of Treaty may yet prove a vast engine of enlargement, when the Monroe doctrine takes its true place as a political fable" (Stoker, *Dracula* 228). We discuss whether Renfield's celebration of an anticipated global American expansion (from "the Pole" to "the Tropics") and the possible repeal of the Monroe Doctrine, established in the United States in 1823 and intended to curb European political interference in the Americas, is ironized here, given that it is voiced by a man Seward refers to as his "pet lunatic" (219).

The full significance of Moretti's reading becomes clear through discussion of other texts by Stoker that reflect on the United States and its growing colonial authority, including extracts from his pamphlet *A Glimpse of America*, the short story "The Squaw," and his novels *The Mystery of the Sea* and *The Lady of the Shroud*. These texts help us account for Moretti's conclusion that Morris "must die" (95). *A Glimpse of America* is based on a speech that Stoker gave in London, reflecting on his travels while touring with the Lyceum Theatre in North America. The speech notes the similarities between Britain and the United States: "Our history is their history—our fame is their pride—their progress is our glory" (47–48). It is also noteworthy that Stoker lectured on Abraham Lincoln from 1886 to 1893 on tours in England and the United States (the US lectures ended in 1887) that praised Lincoln as a man of peace and reconciliation ("Lecture"). However, by the time of "The Squaw," the author's attitude

118   *DRACULA* AND MASCULINITY

toward the United States had changed. The tale centers on the European adventures of Elias P. Hutcheson, from Nebraska, who is a frontiersman anticipating the representation of Quincey Morris. Bored by a peaceful Europe and looking for trouble, Hutcheson joins a British honeymooning couple who are visiting a castle in Nuremberg and tells them about the time he killed an Indigenous woman. His violent nature reappears when he kills, if accidentally, a kitten playing with its mother in the castle. The thrill-seeking Hutcheson asks to be put into an Iron Virgin (also known as an Iron Maiden, a type of vertical torture device with spikes on the inside door), but the cat attacks the man holding the door open so that the door closes and Hutcheson is killed. In effect, Hutcheson is symbolically judged and executed in Europe not only for his killing of the Indigenous woman but also because he signifies a violent, invasive American presence in Europe.

Hutcheson represents a form of masculinity that needs to be punished because of the colonial violence he embodies. In the seminar, we discuss the reasons Stoker's attitudes toward the United States might have changed and explore how the rival colonial attitudes identified by Moretti were reflected in the United States' colonial interest in the Philippines and the Spanish-American War of 1898, in which the United States ousted the Spanish from Cuba. William McKinley's administration in the late nineteenth century was clearly far removed from the type of reconciliations Stoker had extolled in his Lincoln lecture. Stoker's acute consciousness of geopolitical developments is illustrated by *The Mystery of the Sea*, in which the narrator, Archibald Hunter, is attracted to an American holidaymaker in Scotland, Marjory Drake. Marjory is a millionaire who has actively supported the United States in the war against the Spanish in Cuba by buying a battleship for the navy. Her belligerent expression of authority appears in a speech that rhetorically echoes the Count's speech on the lineage of his warlike blood. Marjory tells Archibald, "I come from a race of men who have held their lives in their hands from the cradle to the grave. . . . Their blood is in my veins, and speaks loudly to me when any sense of fear comes near me" (Stoker, *Mystery* 104). This speech, following Moretti, underlines Marjory's colonial threat. We thus note how the language of similarity that characterizes *A Glimpse of America* has now been supplanted by a language of difference. Marjory will not die violently, like Morris, but she is effectively tamed when she becomes Archibald's wife and transfers from a public political world to a private domestic one.

In the seminar, we discuss the gendered aspects of Marjory's threat and the triumph of a type of British masculinity that is represented by Archibald. Finally, we look at the concluding part of Stoker's other vampire novel (or so it would have seemed to its contemporary readership), *The Lady of the Shroud*. At the end of the novel, the seven-foot Rupert Sent Leger, a Scot of Viking descent, has on marriage become the king of the Blue Mountains (set in the Balkans and reflecting the Balkan crisis of the time), and on a boat he and his queen meet the reigning British monarchs. In this moment "the King and Queen of the greatest nation of the earth" are "received by the newest King and Queen—a King and Queen who won empire for themselves" (255). This meeting is recorded by a journalist for the fictitious *Free America* and is subjected to an editorial amendment that changes "greatest nation on earth" to "Greatest *Kingdom*" (255), which implicates the real source of conflict at the time.

By looking at Stoker's changing attitude toward the United States, it becomes possible to see why the frontier man of action, Quincey Morris, is not allowed to survive in *Dracula*. His name may be affectionately recalled in the naming of Jonathan and Mina's child, but he cannot be accommodated within a novel that is keen to eradicate threats to Britain's colonial authority.

Masculinity and constructions of national identity are clearly aligned by Stoker, and this, alongside accounts of degeneration, provides students with a way of thinking about the contexts that shape the representations of masculinity in *Dracula*. The move from passive to aggressive (especially in the instance of Jonathan Harker) can thus be usefully explained by looking at how this journey negotiates theories of degeneration and takes place within a geopolitical context in which Britain's colonial authority had become increasingly challenged.

"She Interest Me Too":
Centering Women in *Dracula*

Patrick R. O'Malley

How should we teach *Dracula* in a classroom responsive to the demands of Me Too and the need to be aware of the effects of pervasive sexual violence, inside and outside the academy? That is, I think, one of the most pressing questions for our pedagogical approach to this gripping, complex, and occasionally traumatic novel today. I have taught *Dracula* more than I've taught any other text, and it's the one that I both most enjoy teaching and feel most anxious about, a fact that speaks to its continued power of haunting. It is also probably the work for which the assumptions guiding my teaching have most changed in recent years, particularly in terms of its representations of gender and sexuality and the student experience of encountering them.

Notwithstanding Nina Auerbach's argument, in *Our Vampires, Ourselves*, that "*Dracula* is in love less with death or sexuality than with hierarchies" broadly conceived (66), it is certainly the case that scholarship and teaching on this novel have frequently emphasized its suggestions of gender and sexual transgression; *Dracula* might as easily appear on the syllabi of courses dedicated to such subjects as Victorian sexualities as on those focusing on nation and empire or the gothic. I've taught this novel in all three of those classes as well as making it the principal test case in a course on methodological approaches to literary analysis, including structuralist, historicist, Marxist, psychoanalytic, deconstructionist, postcolonial, ecocritical, feminist, and queer critique. The keywords of publications over a half century of scholarship on *Dracula* affirm the persistence of readings that emphasize gender and sexuality and track the novel's movement to the center of the literary canon: at the time of writing, four entries with the tags "Stoker," "*Dracula*," and "gender or sex°" appear in the *MLA International Bibliography* in the ten-year period from 1970 to 1979, inclusive (of twenty-seven in total for the novel); forty-five do in the ten-year period from 2010 to 2019 (of 317 in total).

"Gender and sexuality," of course, name many different critical and pedagogical approaches to *Dracula*, from psychoanalytic readings that have been foundational to gothic studies to historical accounts of the rise of the New Woman or Victorian sex work or sexually transmitted diseases or the conjunction of the novel's 1897 publication with Queen Victoria's Diamond Jubilee and the public performance of British womanhood that that event provided. In my course focused on methods of literary study, I have often used that fact of critical history to encourage students to consider how theoretical frameworks that initially seem fundamentally distinct might generatively be put into conversation with each other. I might ask them to characterize the differences between

Patrick R. O'Malley   121

the questions and kinds of evidence in Franco Moretti's *Signs Taken for Wonders* and those in Jennifer Wicke's "Vampiric Typewriting: *Dracula* and Its Media." While each critic brings Marxist or historicist approaches to bear on the novel, together with psychoanalytic accounts of desire, they do so in widely divergent ways.

In a class more specifically dedicated to gender and sexuality, I have placed *Dracula* in the context of some of Stoker's other writing, often "The Censorship of Fiction" along with both his 1872 and 1876 homoerotically charged letters to Walt Whitman. In the first of those letters, for example, Stoker muses to Whitman, "How sweet a thing it is for a strong healthy man with a woman's eyes and a child's wishes to feel that he can speak so to a man who can be if he wishes father, and brother and wife to his soul" (Traubel 185). In "'A Wilde Desire Took Me': The Homoerotic History of *Dracula*," Talia Schaffer has provided an exceptionally readable and engaging account of the suggestions of homoerotic desire in Stoker's life and writing, including the Whitman letters.[1] My students are fascinated by the fact, related in Schaffer's article, that the woman Stoker married, Florence Balcolme, had been enthusiastically courted by Oscar Wilde ("Wilde Desire" 391–92). Given all this—and given what they understand to be the erotically charged rhetoric of *Dracula* itself—they are generally puzzled by Stoker's assertions in "The Censorship of Fiction": "A close analysis will show that the only emotions which in the long run harm are those arising from sex impulses" (483); "such works as are here spoken of deal not merely with natural misdoing based on human weakness, frailty, or passions of the senses, but with vices so flagitious, so opposed to even the decencies of nature in its crudest and lowest forms, that the poignancy of moral disgust is lost in horror"; and "They in their selfish greed tried to deprave where others had striven to elevate. In the language of the pulpit, they have 'crucified Christ afresh'" (485). There's much here that might describe *Dracula* itself; how, I ask my students, might we think of the novel in terms of what Stoker identifies as the sexual politics of popular fiction? Does *Dracula* uphold the morality its author advocates or violate it?

It seems that despite the sexual and gender conservativism of Stoker's "Censorship of Fiction," *Dracula* bursts with images of sexual exploration and fantasies of swapped or nonbinary genders. It repeatedly violates the norms that it putatively upholds. As just one example, Jonathan's concluding note seeks to contain the novel's gothic energies with an appeal to marriage-plot closure: "When we got home we were talking of the old time—which we could all look back on without despair, for Godalming and Seward are both happily married" (Stoker, *Dracula* 344). And yet the novel itself has already narrated the *failure* of the marriage plot to maintain a strict boundary between past and present in Mina's sealing of Jonathan's journal with her wedding ring ("an outward and visible sign for us all our lives that we trusted each other" [Stoker, *Dracula* 108]), a seal that she soon has to break. Apparently, heterosexual marriage is not as efficacious in warding off vampiric infiltration as Jonathan seems to believe.

122   CENTERING WOMEN

At least since the 1980s, many readings of *Dracula* have grounded their analysis of sex and gender in the novel in the juxtaposition of three sensational set pieces that punctuate its plot with erotically or sexually charged horror: the near seduction of Jonathan by the three female vampires in Castle Dracula (46–48); the tracking and staking of vampiric Lucy by Arthur, John, Quincey, and Van Helsing (197–206); and the spectacle of Mina's victimization by Dracula in her bedroom (241–42, 260–63). As a key (and early) example of that analysis, I frequently assign Christopher Craft's influential "Kiss Me with Those Red Lips: Gender and Inversion in Bram Stoker's *Dracula*." My students don't always agree with all Craft's readings of the vampire's mouth as a "subversion of the stable and lucid distinctions of gender" ("Kiss Me" 109), but they tend to find them intriguing (and his coinage of the term "Crew of Light" for the group of vampire hunters can be very helpful). Craft usefully positions his claims about gender and sexuality within the context of the late-nineteenth-century concept of "inversion," a notion that helps to explicate not only Jonathan's desire for penetration by the vampiric women but also his imaginative description of himself, just before that scene, "sitting at a little oak table where in old times possibly some fair lady sat to pen, with much thought and many blushes, her ill-spelt love-letter, and writing in my diary" (Stoker, *Dracula* 45). Similarly, Van Helsing's famous description of Mina as having a "man's brain—a brain that a man should have were he much gifted—and woman's heart" (220) might echo Richard von Krafft-Ebing's description of female sexual inversion as "the masculine soul, heaving in the female bosom" (264).

As important as that critical history is to students' understanding of *Dracula's* representation of homoeroticism and gender transgression, though, I want here to complement it with a different reading and pedagogical practice I have moved toward in recent years. There has been a tendency, both in some of the most influential criticism and in my own teaching, to focus on those tableaux of spectacular gender and sexual anxiety as the key to *Dracula's* sexual politics and aesthetics. They are, to be sure, striking and important scenes. But I have come to believe that too narrow a focus on them delimits our understanding of the range of ways of inhabiting—and querying—gendered and sexual identities that *Dracula* offers. For one thing, that reading tends to center male experience, representing female characters largely as immobilized victims (Mina), near-pornographic fantasies (the vampiric women), or the subjects of what Craft calls "corrective penetration" of vampiric Lucy ("Kiss Me" 118). Sexually agential women quickly become threatening monsters, as in the case of the vampiric women or of Lucy joking to Mina about wanting to marry multiple men (Stoker, *Dracula* 60). By celebrating vampirism as a transgression of oppressive Victorian sexual norms (enforced by Van Helsing and the rest of the "Crew of Light"), Craft downplays the ways in which *Dracula* stresses vampirism's own gendered violence toward women. Whereas Craft reads the bedroom attack on Mina as an "initiation scene," for example, in which "Dracula compels Mina into the pleasure of vampiric appetite" ("Kiss Me" 125), the novel—unlike some adaptations[2]—does not, at least in my reading, figure this as the awakening of sexual agency: "I lay still and endured," Mina says; "that was all" (Stoker, *Dracula* 241). This is not pleasure but sexual assault.

Part of the reason these particular scenes have seized critical and pedagogical attention, I want to suggest, lies in the legacy of psychoanalytic critique that continues to underwrite significant strands of feminist, queer, and gothic studies. Three of the most influential approaches to teaching issues of gender and sexuality in *Dracula*, these critical methods have largely shaped my own scholarship on the novel along with the pedagogy that has arisen from that scholarship. But I was startled into reflection a few years ago when a student asked me why we so often focused our class discussion on *Dracula*'s scenes of sexual violence. To answer, I considered the ways in which the novel produces its phenomenological response, even in the terms of sensationalized reading that Stoker describes in "The Censorship of Fiction." Horror, like Jacques Derrida's *bricoleur*, mobilizes what is available for its effects (Derrida, *Writing and Difference* 285–86). Among all the overdetermined resonances of vampiric attack (economics and class, race and ethnicity, empire and colonialism, religion, disease, technology, women's entry into the worlds of professional life and capitalist consumption, and modernity itself, among others), the eerie awareness of the vulnerability of our bodies to trauma or infiltration ranks high; sexual and gendered violences offer a gold mine of anxieties and fears.

But even acknowledging the importance of those aspects of the novel to the way it mobilizes its gothic affects of fear, is sexual trauma truly the singular master key for deciphering its representation of gender? That is the import of my student's gentle challenge and the area where the insights and ethical demands of the broader Me Too movement have most inspired me to adjust my approach to teaching *Dracula*. For one thing, while I find the rhetoric of a "trigger warning" unhelpful, I have begun to advise students in advance of our sessions on this novel that both the text and our discussion of it may include content that some will find difficult and that I understand that they might not always be able to contribute to those conversations. As Aaron Hanlon has argued, this in no way excludes the consideration of important critical approaches in the classroom but rather establishes a consciously student-centered pedagogical space in which to make those discussions *more* possible. This is, in my experience, even more important for online and hybrid classes, in which it can be significantly more difficult to perceive how students are responding psychologically or emotionally to a text or a class conversation.

Given that, I have found it transformative to recontextualize those scenes of sensational violence within the broader context of the novel's often contradictory representations of gender and desire, a context not always tied to anxiety or trauma. Encouraging students to track Mina's relationship to gender roles, for example, can provide them with a complex set of passages for thinking through what the novel is doing, particularly given that Mina (unlike Lucy) is a professional woman from the start; her very first letter opens with the apology that she

124   CENTERING WOMEN

has "been simply overwhelmed with work," since "[t]he life of an assistant school-mistress is sometimes trying" (Stoker, *Dracula* 60). It is Mina who ridicules New Woman activism and (imputed) sexual politics in a diary entry written in Whitby:

> We had a capital "severe tea" at Robin Hood's Bay in a sweet little old-fashioned inn, with a bow-window right over the seaweed-covered rocks of the strand. I believe we should have shocked the "New Woman" with our appetites. Men are more tolerant, bless them! . . . Lucy is asleep and breathing softly. She has more colour in her cheeks than usual, and looks, oh, so sweet. If Mr. Holmwood fell in love with her seeing her only in the drawing-room, I wonder what he would say if he saw her now. Some of the "New Women" writers will some day start an idea that men and women should be allowed to see each other asleep before proposing or accepting. But I suppose the New Woman won't condescend in future to accept; she will do the proposing herself. And a nice job she will make of it too!   (93–94)

The novel concludes with Van Helsing's reductive description, quoted with apparent approbation by Jonathan, of Mina as a mother and as the recipient of male devotion: "This boy will some day know what a brave and gallant woman his mother is. Already he knows her sweetness and loving care. Later on he will understand how some men so loved her, that they did dare much for her sake" (344). It's a description that minimizes Mina's own agency in the fight against Dracula, something that the men in the novel repeatedly do. She is twice excluded from the group sessions dedicated to planning the assault on Dracula, each time with at least some reference to her gender, and both times that deci-sion leads to disaster (228, 296). In each case, though, it is Mina who figures out the necessary next step, something that she can do only once she is brought back into the group's confidence. The novel itself seems to have difficulty main-taining the gendered assumptions underlying Van Helsing's dichotomy between "man's brain" and "woman's heart," as Mina, often at odds with those assump-tions, keeps solving problems that the other "man's brains" cannot. Providing my students with information about the New Woman—and arguments over the New Woman's role in challenging or reaffirming Victorian notions of gender—I ask them to debate whether Mina, despite her expressed antifeminism, is in fact herself a sort of New Woman.[3] What are the implications of that seeming con-tradiction for the novel's understanding of gender and gender roles?

In fact, *Dracula* presents a different set of gendered representations as well, beyond the victimized "good" woman in need of male protection and the vic-timizing "bad" woman deploying her sexuality to destroy men: that of woman as reader, writer, and problem-solver, not just the recorder of others' words (as Mina at times is) but also the producer of her own. Mina's sleuthing is one example of this, but it is not the only one. An excellent resource for this approach to the novel is Renée Fox's "Building Castles in the Air: Female

Intimacy and Generative Queerness in *Dracula*," which reads women's sexuality not as monstrous threat but as "resuscitating power" (591). Fox argues that "Lucy and Mina's queer female intimacy," articulated in the representation of their friendship in writing, "plays an indispensable role in generating the novel's texts and in bringing little England together to fight Dracula" (606). The essay productively shifts our attention away from the representation of male homoerotics and homosociality that Craft and others have highlighted in *Dracula* and toward the less paranoid female erotics that Sharon Marcus has described in *Between Women: Friendship, Desire, and Marriage in Victorian England*.

What Fox offers is a reading of *Dracula*'s female characters as subjects of their own linguistic construction rather than objects of masculine scripts. In that regard, I have found another passage, Lucy's description of studying herself in the mirror, also generative:

> [John Seward] has a curious habit of looking one straight in the face, as if trying to read one's thoughts. He tries this on very much with me, but I flatter myself he has got a tough nut to crack. I know that from my glass. Do you ever try to read your own face? *I do*, and I can tell you it is not a bad study, and gives you more trouble than you can well fancy if you have never tried it. (Stoker, *Dracula* 62)

As a passage, it is itself a kind of interpretive knot: Lucy recounts studying her face in the mirror and, from that reflected image, trying to interpret what she is thinking. But what else could she be thinking but "What am I thinking?" The entire passage is a fantasia on what it means to think and to know; Lucy's account plays deliriously with the interplay of agency and objectification, with what it means to read and to be read, with resistance to the penetrating gaze of another. In looking at herself, Lucy turns herself into the object of her own interpretation, an act for which she is of course also the agent. All that is relevant to *Dracula*'s representation of gender and sexuality, but one other aspect of this passage strikes me as well: Lucy takes *pleasure* in herself both as a face and as a mind. It is a scene that substitutes a female spectator—and female cognizing subject—for a male one and female pleasure in visuality and epistemological puzzles for male anxiety. This passage is far less frequently written about or taught than the much more celebrated mirror scene of Jonathan's failure to see Dracula in his own looking glass, but I have found that juxtaposing these two scenes can lead to insightful class discussions.

Reading *Dracula* in this way with a class can also open up the relationship between writing and thinking—and writing *as* thinking—and it positions women as the agents of that relationship. While acknowledging and understanding the ways in which the representation of sexual violence is important to *Dracula*'s narrative and phenomenological effects (and the fact that students' personal experiences will make critical engagement with that literary

126   CENTERING WOMEN

representation of violence more or less possible), instructors should point out that those representations are not the only way for women to see themselves in this novel. At a university like Georgetown, where I teach and where the majority of undergraduate students are women, the insight that *Dracula*, for all its Victorianism and all Mina's own snide remarks about New Woman agency and censoriousness, also offers an alternative vision of gender has greatly expanded the ways in which I can help students find themselves in the texts we're reading, not as victims but as writers. It has also generated new approaches for me in terms of using *Dracula* in classes primarily devoted to teaching composition.

Another way to put this is that, in teaching gender and sexuality in *Dracula*, I have come to want to take more seriously and at face value Van Helsing's statement about Lucy: "she interest me too" (116). The rhetoric of sexual violence and the sort of misogyny that Stoker expresses in "The Censorship of Fiction" are important, but so are the ways that the novel itself offers alternatives to a phobic stance, alternatives that might, in Eve Kosofsky Sedgwick's generative framework (*Touching Feeling* 123–51), move past paranoia to a sort of reparative reading.

NOTES

1. The article is extracted in the second Norton Critical Edition of *Dracula* (470–82) but without most of the cultural, historical, and biographical context.

2. For example, the 1979 film *Dracula*, directed by John Badham and starring Frank Langella as Dracula and Kate Nelligan as Lucy (equivalent to Mina in the novel), highlights Lucy's erotic agency and adds at least a suggestion of feminist politics. (Like many adaptations based on John L. Balderston's 1927 revision of Hamilton Deane's 1924 play, the film reverses the names of the two principal female characters [Deane and Balderston].)

3. A good contemporary source for debates over the New Woman is Sarah Grand's "The New Aspect of the Woman Question," in part because it is often credited with coining the term and in part because—while Stoker doesn't name specific writers in "The Censorship of Fiction"—Grand seems to be exactly the sort of novelist he has in mind in his attack on women writers as the "worst offenders" against morality (485).

FILM AND TELEVISION

The Dracula Megatext

Jeffrey Andrew Weinstock

A productive preliminary step when teaching Bram Stoker's *Dracula* is to solicit from students what they know about Dracula, and about vampires in general, and to compile a list. What does Dracula look like? What are his strengths and abilities? What are his weaknesses? The usefulness of such a list will become evident by the time students have finished chapter 2.

As recorded in his journal, when Jonathan Harker first arrived at Castle Dracula after his harrowing coach ride through the Transylvanian darkness, he was greeted by "a tall old man, clean-shaven save for a long white moustache, and clad in black from head to foot" (Stoker, *Dracula* 24). As Harker scrutinized the old man further, he noticed that his face "was a strong—a very strong—aquiline, with high bridge of the thin nose and peculiarly arched nostrils; with lofty domed forehead, and hair growing scantily round the temples, but profusely elsewhere. His eyebrows were massive, almost meeting over the nose, and with bushy hair that seemed to curl in its own profusion." His ears "were pale and at the tops extremely pointed," while his hands were "coarse—broad, with squat fingers" and, "strange to say, there were hairs in the centre of the palm" (27).

Stoker's description of a very hairy Count Dracula—for this is, in fact, who has greeted Jonathan—may be surprising to students and other modern readers of the novel since it does not correspond with the commonplace conception of Dracula as middle-aged, clean-shaven, and dressed for the opera in a white tuxedo shirt and bow tie, with a high-collared black cape and white suit jacket pocket square—the description students are likely to have supplied prior to beginning the book. In the popular imagination, Dracula has a relatively prominent widow's peak, normal-looking ears and eyebrows, piercing eyes, and longish fingers that tend to contort strangely—without any apparent hair on the palms. Ironically, the most famous representation of Stoker's Count appears nowhere in Stoker's novel; it derives instead from Tod Browning's 1931 film's casting of Bela Lugosi in an adaptation that owes more in many respects to

128   DRACULA MEGATEXT

Hamilton Deane and John L. Balderston's stage version of *Dracula* than to Stoker's novel.

There is another version of Dracula in Stoker's text, however. After the funeral for Jonathan Harker's employer, Mr. Hawkins, Mina and Jonathan are walking through London when Jonathan suddenly stops short and turns pale at the sight of "a tall, thin man, with a beaky nose and black moustache and pointed beard" (Stoker, *Dracula* 165–66). "Do you see who it is?" he asks Mina. When she confesses her ignorance, he replies, "I believe it is the Count, but he has grown young" (166). The two walk on together and then, because it is a hot and sunny day, take a seat in the shade of a park to allow Jonathan to recover from the shock. Linger on this moment with your students and ask them what seems odd here.

Stoker's Count in this representation is younger and now sports a Vandyke beard. What is perhaps most startling, though, to students and modern readers who are paying careful attention may not be Dracula's facial hair but that the Count is out and about during the day, despite the fact that prevailing conceptions of vampires understand them to be allergic to sunlight. Van Helsing, in his lecture to the "Crew of Light" (as Christopher Craft ["Kiss Me"] dubs the heroes) after Lucy's second death has proved the existence of vampires, explains that the vampire's "power ceases, as does that of all evil things, at the coming of the day" (Stoker, *Dracula* 224) but not that sunlight destroys the vampire—and, indeed, Dracula is again encountered during the day; as the team is sterilizing Dracula's coffins of earth in his south London lair, they are surprised by the Count himself in the middle of the afternoon.

Noting the fact that Dracula in Stoker's novel can move about during the day, ask your students where they have encountered the idea that sunlight kills vampires. Like the template for the mental picture we have of Dracula himself, this aspect of vampire lore originated in the movies—in this case from F. W. Murnau's silent German Expressionist adaptation, *Nosferatu*. In this unauthorized adaptation, the vampire, having feasted freely upon the female protagonist, who martyrs herself to save those she loves, disappears in a rather disappointing puff of smoke when struck by the dawn's first light. Over time, this properly cinematic special effect has been amplified to such an extent that contemporary cinematic vampires smoke, melt, burst into flames, or even explode when exposed to sunlight. As your students will no doubt insist in your original list of vampire characteristics, it is now widely agreed upon that sunlight destroys vampires, yet this understanding is absent from the literary vampire urtext, Stoker's *Dracula*. This realization then permits instructors to introduce the idea of the "Dracula megatext."

The Dracula Megatext

That when we think of Dracula today we picture Lugosi—or iterations of Dracula based on Lugosi's representation, including Grandpa (Al Lewis) on

The Munsters, Count von Count on *Sesame Street*, Count Dracula in the *Hotel Transylvania* animated films, and so on—and that only some of the qualities we associate with Dracula and vampires are actually present in Stoker's text (while other qualities Stoker attributes to vampires are not present in later adaptions) makes clear that Dracula could be considered "overdetermined" in the Freudian sense—that is, he is an image or idea whose origin is traceable back to multiple sources. Stoker's *Dracula* remains the most obvious and important point of origin but has been supplemented over time by many other representations of the Count that reinforce qualities associated with Stoker's character, reject or revise some aspects, or introduce new ones. As Matthew Crofts observes, "[T]he contemporary version of Dracula is a composite of features from his many textual afterlives" (63). Each new contribution to the growing body of representations of Dracula therefore participates in what, borrowing from science fiction studies, we might refer to as the "Dracula megatext."

In *Science Fiction: A Guide for the Perplexed*, the scholar Sherryl Vint cites Damien Broderick's notion of the megatext as a concept referring to the way that science fiction is "generated and received . . . within a specialised intertextual encyclopaedia of tropes and enabling devices" (Broderick qtd. in Vint 57). The megatext "reveals the way that sf explicitly refers back to earlier instances of itself, each text adding to and playing with the larger body of signs, images, and scenarios that make up sf's shared world." As such, *megatext*

> describes a context in which writers operate within an understanding of a certain set of established images and motifs, such as cyborgs or hyperspace or FTL [faster than light] travel, that do not belong to any single text or author, but are shared, each new iteration both relying upon established meanings and associations, and also opening them up to new possibilities, creating a vast and interconnected web of meanings that exceeds what appears in any single text.

Within the megatext, "[c]ertain prominent texts become dense centers of gravity, inevitably pulling the meaning of icons toward their influential formulations. For example, any created being in sf carries a trace of Frankenstein's Creature" (57).

This idea of the megatext, itself borrowed from science fiction studies, provides a useful framework for students and researchers to think about origination, appropriation, and adaptation over time. Megatext allows us to acknowledge not only Stoker's novel as a "dense center of gravity" at the core of the representation of vampires but also the roles that familiarity with vampire narratives in general and *Dracula* in particular play in the pleasure derived from consumption of contributions to the megatext. In the same way that every science fictive narrative involving created beings (robots, AIs, cyborgs, etc.) finds its roots in Mary Shelley's urtext *Frankenstein*, all twentieth- and twenty-first-century vampire narratives—whether explicitly naming their vampire Dracula or not—unavoidably have as a point of reference Stoker's novel. What is more, creators of

130   DRACULA MEGATEXT

new vampire texts, themselves possessing a general understanding of the "web of meanings" associated with the vampire, can assume, at least to a certain extent, a conversance with the "established meanings and associations" connected to the vampire on the part of their audience. As Stacey Abbott notes, "Dracula's various screen appearances build upon each other, operating as much in dialogue with their cinematic and televisual predecessors as they do with Stoker's original text" (192). Ask your students how protagonists in vampire narratives prepare to do battle with their undead opponents and a pattern will be revealed: research! Myths and legends about vampires will be rehearsed, some of which will be confirmed and others refuted through interaction with the vampire. Each new iteration of the vampire in general and Dracula in particular thus charts a path between the poles of repetition and innovation, and, as Vint suggests of science fiction, much of the enjoyment of Dracula narratives is derived from the interplay of comfortable familiarity and surprising novelty.

Four Draculas

Stoker, of course, did not invent the notion of the vampire any more than Shelley invented the notion of breathing life into inanimate matter. There were literary vampires that preceded *Dracula* in the nineteenth century (e.g., in John Polidori's *The Vampyre*, James Malcolm Rymer's *Varney the Vampire*, Joseph Sheridan Le Fanu's *Carmilla*, and other works) and folkloric accounts of supernatural blood-drinking creatures stretching back to antiquity within many different cultures. *Dracula*, instead of inventing the vampire, functions as a kind of vampire confluence—the place where different past vampire myths and narratives meet and from which they flow forth and diverge again. In thinking about and teaching *Dracula* today, however, we must acknowledge the different paths that *Dracula* has taken since its publication and the ways the intertextual interplay of differing interpretations shapes our reception of the novel itself and its central antagonist—because, as I emphasize to my students, when we read *Dracula* today, there is not just one vampire in our minds but rather many overlapping ones. Stoker's eponymous Count is now less an individual character, I explain, and closer to an archetype—and it is difficult to consider Stoker's vampire in a contemporary context without also having as a point of reference the cinematic tradition. Although there have been hundreds of adaptations of *Dracula* and appropriations of its vampire antagonist, four of the films that I consider most important in terms of shaping the contours of the Dracula megatext, and that I assign as viewing during our unit on Stoker, are Murnau's *Nosferatu*, Browning's *Dracula*, Terence Fisher's *Horror of Dracula*, and Francis Ford Coppola's *Bram Stoker's* Dracula. Each of these four famous adaptations, while unavoidably a product of its historical moment, has nevertheless participated in shaping our understanding of vampires, of Dracula, and, indeed, of Stoker's novel, and consideration of each in coordination with Stoker's novel allows students to perceive how the Dracula megatext functions.

In the same way that Stoker's *Dracula* was not the first vampire story, Murnau's *Nosferatu* was not the first cinematic adaptation of Stoker's *Dracula*—it was preceded by a Turkish film called *Drakula halála* (*Death of Dracula*) and possibly a somewhat earlier silent Soviet adaptation, the existence of which is unconfirmed (see Melton, *Vampire Book* 720). Despite Florence Stoker's attempts to have Murnau's expressionistic adaptation of her husband's novel quashed (Keatley), however, *Nosferatu* is the earliest existing film adaptation and has contributed to the Dracula megatext in several respects—notably by introducing the alternative representation of Dracula as rat-like but also through its use of special effects that have shaped subsequent cinematic representations of the Count and now seem inextricably intertwined with him.

As one of the earliest film adaptations of *Dracula*, *Nosferatu* was not constrained or influenced by previous visual representations of Stoker's Count, and, with his pointed ears and bushy eyebrows, the actor Max Schreck's Count Orlok in *Nosferatu* is actually closer in some respects to Stoker's description of his vampire than the more familiar Lugosi model. What stands out most, however, about Count Orlok, as students will readily appreciate, is his rat-like appearance. Stoker, it is true, does not describe Dracula in this way; however, Orlok's appearance nevertheless finds its basis in the novel, for Dracula is associated with rats and vermin throughout. Memorably, Dracula, seeking to coerce Renfield's allegiance, reveals to him thousands of rats whose appearance is likened to his own: "He moved the mist to the right and left, and I could see that there were thousands of rats with their eyes blazing red—like His, only smaller" (Stoker, *Dracula* 259). Murnau's Count Orlok, amplifying this association with rats, is presented with rat-like incisors and pointed ears, and the coffins of earth he takes with him from Transylvania to Wisborg are swarming with rats as well. The representation of Count Orlok in *Nosferatu* can be considered a minor but important distributary branching off the vampire confluence that is Stoker's novel and contributing to the megatext. Klaus Kinski's version of Orlok in Werner Herzog's remake of *Nosferatu* is, of course, patterned after Schreck's, but so too is the master vampire Barlow (Reggie Halder) in the miniseries *Salem's Lot*, based on a novel by Stephen King. Gary Oldman's Count Dracula in Coppola's *Bram Stoker's* Dracula also assumes a Nosferatu-like appearance as one of his forms.

The makeup used to fashion Max Schreck's representation of the vampire is one aspect of the special effects developed in *Nosferatu* that have influenced later representations. In teaching *Nosferatu*, it is useful to highlight the cinematic tricks Murnau originated or refined to convey the supernatural qualities of his vampire antagonist. He used a dissolve to show his vampire turning to smoke when struck by the dawn's first light, thus introducing the now commonplace belief that sunlight kills vampires; he used a stop-motion sequence to simulate unnatural speed; and, perhaps most significantly, he associated his vampire with shadows that seem to move and stretch on their own—among the film's most famous scenes, one shows Orlok's shadow climbing the stairs

132   DRACULA MEGATEXT

to the female protagonist's room and then stretching shadowy fingers toward her door. That a vampire casts a shadow at all is specifically refuted by Stoker's Van Helsing, who mentions to the Crew of Light that, in the same way that he casts no reflection, the vampire "throws no shadow" (Stoker, *Dracula* 224). Later vampire films have nevertheless appropriated this idea of the vampire's living shadow. In Carl Dreyer's *Vampyr*, for example, there are shadows that dance independently of their owners, while Oldman's Dracula in *Bram Stoker's Dracula* has a shadow that moves on its own (an effect later spoofed by *The Simpsons* in "Treehouse of Horror IV," in which Mr. Burns, patterned after Oldman's Dracula, is given his own living shadow playing with a yo-yo).

If Murnau's adaptation is a minor but important distributary, Browning's adaptation is the main tributary. More so than any other film, as a list of vampire qualities solicited from students is likely to confirm, Browning's adaptation has shaped the conception of the vampire in the contemporary imagination. As noted at the start of this essay, Bela Lugosi's Dracula departs from Stoker's description of him in significant ways; nevertheless, both Lugosi's appearance in the film and the delivery of his lines with his Hungarian accent are the standard by which other representations of Dracula are judged—Dracula is now firmly fixed in contemporary popular culture as a mysterious foreign aristocrat dressed to the nines who delivers lines not in fact present in Stoker, such as "I never drink . . . wine," with ominous foreshadowing.

In addition to fixing his appearance, Browning's *Dracula* emphasizes the vampire's hypnotic gaze. Note for students how Browning fixes his camera on Lugosi's eyes, which are often strategically lit to highlight their mesmeric power; Dracula is thus presented as a Svengali-like figure who controls his victims through the power of his will. Indeed, a key scene in Browning's *Dracula* not present in Stoker involves a kind of contest of wills between Dracula and Van Helsing, played by Edward Van Sloan. Van Helsing has discovered the true nature of the mysterious aristocrat, and Dracula seeks to destroy the man he now perceives as a threat, commanding Van Helsing to "Come . . . here." Van Helsing's success at resisting Dracula's command is pivotal in turning the tables on the monstrous Count. This test of Dracula's mesmeric powers is more an amplification of a theme present in Stoker than a cinematic innovation; Stoker's Dracula is able to bend people to his will—notably, when he forces Mina to drink from his chest. However, Browning's adaptation offers a visceral representation of this power that has become central to the Dracula megatext.

Lugosi's representation of the Count in Browning's film is languorous and relatively restrained. His character doesn't have visible fangs, and the film—in black and white, in keeping with the period—shows no blood and offers little in the way of overt sensuality. All that changes, as students will note, with Hammer Film Productions' version of *Dracula*, distributed in the United States as *Horror of Dracula*, starring Christopher Lee in the role of the Count and Peter Cushing as the intrepid Van Helsing. It is this film, the first in Hammer's series of nine Dracula films, that gives us so much of what we now associate with Dracula

Jeffrey Andrew Weinstock   133

and vampire films in general: a more assertive, dynamic antagonist; sexy vampire brides with heaving bosoms; bared fangs; and, of course, blood. Ask students to compare *Horror of Dracula* to Stoker's *Dracula*, noting where they are parallel and where the story and character representations diverge. While there is much to discuss here, *Horror* amplifies elements of vampire lore present in Stoker (such as the power of the cross to ward off the vampire) or invented by the cinematic tradition (such as the power of the sun to destroy the vampire) while introducing the idea that, as Crofts puts it, "Dracula always comes back" (66).

Christopher Lee's Count Dracula, significantly, is the origin point for all modern vampire action films. Within *Horror of Dracula*, he is active and assertive, flashing his fangs and, as Crofts observes, "launching into savage bursts of movement" (64). With eyes ablaze and red, Technicolor blood staining his face, he interrupts his sexy vampire bride early in the film as she is poised to snack on Jonathan Harker, forcefully throwing her to the ground. Later, as he is pursued back to his very modern castle, he runs, jumps, and attacks. This muscular kineticism is also connected to a more explicit sensuality. Lee's Dracula is commanding, and his female victims await his coming with equal measures of dread and desire. Through *Horror of Dracula* and the later Hammer Dracula contributions, "Dracula becomes more associated with his sexuality, allure, and violence than any of his other qualities—paving the way for future variations" (65).

What students may also observe about *Horror of Dracula* is its early elaboration of motifs that are now fully entrenched in vampire lore. During the final confrontation with Dracula, Peter Cushing's Van Helsing rips down the curtains over a large window. He then pins Dracula in place using a cross made from two heavy iron candlesticks as the streaming sunlight causes Dracula to rapidly and dramatically decay and turn to dust before the viewer's eyes. In Stoker's novel, of course, Dracula cannot abide religious icons such as the crucifix and communion wafer. Hammer's *Horror of Dracula* takes this motif a step further by introducing the idea that makeshift religious icons, if wielded with film belief in their efficacy, can function similarly as vampire prophylactics; it additionally renders the power of the sun over the vampire, introduced in *Nosferatu*, far more explicitly. As Crofts notes, the Hammer Dracula films also contribute to the "composite Dracula" megatext the now-familiar conceit that Dracula *always* comes back as a "recurring menace" (66–67). Contemporary viewers know that you just can't keep a good vampire down.

It's not just Dracula who always comes back, though—at least, that's among the main additions to Dracula lore students may discern in Coppola's big-budget, big-name-cast version of *Dracula*, misleadingly titled *Bram Stoker's* Dracula. This adaptation of Stoker's novel, with Oldman as the eponymous Count, completes the transformation of Dracula from mysterious, demonic antagonist into sensual, romantic antihero by introducing a reincarnation subplot students will note is nowhere present—or even implied—in Stoker's novel.

Amplifying the association between Stoker's Count and Vlad the Impaler, Coppola creates a backstory for Dracula in which his young bride, Elisabeta

134 DRACULA MEGATEXT

(Winona Ryder), after receiving a false report that her husband, Dracula, has died in battle, commits suicide. Enraged, Dracula curses God and embraces darkness. Flash forward several centuries: when Dracula glimpses a photograph carried by Jonathan Harker (Keanu Reeves) of his fiancée, Mina Murray, also played by Ryder, he recognizes her as his reincarnated bride. What follows then is the sensual reunion of the melancholic vampire and his lost love, who admits to the Crew of Light that she remembers her past life and loves the Count, even as she acknowledges that he has become a monster who must be destroyed. In the final scene of the film, Mina's love releases Dracula from his curse and allows him to go to his eternal rest.

Of course, as students who have read the novel will be in a position to observe, Stoker does not present Dracula as a melancholic lover or suggest that Mina is somehow his reincarnated wife—this subplot (involving vampires if not Dracula explicitly) may well have originated with the 1960s supernaturally themed soap opera *Dark Shadows* and turns up in later films, such as the American blaxploitation film *Blacula* and the comedy *Love at First Bite*. Its presence in *Bram Stoker's Dracula*, however, is the logical culmination of a developmental arc in which Dracula increasingly is presented as far more dynamic, charismatic, and desirable than the prudish Crew of Light that pursues him. This transformation testifies to important conclusions: first, that Stoker's vampire inevitably serves as a kind of Rorschach test for different audiences in different contexts. To riff on Nina Auerbach's study of vampire films, each era embraces the Dracula it needs and gets the Dracula it deserves (145). But what the many transformations of Stoker's monstrous Count also foreground is that Dracula in the popular imagination is legion—a composite amalgamation of many representations over time, all tethered to Stoker's text, but with varying degrees of strength. Returning then to the preliminary list of Dracula characteristics and vampire features compiled at the start, the concept of the Dracula megatext is thus one that allows students and vampire researchers to acknowledge that Stoker's undead creation now has many authors.

Vampires in a Virtually Flipped Classroom

Peter Gölz

Vampires are more popular than ever. "Students love vampires" (Ormandy 204), and there really is a vampire for everyone and every interest. Despite their undead state, vampires are some of the most lively figures in our "myth pool" and "cultural echo chamber" (Kooyman 260), and "Dracula has reached the point of pop culture osmosis that rivals Santa Claus or Sherlock Holmes" (Leeder 146). After all, which other fictional character has seen so many variations and adaptations, has expanded into so many new directions, has appealed to all age groups, and has remained popular for such a long time? It took a long time before vampires and vampire studies were accepted as serious topics, but now they have finally been allowed to enter the halls of academia.

Popular culture courses, or, more specifically, horror or vampire studies courses, had to fight the traditional canon for a long time because of the modernist distinction of high versus low culture. Many "dream courses" were dead on arrival because of this attitude, doomed by an academic anti-pop stance like the one described by W. Scott Poole: "Skepticism about the pedagogy and study of monsters comes, knowingly or unknowingly, from scholars influenced very much by the Frankfurt School's grumpy evaluation of pop culture as mind-numbing, apolitical mass culture" (2). This "Great Divide" (Huyssen) between so-called "low" and "high" culture also played a role at my university. It took almost ten years for my course A Cultural History of Vampires in Literature and Film to be offered in the catalog. Many instructors have encountered initial criticism of such course topics as not academically "serious" enough. In "Legitimizing Vampire Fiction as an Area of Literary Study," Sue Weaver Schopf describes the reactions to her new course at Harvard when it was first proposed, in 2010: "In contrast to these mixed attitudes inside the University, I encountered unbridled enthusiasm from the general public" (9). When the course was finally offered, almost two hundred students enrolled. Nowadays, "the assumption that literary and cinematic horror texts are low cultural forms unworthy of serious critical attention has been successfully challenged on a number of fronts" (Ahmad and Moreland 5).

It seems easy to attract students with courses on vampires and other monsters; indeed, many "may enter our classes assuming that nothing could be easier than thinking and talking about zombies, vampires, and Frankenstein's monsters. . . . So, our students come sometimes giddy with excitement but uncertain of what we will actually do" (Poole 1). What we do in our classrooms has been discussed in a number of recent publications, most notably *Monsters in the Classroom* (Golub and Hayton), *Buffy in the Classroom* (Kreider and Winchell), *The Vampire Goes to College* (Nevárez), and *Fear and Learning* (Ahmad and Moreland).

136   VIRTUALLY FLIPPED CLASSROOM

Vampires finally have a chance to demonstrate that they are a "kind of pedagogical Rosetta Stone" (Leeder 152) and that they can be used to teach almost anything.

I have been teaching A Cultural History of Vampires in Literature and Film at the University of Victoria, in British Columbia, since 2001. The first time the course was offered, it had 70 students. Over the years it has had an average of close to 300 students in the fall and 130 in the summer term. In May 2020, the course was offered completely online for the first time and attracted 180 students, which was the highest enrollment in any summer term.

As we finished the spring term online and rushed to prepare for completely online offerings in May, I searched for an appropriate image for our learning management system (LMS) site. I chose a still from *Nosferatu: A Symphony of Horror* that shows Ellen throwing up her hands at the very end of the film. It seemed an apt visualization of what teaching in the summer of 2020 might be like.

General Course Structure

Before the start of the 2020 summer term, a large number of students had contacted me to inquire about the format and content of the course. Instead of waiting for the first class to share this information, the department posted a video introducing the course outline and the instructor on *YouTube*. Previously, courses had been advertised locally on digital displays on campus; however, sharing information on *YouTube* allowed for broader, public access because one did not have to log into the university's LMS or any other password-protected site to watch the video. Students took a close look, and when the term started, there had been twice as many hits for the course outline video as there were registered students in the class.

The course began with two synchronous sessions, one in the morning and one in the late afternoon, and students from Asia, Europe, and North America joined in on *Zoom*. While this first session was mostly a meet-and-greet, it is highly recommended to organize students into groups for collaborative work as soon as possible, since "[s]tudies suggest that small-group activities promote student mastery of material, enhance critical thinking skills, provide rapid feedback for the instructor, and facilitate the development of affective dimensions in students, such as students' sense of self-efficacy and learner empowerment" ("Teaching"). In order to establish a sense of community, we also had a presentation and Q and A with a guest speaker on the second day of class. Since this was a *Zoom* meeting, it added value for students at no cost to the department, and students were very excited to meet David Skal, who talked about Bram Stoker, *Dracula*, and Tod Browning's film (*Dracula*).

The course itself presents a historical overview and focuses on questions of genre, gender, and intertextuality. Stoker's *Dracula* and Patrick Süskind's *Perfume: The Story of a Murderer* are the assigned novels, and the movies are presented chronologically in three modules: the Classics module consists of

Nosferatu: A Symphony of Horror and Browning's *Dracula*; Remakes and Retakes includes *Nosferatu the Vampyre, Bram Stoker's* Dracula, *Interview with the Vampire*, and *Perfume*; and New Generations contains *The Lost Boys*, "Buffy vs. Dracula," and *Let the Right One In*. Normally, *We Are the Night* and *What We Do in the Shadows* are also included, but unfortunately there were no streaming rights available for them in Canada the summer I taught this iteration of the course. At the beginning of every week, prerecorded lecture videos introduced the films as well as the central topics and themes for the week. While there seems to be a general agreement that recorded lectures should be very short—ideally, just "cliplets"—students did not complain about videos that were longer than ten minutes, because they could stop and replay them at any time. In fact, they reported liking this format more than attending an in-person lecture and then consulting a posted summary of the lecture in note form. Now they could watch the lecture in their own time and at their own speed and had access to all *PowerPoint* slides rather than just a posted summary.

The Virtually Flipped Classroom

The vampire course was a traditional lecture course until two years ago. The topic and, initially, the lecture format appealed to students who were looking for elective courses, and the goal was to offer an attractive course that would help balance low enrollment numbers in the department. Anne Daugherty and Jerri L. Miller refer to this as "luring online students with the power of the vampire." While the course has been popular for almost twenty years, lectures and exams did not give students many opportunities to work with the movies and the readings. When students completed their course experience surveys at the end of the term, they often stated that they would have preferred to actively engage with the material, which was not possible in the large lecture class. After various unsuccessful attempts to give students more opportunities to talk and actively participate in class, the course was redesigned as a "flipped" classroom:

> In the flipped classroom, students are required to engage in or complete some form of preliminary learning online in preparation for a structurally aligned learning activity on campus with their instructors and peers. The structural alignment between these two activities is an important distinction for those who may think that simply uploading their lecture recordings will suffice. In flipped mode, students will be meeting a topic for the first time online, usually via short and to-the-point videos, rather than through attending a lecture as has been traditionally the case. This sudden change in direction (often referred to as "reverse teaching") can be quite confronting to students whose conceptions of university teaching are that new material should be presented by a professor in a lecture that they have paid good money to attend. (Reidsema et al., Introduction 6)

138   VIRTUALLY FLIPPED CLASSROOM

To allow for more student-engaged classes, regular completion tasks were introduced. These tasks were divided into individual and group completion tasks that students had to submit every week. The group meetings in particular were instrumental in breaking the instructor-student barrier that had existed in the large lecture class.

In order to ensure that students had read the outline and were aware of all assignments and tasks, a short multiple-choice test based on the outline was also posted in the first week. Especially in a large class, one could assign such a test as a required completion task that students have to pass before they can access further sections of the LMS. Students also had the option of completing various other introductory multiple-choice tests based on *YouTube* videos such as "How Did Dracula Become the World's Most Famous Vampire?—Stanley Stepanic," "Vampires: Folklore, Fantasy, and Fact—Michael Molina," and "German Expressionism: Crash Course Film History #7." The videos offered a general introduction to the topic in addition to what was discussed in the course lectures, and the tests introduced students to the format and kind of multiple-choice questions that would be used in the midterm and final exam.

Of the regular weekly completion tasks, the only recurring task was to write multiple-choice questions and answers about the assigned films. Students submitted their individual questions and answers by Wednesday, and the groups met on Thursday or Friday to select the five best questions and answers from everybody's submissions. Students were aware that these questions could and would also be used in upcoming exams. According to Jennifer Jones, "[T]o ask students to develop questions for a quiz or examination [is] one strategy to encourage self-regulated learning. The process of developing questions scaffolds higher-order thinking. Rather than just memorize or apply the material, students must think about how to evaluate their knowledge of the material." This recurring task and its two-stage process were central to shifting to a student-centered setting. When they met in their groups, students took turns as facilitators who were also responsible for posting a summary of their discussions. Adam Wilsman affirms, "Assigning group members roles (like facilitator, recorder, divergent thinker, etc.) or distributing a group assessment rubric can keep groups relatively balanced and fair and help ensure participation by all group members."

Introductory Group Task: Film Sequence

The first group task of the term was a sequence analysis of *Nosferatu: A Symphony of Horror*'s first six minutes. In preparation, students had watched a video chapter from Richard Barsam and Dave Monahan's *Looking at Movies* that introduced them to basic cultural and formal analyses, exemplified by a reading of a scene from *Harry Potter and the Deathly Hallows: Part 1* (22–31). Students were also given this short set of questions based on a critical approach developed by Anton Kaes and Eric Rentschler before they met in their groups to discuss narrative, staging, sound, or cinematography.

Narrative

Does the sequence encapsulate the major oppositions at work in the film?

Which channel of information (image, music, writing) dominates in this sequence?

Does the film forward a sense of itself as a framed view of things?

Are we made to respond in certain ways?

How are women portrayed? Are they shown as passive objects of the male gaze?

Staging

How does the staging visualize the main conflicts?

Do props take on symbolic meaning? How do sets and props comment on the narrative?

Is space used as an indirect comment on a character's inner state of mind?

What do appearance, gestures, facial expressions, voice signify? Movement of characters: toward or away from camera, left to right or vice versa? Who looks at whom?

Sound

What kinds of sounds are used? What do they signify?

Is the source part of the story (diegetic) or added on (nondiegetic)?

What kind of music is being used? Is it typical for the period depicted?

Does the music comment (foreshadow or contradict) the action? Does it irritate/alienate?

What is the music's purpose in the film? How does it direct our attention? How does it shape our interpretation?

Are there sound bridges (sounds connecting scenes)? What do they signify?

Cinematography

What information do the camera movements convey? Are they subjective (POV)?

What kind of angle is used? High, low, straight-on, eye-level shot?

Are there gradual changes, cuts, abrupt shifts and disjunctions?

Is the rhythm flowing, jerky, disjointed, fast- or slow-paced?

140 VIRTUALLY FLIPPED CLASSROOM

My teaching assistants and I took turns joining the groups to discuss their readings of the *Nosferatu* sequence. Related topics like the film's main binaries, gender roles, and stereotypes, as well as questions of genre and intertextuality, had already been introduced in the posted lecture. *Nosferatu* was also discussed as an example of the first of four stages of genre evolution defined by Thomas Schatz: experimental, classical, refinement, and baroque. Long before the term *horror film* was used, this film by F. W. Murnau was the first cinematic adaptation of Stoker's novel, attributed in the film's opening titles: "Nach dem Roman 'Dracula' von Bram Stoker—Frei verfaßt von Henrik Galeen" ("From the novel 'Dracula' by Bram Stoker. Adapted by Henrik Galeen"). Since the filmmakers had not sought or paid for permission to use Stoker's material, the author's widow, Florence, sued Murnau's company for copyright infringement in a Berlin court that ruled that all copies of the film had to be destroyed: "F.W. Murnau's 1922 *Nosferatu* changed Bram Stoker's *Dracula* in terms of time (dating it back 50 years), place (moving it from Transylvania to Germany and from London to Bremen), and even names (Dracula became Count Orlok). Today those changes would likely be enough to escape copyright infringement suits, but they were not sufficient at the time" (Hutcheon and O'Flynn 146). This history can also serve as a poignant introduction to questions of originality, fidelity, and theories of adaptations in addition to positioning *Nosferatu* as an early horror film.

Nosferatu's opening sequence was also used to show students the importance of sound in horror films. The Kino edition with the restored Hans Erdmann score was contrasted with the heavy metal soundtrack of Front Row Entertainment's *Nosferatu: The First Vampire*. Watching what for most was their first experience of a silent movie, students learned to appreciate the film as an example of the experimental stage not only of horror but also of filmmaking in general. Murray Leeder had a similar experience: "Students almost always respond well to *Nosferatu*, in part because of the lasting effectiveness of Max Schreck's performance, and the film's formal ostentation (the use of sped-up footage, negative footage etc.). With the possible exception of the films of Buster Keaton, I have found no better film than *Nosferatu* in breaking through the built-in resistance many students have to silent films" (148).

Capstone Group Task: Intertexts and Adaptations

At the end of the term, students returned to another sequence analysis, this time looking at clips from six versions of what is arguably the novel's most famous scene—Jonathan's encounter with the "three young women, ladies by their dress and manner" in chapter 3 (Stoker, *Dracula* 46). Comparing the six versions provided students an opportunity to reflect on their own preconceptions and how those would influence or predetermine their reading of the scenes. As Ben Kooyman points out, "When readers demand fidelity from a film adaptation of a text, they are demanding fidelity to their own interpretation of that text" (248). Students also noticed that, as Linda Hutcheon and Siobhan O'Flynn observe, "films about Dracula today are as often seen as adaptations of other earlier films as they are of Bram Stoker's novel" (21). The six clips were taken from media that had been categorized according to Schatz's four stages; the experimental stage was represented by *Nosferatu*, the classic by *Dracula*, the refined by three Hammer House of Horror films, and the baroque by "Buffy vs. Dracula," in a postmodern take.

To review the plot and as an introduction to analyzing the novel (Daugherty and Miller note that "the trickiest part of including *Dracula* in an online literature course" can be "encouraging the students to actually read the novel" [193]), students watched a *YouTube* video that presented a "summary and analysis" of the novel ("*Dracula*: Summary and Analysis"). Individually and in their groups, students were asked to comment on this review and to assign it a grade. This exercise helped students reflect on their criteria for their own analysis and was also a fun task, especially when students discussed their assigned grades (which ranged from C+ to A+) within their groups. The exercise also helped students move beyond "the notion that adaptations ought to be faithful to their ostensible source texts" (Kooyman 245) because "the act of adaptation always involves both (re-)interpretation and then (re-)creation [and is best seen as] a form of intertextuality" (Hutcheon and O'Flynn 247). In the students' developing critical approach, fidelity became an unreliable indicator of successful adaptations. Rather than look for authenticity, students came to see the intertextual dialogue between the novel and its cinematic variations as palimpsests that connect and challenge our readings.

Outcomes

Flipping the class, assigning two-step tasks, and using an online format allowed for significant and meaningful communicative interactions in a large class. The new structure also allowed me as the instructor to "[move] from the role of lecturer ('Sage on the stage') to facilitator ('Guide on the side')" and to cocreate with students a course that "explicitly define[d] learning as mutually constructed meaning" (Kavanaugh et al. 17). While the course will continue as a flipped, online course, there are two elements that will be added next time it is offered. In addition to posting prerecorded lectures online for the students to view and review before group meetings, I will add a simulive component so students can interact with the instructor and the teaching assistants during the streaming lecture through chat.

The final course component was an analytical essay about one of the films discussed in class. For a class where most students came from science departments rather than the humanities, a traditional essay was a challenging task, but the regular completion tasks throughout the term helped students build the skills to practice a more rewarding form of analysis in the form of "digital storytelling," consisting of "short personal digital narratives, typically less than three-minute

142 VIRTUALLY FLIPPED CLASSROOM

multimedia movies, employing a combination of photographs, video, animation, sound, music, text, and narration" (Frazel 197).

Adapting the vampire course to an online format and introducing regular completion tasks reshaped the course and allowed for a significant amount of teacher-student and student-student interaction, which had not been possible when the course was offered as a lecture class. Maybe this is also something we can learn from vampires: that we need to be ready to adapt to cultural paradigm shifts—and that the results might be extremely satisfying.

NEW MEDIA AND DIGITAL HUMANITIES

Dracula in the Undergraduate Digital Classroom

Christopher G. Diller

If there is a novel that undergraduates likely have not read but think they already know, *Dracula* is it. Exposed to contemporary television and film adaptations—most recently the comedy horror film *Renfield*—as well as other large- and small-screen fare, students come to class familiar with typical vampiric traits as well as sometimes unfounded expectations regarding youthful angst and attractiveness. They are often surprised by the pleasures of delving into the *Dracula* text itself for a more thorough understanding of the particular historical world of the novel and the imaginative world of its author. As scholars have noted, the chronological events of this epistolary novel date exactly to 1893, and Stoker was "evidently keen to establish an aura of 'authenticity' around his story, by getting all the dates and [train] timetables right, so that, as he put it in the opening words to *Dracula*, its history 'may stand forth as simple fact'" (Frayling, "Bram Stoker's Working Papers" 350). Indeed, one enterprising European scholar, Hans Corneel de Roos, using geographic information system (GIS) maps as well as comparative descriptions of Transylvanian mountain views from the novel, has pinpointed the "real" location of Dracula's castle, and Stoker himself integrated many other real-world referents, including cities, neighborhoods, buildings, graveyards, and land and sea routes (if sometimes with ambiguity).

Dracula therefore lends itself to geospatial and other visual methods of mapping and analysis. In what follows, I describe an upper-division (capstone) course for literature majors that takes *Dracula* as its only primary text and offers a modest introduction to the digital humanities in both theory and practice, using selected readings and two web-based tools that require no knowledge of coding. Specifically, students use *Voyant Tools*, a free-access digital reading and analysis environment, to generate empirical and visual data reflecting word frequencies and correlations. Then they collaboratively use *ZeeMaps*, an inexpensive mapping tool based on a *Google Maps* template, to pinpoint and annotate the novel's place names and routes according to the movement of its major characters.[1] I have found this approach beneficial to majors who are intrigued

144   DIGITAL CLASSROOM

by visual and quantitative literary analysis rather than just the close reading practice with which they are so familiar; students who peer-review not only one another's writing but also their readings and spatial plotting of the novel; students who integrate empirical and visual data in their essays to support or qualify close reading evidence; and, not least, students whose digital reading and mapping experiences spark new questions and a return to the novel with fresh eyes.

Readings and Materials

Even in this Internet age, where text is text (making the idea of genre a head-scratcher for many students), most undergraduates in my classes have not heard of digital humanities—an umbrella term that encompasses computational methods in the humanities and textual analysis more generally. The literary study potentials of digital humanities, an approach with origins in linguistics and computational science, are fairly easy to introduce by using, for example, the confirmation through computational stylistic analysis that Christopher Marlowe is now officially a coauthor of the *Henry VI* plays or that best-selling genre fiction has an underlying "code" of thematic and stylistic attributes (see Alberge and Archer and Jockers, respectively). An instructor can wade deep into the history and theory of digital humanities using such rich resources as the *Debates in the Digital Humanities* series, but in my experience, students find such readings only mildly interesting even after their initial shock regarding the incredible smallness of the literary canons we teach and ask them to value. In this regard, Franco Moretti, who coined the term *distant reading*, recalls that when he began to study national bibliographies, it made him

> realize what a minimal fraction of the literary field we all work on: a canon of two hundred novels, for instance, sounds very large for nineteenth-century Britain (and is much larger than the current one), but is still less than one per cent of the novels that were actually published: Twenty thousand, thirty, more, no one really knows—and close reading won't help here, a novel a day every day of the year would take a century or so.
>
> (*Graphs* 3–4; see also Wilkens)

Similarly, Jodie Archer and Matthew L. Jockers estimate that "approximately fifty to fifty-five thousand new works of fiction are published every year" but of those only "about two hundred to two hundred and twenty novels make the *New York Times* bestseller list" (3).

Given the expertise needed to assemble and analyze a large corpus of literary texts, however, a hybrid approach to digital humanities in the undergraduate classroom can combine close and distant reading methods to create a comforting yet unfamiliar and therefore intriguing learning space. In the spirit of reading and writing less to say more, the singular focus on *Dracula* for an entire term allowed us to move, in good pedagogical fashion, from traditional close reading and writing practices to complementary ones based on quantitative analysis and visual presentation. One prerequisite for this approach is a "clean" digital copy of *Dracula* transcribed from the reliable *Project Gutenberg* website—that is, a copy pruned of any metadiscourse such as publishing information; Stoker's dedication, "To my dear friend Hommy-Beg"; and chapter and page numbers if not titles (as character names and genres like "diary" are intrinsic to the novel and its word count). The goal here is to create a text ready to upload to *Voyant Tools*. Another prerequisite is a common printed edition of *Dracula*—the Norton Critical Editions are a good choice—so that students can quite literally be on the same page when they peer-review not only one another's readings but also their plotting of the novel's place names, character movements, and geographical routes.

In good contrastive rhetoric fashion, students engage *Dracula* traditionally in the first part of the term—that is to say, by close reading and rhetorical analysis. Students write daily discussion cards in class that analyze, for instance, a specific moment or turning point in the text, an extended metaphor, or interconnected scenes (such as the developmental logic of Lucy's four blood transfusions) and write a medium-length essay that relies primarily upon textual evidence and little if any secondary research. In addition to reinforcing familiar skills—repetition is never redundancy when it comes to teaching and learning—the first part of the class thereby builds familiarity with the novel's characters, plot, and thematic emphases that the second half of the term both assumes and questions with its digital approach. At a glance, here is the assignment arc of the class:

- traditional analysis essay
- digital archive presentation
- *Voyant Tools* exploration and analysis
- *ZeeMaps* collaborative project
- close/distant reading argumentative essay
- short reflection essay

As a transition to the digital analysis portion of the class, students prepare presentations on a single digital archive of their choice (such as the Walt Whitman or Kate Chopin or John Muir archives) to dip their toes into digital resources and scholarship beyond familiar databases like *Project Muse* and the *MLA International Bibliography*. After the presentations, we turn to a tutorial housed on the *Voyant Tools* website, a streamlined introduction to the *Voyant Tools* home page I wrote in collaboration with a student worker, and an instructor-led demo of its home page tools.

146   DIGITAL CLASSROOM

Voyant Tools

Having read the entire novel once and written a critical inquiry, students return to *Dracula* and become familiar with the primary tools on *Voyant*'s home page that foster interplay between close and distant reading. To create the *Voyant* home page of the novel, one just needs to upload a clean file of the text to find (from left to right and top to bottom) a Cirrus word cloud, a Reader pane for reading and searching the text, a Trends graph dividing the novel into ten equal tranches (approximately 16,200 words each) with an initial plotting of its five most frequently used words and a search feature, and a Summary section of metadata about the novel, including the total number of words, the number of unique word forms used, and the average number of words per sentence (a potential historical and stylistic comparative point with other authors and time periods or genres).[2] The Phrases tab in the summary documents verbatim word phrases—testament to the fact that even the best writers often have stylistic tics—whose incidence is illustrated in the Trends window. Clicking on any node in the Trends window itself takes the viewer back to the Reader pane to see where that phrase occurs in the novel, a function that epitomizes the inside/outside nature of *Voyant*. Finally, for the purpose of this brief overview, the bottom right of the home page provides a Contexts tool that displays collocates surrounding a chosen word and a Correlations tool that provides a statistical measure of the relative convergence of two words. Each tool is accompanied by a question mark icon that, when clicked, provides a brief explanation of the tool's capabilities.

Voyant's search function allows users to play around, enter keywords of interest from prior interpretations of the novel, and use the tools as a kind of heuristic to try out hunches based on intuition or striking passages. The visual results of *Voyant*, especially, help students feel free to question prior assumptions and arguments as well as pose new lines of inquiry in an experimental, nonintimidating environment. For example, if one searches for the word *mouth* after reading Christopher Craft's essential essay "'Kiss Me with Those Red Lips:' Gender and Inversion in Bram Stoker's *Dracula*" in the first Norton edition (Craft, Excerpt), one might expect to find the words *lips* and *red* and perhaps *bone* in proximity with that keyword. And while one does find the former, the collocates mapped under the Links tab located on the upper left of the home page suggests that at least equal weight should be given to *chin* and *gums* and *pale* as well as *blood*; *chin*, for example, occurs in the passages where Jonathan Harker encounters the female vampires, where he views the blood-bloated Dracula in his coffin, during Lucy's illness and slow transformation into a vampire, when the vampire Lucy has fed and is found in her coffin, and after Dracula's attack on Mina. Thus, the keyword in context suggests an intersection of sexual and medical discourses and the gendering of the latter regarding Lucy and Mina's illnesses.

Voyant's simple interface, multiple and intuitive utility panes, and ability to export data and create a persistent link such as the one I created for *Dracula* are some of its most attractive features. Nevertheless, there are inherent assumptions and restrictions in *Voyant*, as there are in all other software applications. The keyword *Dracula*, for instance, can be traced for its collocates and distribution across the text, and it predictably ascends early in the novel, when readers are introduced to the character with his handwritten note to Jonathan Harker, and later, when the plot returns to Transylvania and reaches its dramatic resolution. However, Dracula is also embodied as a historical personage, as a dog, as a bat, as mist, as red eyes, and as "coffins" that move into and out of England. Dracula himself therefore does not neatly match the keyword *Dracula*, although his various incarnations can be compared for closer or more distant affiliations. The key question *Voyant* cannot answer, despite showing patterns the human eye usually cannot catch, creating data but not meaning, is, What is the significance of these different forms of embodiment (if any) at particular moments in the novel?

ZeeMaps

If *Voyant Tools* offers a kind of inside/outside perspective for analyzing and visualizing *Dracula*, *ZeeMaps* does so differently: the process of re-creating the plot of the novel and annotating places, routes, and character movements asks students to create an implied argument about its most important turning points and to represent their interpretive decisions through the place markers, annotations, and routes that *ZeeMaps* enables. Like *Voyant*, *ZeeMaps* has its own set of embedded assumptions and constraints in producing visual data, and I have therefore found it useful to assign Tyechia Lynn Thompson's "Mapping Narratives of Reversal in 'Baldwin's Paris'" to highlight the potentials and limitations of geospatial mapping before students engage with the tool. Thompson uses *Google Earth* to map 104 place names in Paris that appear across Baldwin's oeuvre, and she persuasively traces patterns of character contact and intimacy, or the lack of it, in liminal spaces such as Montparnasse. Her primary takeaway is that Paris is a more perduring conceptual ground in Baldwin's post-1963 writing than has commonly been assumed. Nevertheless, Thompson acknowledges that "the limitations of my methods and my tool (Google Earth) . . . [are] geographical approximation and photographically [sic] inaccuracy . . . [and they] influence my interpretation of context and culture in Baldwin's work" (290). Specifically, twenty-six percent of the geography of "Baldwin's Paris" is predicated upon interpretive inferences derived from textual context and clues; close reading, then, is crucial both as an evidentiary resource and sometimes as a corrective to distant reading data. As Katayoun Torabi notes, "[C]omputer-aided analysis cannot replace a close reading of the text itself, and rigorous scholarship is always needed to interpret the results of such analyses" (42).

In the classroom, the replotting and geospatial mapping of *Dracula* become a truly collaborative act that depends on the norming of interpretive assumptions and criteria as students move from close readings to decisions about what

148   DIGITAL CLASSROOM

is significant enough to map. To begin their collaboration, small groups of students—usually three per group—tackle a tranche from the novel and reread it individually first for dates, places, and character movements (which are sometimes reported within other characters' entries in this epistolary novel). Then they review their respective inventories, forge consensus about what to map for their part of the novel, and share and compare that knowledge with the rest of the class. In the first iteration of the course, students transcribed the results of their small-group peer reviews onto a single physical "scroll" of taped construction paper sheets to assemble the novel's time line and to make initial collective decisions about the primary or secondary importance of characters' itineraries and places and routes. This scroll, like Jack Kerouac's legendary 120-foot first full draft of *On the Road*, captured the improvisatory and creative aspects of the small-group collaborations, and it gave the entire class's decision-making physical form. In the second iteration of the course, however, in response to COVID-19 and the need for social distancing in the classroom, students created a common *Google Docs* file to house the results of their small-group and class collaborations; what was lost in terms of physical interaction and play was, perhaps, compensated by the ease of collective revision and dissemination this platform provides.

To guide class discussion and decision-making, the following list of criteria and questions helped us to move from the scroll or *Google Doc* to *ZeeMaps* itself:

> The primary goal is to chronologically and spatially organize the major characters' movements and routes.

> Define the major characters and routes. For example, are Dracula's coffins a character or part of one? What colors will represent whom on *ZeeMaps*?

> Carefully note and peer-review dates, days, and times of day, remembering that the novel's action isn't strictly chronological but is sometimes retrospective.

> Document place names and routes but also similar *types* of places (different hotels, for example, are in more or less posh neighborhoods). At least initially, also note modes of transportation and geographical transition points to final destinations, since not all carriage rides, for example, are as richly described and symbolically fraught as Harker's journey to Dracula's castle.

> Mark with an asterisk uncertain or clearly inferential data, such as when there is no clear temporal or physical referent in the novel or, if there are clues, they are subject to interpretation (à la "Baldwin's Paris").

> Research relevant historical information and images for the map's annotations—for example, from historical travel guides, London Tube maps, graveyards, and so on.

What are the common criteria for annotation? Although we will evolve these along the way, marking and annotating everything on the map would clutter it, and therefore referential accuracy and historical relevance should be primary considerations.

Finally, who will be the *ZeeMaps* and *Google Docs* manager?

Once the class had collated each small group's work, the next task was to agree upon the relative importance of Tier 1 and Tier 2 places and routes (with common agreement that London could and should be primarily composed of Tier 1 place markers and annotations). Like its *Google Maps* template, *ZeeMaps* enables users to toggle between micro and macro and even global perspectives, the broader of which might be missed in the fast-flowing narrative. For example, a brief but suggestive letter from "Quincey P. Morris to Hon. Arthur Holmwood" reminds the latter of their adventures together in the Marquesas Islands, where Quincy and Arthur "dressed each other's wounds" (suggesting a military engagement but also a form of intimacy), and at Lake Titicaca (Stoker, *Dracula* [Auerbach and Skal] 62). Despite the centrality of Europe to Stoker's imagination, then, the visual mapping of these two places associates the men with global, imperialist adventure. (Even Texas, which one of my students drily characterized as "the best country in the United States of America," made the cut.) Unlike the editors of the first Norton Critical Edition, my students questioned whether Quincey's reference to "the Korea" (62) denotes the country itself (rather than the Korea Strait or even a hotel) and did not map that location—an example of how the geospatial perspective helped students reassess the Norton edition's footnotes as well as moments in the novel itself.

If *ZeeMaps*'s toggling of visual perspectives is familiar to almost everyone with a cell phone and GPS today, it does restrict detailed viewing to one place marker at a time, albeit with rich ways to contextualize and interpret relevant moments in the novel: after creating and pinpointing a place marker and titling it, one can add descriptive text, photos, URLs, and other visual and auditory resources. These capabilities once again entail collective decision-making in terms of how dense an annotation could or should be, given its relationship to a particular passage in the novel or a character's developing identity. For example, when Dracula attacks Lucy near the Whitby Abbey churchyard, Mina minutely describes her multiple perspectives:

> The clock was striking one as I was in the Crescent, and there was not a soul in sight. I ran along the North Terrace, but could see no sign of the white figure which I expected. At the edge of the West Cliff above the pier I looked across the harbor to the East Cliff in hope or fear—I don't know which—of seeing Lucy in our favourite seat. There was a bright full moon, with heavy black, driving clouds, which threw the whole scene into a fleeting diorama of light and shade as they sailed across. For a moment

150   DIGITAL CLASSROOM

> or two I could see nothing, as the shadow of a cloud obscured St. Mary's Church and all around it. Then as the cloud passed I could see the ruins of the Abbey coming into view; and as the edge of a narrow band of light as sharp as a sword-cut moved along, the church and the churchyard became gradually visible.   (Stoker, *Dracula* 94–95)

Each of these carefully noted places and viewpoints could be mapped and annotated, but it would be more efficient to create a single place marker that notes how Stoker combines stereotypical Romantic and gothic imagery with precise topographical referents to create visual movement even before Mina rushes to Lucy.

As noted above, the traditional reading of *Dracula* and its digital rendering each take about a half semester, but the syllabus did leave time for a single-spaced, single-page reflection essay and for student evaluations. What is admittedly a small sample of students' anonymous responses in these evaluations over two years suggests that students seem aware of four primary outcomes: the benefits of focusing upon a single primary text, the complementarity of close reading and distant reading and the importance of place and movement in literature, the unique role of the course in the English major, and the experience of true collaboration and teamwork.

At the start of this essay, I noted that students are surprised by the benefits of focusing for an entire course on a single albeit relatively long and now canonical literary text. Given that most of our students take three to four or even more classes per term, and that the end of the semester therefore becomes a time of stress for them (and of unintended competition among instructors for their best work), the semester-long focus on *Dracula* is refreshing to them and for more than mercenary reasons: although they may first think that studying only one novel makes for light work, students quickly realize that deep immersion in a single text induces critical cross-fertilization between reading, research, peer review, and writing tasks.

Second, students notice how important physical contexts and movements are in the novel. Between the spatial bookends of Dracula's journey to London and flight back to Transylvania (a narrative arc that Stephen Arata describes as an anxiety of "reverse colonization"), for instance, students explore how gender inflects freedom of movement. In comparison to the male characters, Lucy is the most constricted in her movement; the more independent Mina is also relatively constricted, even when accompanied by a male companion such as Van Helsing. One student noted that her digital *Dracula* experience helped her see how in a novel studied in a different class, Kazuo Ishiguro's *The Remains of the Day*, movement is the story's catalyst and affects the narrator's memories in the moment. Critical and curricular comparisons like this one thus enable a more syncretic view for students in regard to their experiences and development as English majors.

Last, the digital approach of the course fosters real collaboration both among students and between students and the instructor. In particular, the single common text and the collective mapping project distinguish the course from students' prior experiences. According to one student, many literature classes remain "stuck" in a process of reading a book, discussing its historical and cultural significance, and then discussing close readings that pique a professor's interest. Another student compared the class to a "team," discerning a dynamic that "allowed for freely expressed ideas" and lively discussions "because we were all fully consumed by this book, knowing it was the only focus." If we think of digital humanities in terms of pedagogy first rather than literary canons or even literary history, a reciprocal relationship emerges between "close" and "distant" reading that English majors and even nonmajors find energizing and enlightening. And teaching, after all, is finally what we do on Monday morning.

NOTES

1. A new and even more intuitive and flexible mapping tool can be found at Felt.com.
2. A permanent URL for the *Voyant Tools* home page of *Dracula* is voyant-tools.org/?corpus=9815074ce5a575f05774e26d6e1ad2.

Dracula and New Media

Zan Cammack

Directly after the dedication and before the table of contents, *Dracula* opens with an anonymous note that assures readers that all the disparate accounts that make up the novel's narrative are "exactly contemporary" and each record collated precisely to avoid imprecision in its delivery and to enhance the "simple facts" of the narrative (Stoker, *Dracula* 7). At the end of the novel, Jonathan Harker provides a similar note in which he marvels that "in all the mass of material of which the record is composed, there is hardly one authentic document; nothing but a mass of type-writing, except the later notebooks of Mina, Seward, and myself, and Van Helsing's memorandum" (344). These two addenda to the novel proper tacitly imply that the novel's construction, an assemblage of shorthand journals, newspaper clippings, telegrams, phonograph records, and other media, is essential to the narrative's success and veracity. At the same time, by protesting overmuch, these addenda force us to view the novel's narrative with suspicion and its amalgamation of new-to-the-era media with reservation. It is a novel of aggressive technological progress: "nineteenth century up-to-date with a vengeance," as Harker writes in his shorthand diary (45). And I have to admire Stoker's audacity in creating a narrative in which he tells his audience that they are accessing a phonograph recording, for instance, all while they are likely handling, physically, a bound collection of paper and type and therefore implicitly understanding the work to be a largely traditional physical novel. Stoker brazens out his media-based narrative gambit as an experiment in hypothetical, pre-Internet multimodality.

Dracula, as a result, is remarkable for its potential to be examined by means of digital humanities and new media studies. The structure of the novel is often a surprise to students, who are generally immune to the dramatic vampiric plot twist that Stoker works so hard to simultaneously obscure and reveal through the multimedia accounts. After all, *Dracula* equals *vampire* for modern audiences, so the reveal doesn't work in the same way it would have for Stoker's contemporaries (though a 2019 live-tweeting of reading *Dracula* for the first time demonstrates that the novel still "slaps" with modern audiences, even if the thread might be too salty for classroom consumption [Cerveza Cristal]). In the past, I have heard students grumble that the structure of the novel is a bit of a hang-up for them since it does not smoothly flow in the way they expect from more traditional novels. But introducing them to the text with these opening and closing addenda, as well as a scan through the table of contents, helps the structure of the narrative begin to take shape. And once students understand the novel as a media-driven narrative, they are instantly able to make the connection between Stoker's way of constructing a larger narrative from disparate technologies and their own daily digitally driven, multiplatform communications.

Inherent in this contemporary media connection is the realization that individual platforms have specific abilities and limitations in the way messages are conveyed. At the risk of dating this chapter with a specific example, I point out that a text message serves a different purpose than an *Instagram* post. Both platforms allow images and text, but the first is sent to specific audiences whereas the latter is generally available for more public consumption. Texting does not have the same inherent photo-editing abilities as *Instagram*. Text messaging assumes a somewhat immediate and direct response from those to whom the text is sent, creating a form of exchange or conversation. And texting doesn't always allow for editing after you press Send, which makes us all victims of autocorrect, compelling us to draft a string of subsequent texts to try to undo the awkwardness we've just sent out. *Instagram*'s platform allows for a cropped, filtered, edited image to go with a caption that is meant to elicit "likes" and comments rather than conversation. And *Instagram*'s platform offers several other methods of communication, including direct messaging, "stories" and "reels." So how does this relate to *Dracula*? Stoker is using the cutting-edge media technology of his day, and he is navigating these same questions of platform capabilities. Some platforms work better for certain kinds of communications than others, and each platform has its own challenges and limitations. This media-based discussion with students then leads me to the major objectives and assignments that accompany our exploration of *Dracula*.

I tend to teach *Dracula* as part of a broad survey course in which I thematically emphasize narrative innovation and its spread. I also tend to emphasize the role that digital humanities and new media play in enabling us to quantify and create parallel contemporary connections to these narratives. I spend three to four weeks on *Dracula* as a form of capstone for the innovations of the Victorian era. My objective in teaching *Dracula* is twofold. First, I aim to acquaint students with new media studies as a historical phenomenon. The novel is a fascinating case study in late Victorian media productions and how they inform the spread of information and the construction of social narrative, potentially creating as many narrative problems as they solve. This feeds into the second objective, which is to discuss the novel as an intensely relevant and reflective analysis of contemporary media consumption and narrative construction. To that end, I have created a series of assignments that, first, collaboratively identify the different technologies in *Dracula* as they crop up; second, explicate those technologies' uses and functions in the story; and, third, convey the importance of that new information through two different options for multimodal projects.

As a note on methodology, in a COVID-era teaching environment, where online modalities and platforms are crucial to student success, I tend to use several different open access online resources to accomplish these objectives. I cite

154   NEW MEDIA

specific examples, though I am sure such resources will continue to evolve and each instructor will find what best suits their purposes and the fluctuations of digital humanities and new media technologies. The resources I mention work well in both face-to-face and online teaching modalities.

To teach the novel from this new media perspective, we take the cautions from the addenda at face value; they signal that we should be alert to any kind of media that might be used to tell the story and should be wary of trusting the narrative media implicitly. So, before we move into the novel proper, I ask students to watch for and collectively identify the different types of media within the text as they read. (I use a digital copy of *Dracula*, such as the one provided by *Project Gutenberg*; the Norton Critical Edition [Browning and Skal] is available digitally through Norton and VitalSource, and the second Bedford / St. Martin's critical edition is available digitally through Perusall [Riquelme].) Students tag any media-based technologies they come across. This initially starts out with noting each of the media platforms listed in the headings of each narrative section: Jonathan Harker's journal, a letter from Mina to Lucy, and so on. But beyond these examples, there are smaller, more buried references to media, like a telephone call, myriad telegrams, newspaper clippings, and memoranda. And an even deeper dive finds the specific machines that make some of these communications possible: the Kodak camera Jonathan takes with him to Transylvania (which we never see again), Mina's typewriter, the telegraph machines, and even two different phonographs—one owned by Seward at the asylum and one owned by Lucy, which she never uses (but Seward does). With a collective set of eyes working to track down different types of media, the list becomes extensive.

I also ask students to color-code the novel by the media platform whereby each section of the narrative is delivered. For example, all the telegrams could be purple, traditional letters could be orange, and so forth. The primary purpose of this activity is to demonstrate how complex media distinctions are; a secondary one is to help students begin to visually quantify the range and breadth of different media choices in the text. The first instance very quickly becomes a complex conversation about nuance. For instance, is there a difference between a journal and a diary? Stoker seems to think so. Jonathan and Mina both keep journals, whereas Seward and Lucy keep diaries. Furthermore, Jonathan's journal is kept in shorthand, and Mina's is not; Lucy writes her diary by hand, but Seward keeps his in phonograph for the first two-thirds of the novel and is forced to switch to a written diary only once he leaves London. By color-coding the text, students are able to start spotting trends in the narrative and interrogating them further. What medium is primarily in control at key moments in the plot? Do specific characters vary in their media delivery methods, and why? And why do these nuanced media choices matter?

To answer that last question, we move on to the next part of the project, which is to explicate those technologies' uses and functions in the story. Students are likely still reading and annotating the novel as they begin this process, but relatively early on they will have a foundation in the major media technologies of the text. I split students into small groups to become specialists on a specific form of media or technology from the narrative as well as its impact on the novel. This is a multipronged project. First, students will dig into the history of their selected media technology. Next, they will contextualize the media within the novel by examining how the characters engage with the media. And, finally, they will quantify the media's influences on the larger narrative.

These steps of exploration stem from what Leanne Page identifies as the "techno-performance" of these technologies in *Dracula*: how the media acts in expected and unexpected ways and creates relationships between characters and the technology's performance. Page describes a techno-performative reading as one that "allows us to foreground the role of technology in literature, shifting its function from that of background object to central character. In some ways, techno-performance is an anthropomorphization of technology" (104). Page specifically examines the phonograph, shorthand, and the typewriter as examples of techno-performances in *Dracula* and provides an excellent, though not exhaustive, context for these technologies. Using Page's essay as a jumping-off point, I explain that, although shorthand, in which short and abbreviated symbols represent speech-based sounds, has been around for centuries, in the Victorian era two different new and popular forms of shorthand emerged: the Pitman system, published in 1837, and Gregg system, published in 1888. It is most likely that Jonathan Harker wrote in the Gregg system, since it was the newest innovation. Dracula does not understand Jonathan's letter to Mina because it is written in the innovative shorthand format, so he destroys it, suggesting that new technologies are a threat to the old vampire. Why, then, does Harker abandon that method of writing once he leaves Transylvania?

By examining the typewriter, we learn that it was a keystone of business and office work by the time of *Dracula*'s publication, as were the women who in growing numbers were taking typing courses and joining the workforce. Mina's use of the typewriter (and shorthand) demonstrates her ability to support herself as an educated, independent working woman. Her use of the typewriter by the middle of the novel becomes the most important work of the narrative since we are theoretically reading her "mass of type-writing" that collates all the narratives of the vampire's attacks and allows her to see how they all fit together (Stoker, *Dracula* 344). It is also Mina's typewriter that saves the collective story from the fire that ravages the asylum and destroys all the other clippings and forms of media. Is the typewriter the hero of the narrative, then? Or, as Friedrich Kittler posits, is it an emblem of "our bureaucratization [which a]nyone is free to call . . . a horror novel as well" ("Dracula's Legacy" 73)?

The phonograph, as a final example, was patented by Thomas Edison in 1878 but was not in prominent popular use until near the end of the century. Edison got the idea for the machine when he pierced his finger with a stylus that moved under the vibrations of his own voice. The machine uses a needle to

156   NEW MEDIA

pierce soft wax cylinders when recording and replaying sound, then amplifies the grooves of embedded sound. (Students should be getting vampiric vibes from this technology at this point.) What do we make of the fact that there are so many parallels between machine and monster? Seward's use of the machine is also worth examining. He is talking to a machine, and his language and syntax are supposed to imitate a verbal delivery. The short and choppy sentences of his first entry are meant to replicate that: "Ebb tide in appetite today. Cannot hear, cannot rest, so diary instead." And yet, in the same entry, he starts to use abbreviations of Latin phrases, which make no sense in a verbal delivery. Why would he use the full Latin phrase "*Omnia Romæ venalia sunt*" in one sentence and then directly after that use the abbreviation "*verb. sap*" (Stoker, *Dracula* 67)? He also later tells Mina he has no real organization or labeling system in place for his phonograph records, which seems problematic for a man of science. And Stoker seems to underestimate how many wax cylinders Seward would have produced and has the doctor storing the cylinders in a desk drawer when really he would have amassed nearly an entire modern filing cabinet's worth. And in a rather climactic scene for the phonograph cylinders, when Dracula invades the asylum and sets fire to Seward's office, the cylinders are not just melted in the fire; they further the conflagration. The paraffin wax is said to have "helped the flames" in destroying nearly every other form of media the vampire hunters have amassed (264). Is the phonograph villainous at this moment? It is a counterpart to the typewriter, but what does Stoker imply by setting up a seeming rivalry between these two media?

At this point in the class, there are two different multimodal project options that I have pursued. The first project, which I have used in lower-division courses, asks students to collaborate in remixed (jigsaw) groups to create their own multimodal retelling of a section of *Dracula*. This project reconnects our opening discussions about the intricacies of modality with the text message and *Instagram* example. It also leverages students' newfound, specialized understanding of the complexity of Stoker's specific media technology choices to create a modern narrative that further demonstrates intersections of culture, communication, and technology. The objective is to get students engaged with the cultural creation of a narrative and to demonstrate how the platform is nearly as important as the message.

I divide the novel into sections based on the number of student groups, and each group selects a section for adaptation. I do not require a literal entry-to-entry adaptation (every entry from the novel does not need to be represented), but I do require students to integrate at least three different new media platforms to create a new iteration of the novel section. This is largely in the same spirit as the Emmy-winning series *The Lizzie Bennet Diaries*, a 2013 adaptation of *Pride and Prejudice* that used vlog, *Facebook*, *Instagram*, and *Twitter* accounts from a range of characters to create an interactive real-time telling of a novel. So is this Mina's true-crime podcast with accompanying website and social media accounts? Jonathan Harker's coded *Spotify* playlist for Mina from Transylvania? A *Google Maps* trip planner for London where the vampire hunters document their tasks and finds? The options are quite literally limitless. All I require is that the new media that students use communicate the story in a collaborative way. We also share these new media adaptations as a class so that we can get a relatively comprehensive retelling of the novel. Students finish out the project by writing up individual explanations of where the text of *Dracula* and the media of their projects converge as well as their experience of techno-performance.

The second multimodal project option leans further into a digital humanities exploration of *Dracula* and is one I use in upper-division classes. To facilitate further quantifiable connections between media technologies, their techno-performances, and the characters of *Dracula*, I ask that the small student groups that specialized in a specific media exploration further their exploration of the media in the text using *Voyant Tools*, which is a web-based text reading and analysis environment. Students import the digital text of *Dracula* into the tool and are then able to use the wide range of functions to trace trends or lines of influence for their media. For example, students can quantify how many times *telegram* and *telegraph* are mentioned, then contextualize those uses in the text (and by character, sender, and receiver). They can trace the frequency of these terms within segments of the novel, create a collocated graph of occurrences in close proximity as a force-directed network graph, or even physically map where the technologies are used in the novel. The goal here is to quantify the media's impact on the narrative with datasets that can be represented visually and then further interpreted by students. *Voyant Tools* is very user-friendly with plenty of tutorials and resources embedded in it. I tend to spend a full class period demonstrating the tool using individual group examples and technologies so students can break the ice and get comfortable in a live and interactive setting, whether in a face-to-face setting or a live-stream online session.

After students complete the three components of their group work (history, context, and quantifying influence), I ask that they share their findings in the form of an infographic, generated by sources like *Piktochart*, *Venngage*, or *Canva*. The infographic incorporates all three forms of research in a visually digestible format while still making an argument about the media's larger role in the novel. As a class, then, we have quick, easy access to a large amount of data about how the media in the novel represent late Victorian media networks, narrative construction, and the spread of information.

In presenting these ways of reading media in *Dracula* I recognize the potential concerns about losing sight of the plot and nuanced close readings of the novel, or losing sight of the vampire, for the volume of media. That is a risk, but it is a calculated one. Scholars since the 1980s, starting with Kittler, have found the media of the novel inescapable, and the body of work dedicated to specific technologies in *Dracula* is legion. At the center of these works sits a core of questions concerned about media performance, engagement with media, and media's physical and metaphorical impact in hunting a vampire.

158   NEW MEDIA

Are new media technologies heroes of the narrative, helping to systematically track down the ancient evil, as Kittler suggests (with his wry commentary on the novel's bureaucratization)? Or do the clamoring media obscure the vampire's presence almost to the vampire hunters' undoing, as Jennifer Wicke posits? Leah Richards wonders how the production of so much media tandemly demonstrates the ingenuity of the age while also revealing cultural anxieties about authenticity through media. Each of these questions finds relevant echoes in our students' continually evolving engagement with new media. How are disinformation and misinformation on media platforms obscuring narratives of local, national, and international importance? How is the platform both problem and solution? What do new media reveal about cultural anxieties and modern innovation? Engaging with these questions ensures that an exploration of *Dracula* has direct, palpable, and quantifiable application beyond the classroom. These explorations reinforce Marshall McLuhan's thesis that "the medium is the message" (7). Ultimately, the experience of reading Stoker's *Dracula* as a new media experiment in multimodality may reveal as much as it obscures, but it is literally the narrative we have been handed. New media is the message in *Dracula*.

Exploring the Transmedia *Dracula*

Shari Hodges Holt

I regularly teach *Dracula* in college literature courses through the lens of its "culture-text" (P. Davis 4) to enhance students' engagement with the novel through popular entertainment formats with which they are already familiar while cultivating their awareness of their own reading processes by modeling interpretive strategies. Whether or not students have read Stoker's novel or seen a *Dracula* film, they arrive in our classrooms with preconceptions of the Transylvanian Count rooted in the novel's culture-text, that kaleidoscopic body of appropriations and adaptations that range from children's literature to television shows, graphic novels to video games. Providing a space in the classroom for *Dracula*'s many pop-culture reincarnations is an effective way to turn students' attention to Stoker's original text, illustrating its evolving significance and "permitting a redefinition of anxiety-provoking issues" for new audiences in new media (Rose 2). The study of how such "transmedia storytelling" across multiple media platforms is accompanied by significant audience input (H. Jenkins, *Convergence Culture* 97) enhances students' media literacy skills in an era of "media convergence" that "depends heavily on active consumer participation" and blurs the boundaries between media producers and consumers (1–2). As a diverse culture-text, *Dracula* can therefore be particularly rewarding to teach in a world dominated by mash-ups, reboots, and transmedia franchises. Students who are accustomed to producing and consuming narratives in a variety of reincarnations can take ownership of the literature they study through critical interpretation and creative appropriation, often resulting in discoveries of new relevance in Stoker's novel. To illustrate this approach, I examine how a video game and two television adaptations of *Dracula* that have expanded into transmedia narratives can serve as catalysts for classroom discussion of Stoker's novel while placing it within a framework of related narratives that demonstrate its shifting cultural impact.

Studying contemporary reboots of the *Castlevania* series, a popular 1980s video game available for a variety of gaming platforms and adapted into both graphic novels and a *Netflix* television series, allows student participants to read *Dracula* anew by constructing and consuming a variety of popular entertainment's culture-texts. For those students interested in gaming, and it is worth noting that not all students are, I have suggested the *Castlevania: Lords of Shadow* series and its spin-offs as an optional topic for classroom presentations and writing assignments. In order to participate, students must purchase the games compatible with their preferred gaming platforms; however, even if classroom access to gaming consoles or PCs is not available, students can easily illustrate the game's narrative for the class through fan-produced videos of

160 TRANSMEDIA *DRACULA*

gameplay widely available on *YouTube*. The series' three-part story arc follows the adventures of the medieval knight Gabriel Belmont, who fights to protect Europe from a malevolent order of supernatural creatures that purportedly murdered his wife. *Castlevania: Lords of Shadow*, the first game in the series, recounts Belmont's vengeful quest to resurrect his wife, resulting in his eventual transformation into Dracula, and the second game, *Castlevania: Lords of Shadow—Mirror of Fate*, introduces Belmont's son, who will become a central figure in the series' final installment. *Castlevania: Lords of Shadow 2*, the concluding game in the series, allows the game player to assume the Dracula role in both medieval and modern settings, exploring Dracula's castle and a twenty-first-century city constructed on its ruins through 3D open-world gameplay, in which players choose their own paths toward achieving the game's objectives. While the game's cinematic sequences elaborate the tragic backstory of Gabriel's vampiric transformation into Dracula, detailing the death of his wife and his subsequent enmity with his son, the combat sequences, in which the player as Dracula fights monsters inhabiting the *Castlevania* world, allow the player to wield the former vampire hunter's demon-destroying weapons (such as the Shadow Whip and the Void Sword), as well as Dracula's vampiric powers, including draining opponents of blood to regain strength, shape-shifting into rats to avoid detection, and directing swarms of bats to distract opponents. The game's main mission eventually forces Dracula to confront his past identity as Gabriel Belmont, eschew his quest for vengeance, reunite with his estranged son, and save humanity from the game's "final boss," Satan, who rises from hell in the form of Dracula's dark double, resolved to either dominate or destroy the earth.

The moral conflict between Gabriel's human and vampire identities makes a fine comparison for readings of Stoker's narrative that interpret the vampire as a doppelgänger for the vampire hunters in "a tale, not of overcoming Evil by Good, but of the similarities between the two" (Senf, *"Dracula"* 475). I ask students who write about *Castlevania* to discuss, using the following discussion prompts, how it humanizes the vampire by incorporating the tropes of popular superhero and medieval fantasy franchises:

> How does becoming Dracula through interactive gameplay create empathy for the vampire while echoing the novel's moral ambiguity?
>
> How do you explain the need to sympathize with the vampire expressed in many adaptations of Stoker's novel, and how does that relate to the cultural need to depict the vampire as monstrous for Stoker's original Victorian readers?

The *Castlevania* game series can also introduce the tenuous connection between Stoker's Dracula and his historical namesake, which can lead students from Stoker's working notes for the novel, illustrating his "scanty" knowledge of the medieval prince Vlad Dracula (Miller, "Filing" 215), to the historical research of Raymond T. McNally and Radu Florescu that exaggerated and popularized the connection, which has been subsequently mythologized in television and film. Students can trace the *Castlevania* origin story that depicts Dracula's vampirism as an act of rebellion against his wife's death to other sympathetic adaptations of Stoker's vampire, including Dan Curtis's television movie *Dracula*, which introduced this popular narrative trope (Joslin 88); Francis Ford Coppola's film *Bram Stoker's* Dracula, which integrates this trope with Stoker's Victorian narrative to transform it into a tragic romance; and *Dracula Untold*, which creates a feature-length medieval backstory for Vlad Dracula as a vampiric superhero. The interactivity and intertextuality of the *Castlevania* franchise thus makes it an effective vehicle for exploring the moral evolution of Stoker's vampire throughout the *Dracula* culture-text.

While *Castlevania* illustrates *Dracula*'s role in the history of the sympathetic vampire, the television series *Penny Dreadful*—a neo-Victorian mash-up of canonical nineteenth-century gothic novels, Victorian penny dreadfuls, and horror cinema—can be particularly useful for contextualizing *Dracula* within the gothic tradition's complex negotiation of gender paradigms. In 1890s London, Vanessa Ives, a woman with occult powers, is targeted by a demonic force for seduction. Characters drawn from nineteenth-century gothic fiction (including *Dracula, Frankenstein, The Picture of Dorian Gray*, and *Dr. Jekyll and Mr. Hyde*) join Vanessa in her fight against supernatural evil while wrestling with their own inner demons. The first season focuses on Vanessa's quest to rescue her best friend, Mina Murray Harker, from abduction by "the Master," a demonic creature later revealed to be Dracula, who is also pursuing the supernaturally gifted Vanessa to claim her as his bride and transform her into the "Mother of Evil." The fifth episode of season 1, "Closer Than Sisters," which provides a backstory for Vanessa and Mina's relationship that in many ways mirrors that of Lucy Westenra and Mina Murray in Stoker's novel, is an excellent catalyst for discussing Stoker's female characters through the lens of nineteenth-century gender stereotypes.

Depicting their friendship from childhood, the episode reveals that Vanessa and Mina have been targeted by Dracula because they share a lifelong dissatisfaction with the limitations of the Victorian domestic ideal. When the more conventional Mina succumbs to the ideal and accepts a marriage proposal, the rebellious Vanessa breaks her friend's engagement by seducing her fiancé, a transgression that leads to Vanessa's demonic possession, her incarceration in an asylum, and Mina's abduction by Dracula. I have screened this episode in gothic fiction courses to facilitate comparison of female stereotypes in *Dracula* to those in several additional texts, including *Carmilla* (Le Fanu), "Goblin Market" (Rossetti), *Wuthering Heights* (Brontë), and *Lady Audley's Secret* (Braddon). I preface class discussion with a series of lectures about Victorian bourgeois domestic ideology, nineteenth-century women's legal and economic status, the treatment of female "madness," and the fin-de-siècle New Woman

162   TRANSMEDIA *DRACULA*

debate. Discussion prompts also prepare students to draw connections between the television episode and the literary texts:

> How does the episode's use of the "devoted sisters" trope echo the doubling of female characters in *Dracula*, *Carmilla*, and "Goblin Market" to express alternative approaches to female desire?
>
> How would you compare *Penny Dreadful*'s Mina and Vanessa to Stoker's Mina and Lucy as embodiments of the domestic angel, the fallen woman, and the New Woman?
>
> How would you compare Renfield in *Dracula* to the female characters of *Wuthering Heights*, *Lady Audley's Secret*, and *Penny Dreadful* as gendered articulations of the gothic "madness" trope?

My classes explore how *Dracula* and the "Closer Than Sisters" episode make metaphorical use of sisters in Victorian narratives to express the "multiple contradictions" inherent in Victorian domestic ideology (May 200) through "sisterly difference" (May 198) between "one girl who is passionate, creative, and uncontrolled" and "her more restrained, conventional" counterpart (S. Brown 6). Students note how the "sisters" in both narratives articulate their ambivalent responses to female agency through letter writing. Lucy's and Mina's letters in chapter 5 of *Dracula* reveal that Lucy plans her marriage to Arthur Holmwood while wishing a girl could "marry three men, or as many as want her" (Stoker, *Dracula* 65), whereas Mina studies stenography and typewriting in the hope of being "useful to Jonathan" when they are married, although her desire to mimic "lady journalists" (61) suggests a need for autonomous self-expression at odds with her later criticism of the New Woman. Similarly, "Closer Than Sisters" frames the story as a letter Vanessa writes to Mina exploring their past relationship, which Vanessa narrates through a succession of flashbacks in which she characterizes herself as more overtly associated with the fallen woman, while her friend Mina reluctantly adheres to the domestic ideal. Vanessa's first flashback introduces the adolescent girls at a seaside locale evocative of *Dracula*'s Whitby setting, where the sea represents the tempestuous passions the vampire will unleash upon his arrival. Mina longs to succumb to Vanessa's suggestion that they swim into the ocean "as far out as we can see" ("Closer Than Sisters" 00:04:30–33) but finally refuses out of fear, suggesting the unsustainable tension between compliance with and defiance of the passive feminine ideal.

The rift between the "sisters" is accentuated by the homecoming of Mina's father, Sir Malcom Murray, from his latest expedition to Africa. Sir Malcolm is a predatory invader whose arrival, like Dracula's arrival in Whitby, disrupts the traditional marriage plot for the "sisters" by arousing transgressive sexual desires. When Vanessa secretly witnesses her mother committing adultery with Sir Malcolm, her inner "demon" awakens, dramatized in moments when Vanessa senses the unseen demon behind her while gazing at herself in a mirror, inviting comparisons to Jonathan Harker's encounter with Dracula as his own uncanny double in the shaving mirror scene in chapter 2 of Stoker's novel. Vanessa's subsequent seduction of Mina's fiancé, which is cast as an act of passion by proxy for the "sister" she is about to lose to marriage, similarly evokes analysis of Lucy and Mina's "passionate friendship" (Prescott and Giorgio 487) in comparison to hints of "lesbian incest" in other gothic texts such as "Goblin Market" and *Carmilla* to point up "the sisters' resistance to being the object of male choice" (S. Brown 11). But the episode's graphic portrayal of Vanessa's suffering in an asylum, where she is incarcerated after her act of betrayal, often prompts the most discussion. Vanessa's treatment for "psychosexual hysteria" ("Closer Than Sisters" 00:29:06–08) is dramatized in gendered imagery—the shearing of her hair as a symbolic suppression of her sexuality, hydrotherapy by a phallic hose in a violent cleansing act, and the phallic penetration of her brain in a trepanning operation, which calls to mind, in Stoker's novel, not only Lucy's violent staking but also, in a neat contrast, Renfield's operation. Renfield's trepanation frees him to speak against the Master, whereas Vanessa's operation silences her protest, allowing her to return home a chastened figure. Comparing Vanessa's "hysteria" with Renfield's "zoophagous" madness (Stoker, *Dracula* 77), which results from his affinity with Dracula's insanely egotistical ambition for immortality, can also illustrate for students a fundamental contrast between male and female transgressors in gothic texts; the mad acts of male protagonists usually result from the hubris of power and privilege, whereas female transgression arises from imprisonment in a culture that demands absolute self-negation as the feminine ideal.

"Closer Than Sisters" concludes with Vanessa's discovery that although Mina married Jonathan Harker as a "safe" alternative to the fiancé who betrayed her, her marital unhappiness made her prey to Dracula, who seduced and abducted Mina in an attempt to lure Vanessa into his possession. Vanessa launches a quest to rescue her "sister," signifying her resistance to patriarchal control and her determination to reclaim her agency. Although "Closer Than Sisters" sympathetically dramatizes the plight of Victorian women, instructors should direct students who are interested in completing the television series and its subsequent graphic novels to feminist criticism arguing that the series ultimately perpetuates the gender stereotypes it critiques (e.g., Primorac; Kohlke). In the series finale, Vanessa finally succumbs to Dracula's advances and must beg for death from her former lover Ethan Chandler, an American sharpshooter patterned in part on Stoker's Quincey Morris. Feminist controversy surrounding the series can likewise lead students to similar debates sparked by other *Dracula* adaptations and related vampire fiction, such as the graphic novel series *The League of Extraordinary Gentleman*, which depicts Mina Murray as a strong survivor of Dracula's sexual assault even as the series repeatedly sexualizes her, or the postfeminist depiction of vampire marriage in the popular *Twilight* franchise, which many feminist critics have decried as a return to damaging Victorian gender paradigms. *Penny Dreadful* can thus be a valuable tool for introducing students to gender controversies in the *Dracula*

164   TRANSMEDIA *DRACULA*

culture-text, other related gothic fiction, and the larger field of feminist literary theory.

The complex evolution of Count Dracula himself as a signifier of cultural anxieties can be effectively illustrated for students by the 2013 NBC television adaptation of *Dracula*. The series' first episode, "The Blood Is the Life," surprises students with creative changes to the source material and prompts enlightening discussions of the novel and its adaptation history. While maintaining Stoker's central characters and period setting, the graphic novelist and screenwriter Cole Haddon playfully adapts *Dracula* into the steampunk subgenre of science fiction, combining nineteenth-century industrial steam technology with current science to unite Victorian and twenty-first-century cultural apprehensions.[1] After the medieval Christian organization the Order of the Dragon transforms Prince Vlad Dracula into a vampire and executes his wife as a punishment for heresy, Dracula vows revenge on the Order as it expands its power throughout the ensuing centuries. Resurrected in the nineteenth century by Professor Van Helsing, with whom he forms an uneasy alliance against the Order, Dracula arrives in 1890s London, where the secret society has survived into the Victorian age in the form of the British Imperial Company, which threatens to solidify the Order's power abroad through religious oppression, imperialist expansion, and capitalist investment in oil futures. Disguised as an American entrepreneur, Alexander Grayson, Dracula devotes himself to developing a wireless electricity source to destroy the Order's financial interests in oil as the Christian terrorist organization plots a coming war in the Middle East that will destroy "the Ottoman" and ensure their own global domination. Highlighting the novel's anxieties about colonialism, capitalism, and the conflict between religion and science, the show's revision of Stoker's narrative likewise evokes twenty-first-century concerns about religious extremism, terrorism, corporate greed, and environmentalism.

When discussing character revisions in the series, students express particular shock at the transformation of Van Helsing. Although motivated by vengeance for his children, who were murdered by the Order when he broke from their ranks, Van Helsing's brutality (he cuts his partner's throat to resurrect Dracula and later kidnaps, mutilates, and vamps the children of the Order's leader) can underscore for students the similarity between Van Helsing's and Dracula's methods in the novel that evince the novel's moral ambiguity. Renfield undergoes a similarly striking transmogrification as Dracula's closest friend, formerly enslaved and now a lawyer, who meticulously manages Dracula's campaign against the Order while providing a calming check to the vampire's more vengeful and violent impulses. Their deep friendship, which subverts the novel's master-slave dynamic and exposes imperialism's racist underpinnings, can prompt classroom exploration of the racism inherent in Stoker's narrative of "reverse colonization" (Arata 623).

The female characters similarly take the novel's gender dynamics in more postmodern directions. The series accentuates Lucy's transgressive sexuality

Shari Hodges Holt   165

through her sympathetic depiction as a closet lesbian who uses heterosexual flirtations to mask her growing attraction to her best friend, Mina. As the reincarnation of Dracula's beloved wife, Mina evinces the domestic angel qualities of the character in Stoker's text, whereas her role as an ambitious medical student exaggerates her New Woman features. The series contemporizes the novel's anxieties about female agency through Mina's relationship with her fiancé, Jonathan Harker, an ambitious reporter for the *London Inquisitor*, who evinces growing professional jealousy of Mina while Dracula/Grayson supports Mina's career goals.

However, Dracula/Grayson usually provokes the most classroom conversation, providing an effective tool for exploring *Dracula* as an "Imperial Gothic" work (Brantlinger 243). Jonathan Rhys Meyers's performance combines the aristocratic finesse, animal ferocity, and tragic loneliness of past screen portrayals of the vampire with the brashness, virility, and combat skills of Stoker's Quincey Morris, evinced in a spectacular combat scene in which Dracula/Grayson defeats one of the Order's vampire hunters. But unlike Morris, who represents the burgeoning power of American democracy to save Western civilization from the incursion of the eastern European vampire, Dracula/Grayson turns his skills against Western colonialism in the form of the British Imperial Company. While scholars such as Stephen D. Arata and Franco Moretti have interpreted Dracula's invasion of England as an expression of nineteenth-century anxiety about the vampiric nature of colonialism and bourgeois capitalism, my students and I discuss how Dracula/Grayson attacks crony capitalism in a manner relevant to those audiences living in the wake of the 2008 Great Recession and the Occupy Wall Street protests. As an intrepid inventor-scientist in the style of Nikola Tesla, Dracula/Grayson also engages with contemporary environmental concerns about climate change and green energy, as is illustrated in two scenes that can be contrasted effectively with those between Dracula and Jonathan Harker in the novel's opening chapters. In a stunning inversion of the darkness and horror of Jonathan's visit to Castle Dracula, Dracula/Grayson invites Jonathan and London's elite to his mansion to demonstrate his new technology, offering "a way out . . . of the darkness" through "free, safe wireless power" ("The Blood Is the Life" 00:12:09–13, 00:12:47–54) as generators in his steampunk laboratory set alight a collection of wireless light bulbs. The spectacular display radically reimagines Stoker's "Crew of Light" (Craft, Excerpt 445), now headed by Dracula himself as a champion of democratic entrepreneurship against feudal privilege and scientific denialism. In a subsequent interview with Jonathan that makes a striking contrast to Dracula's regal pride in his "ancestors" as a "conquering race" in the novel (Stoker, *Dracula* 38), Dracula/Grayson asserts he is "always fixed on the future," standing against "the privileged" and "vested interests." He declares, "We have it within ourselves to redefine our species," pointing out that "Darwin taught us . . . [t]hat man evolves. That is what I have come here to accomplish. To facilitate that evolution" ("The Blood Is the Life" 00:27:40–00:29:09). Whereas Stoker's Dracula embodies Victorian

166   TRANSMEDIA *DRACULA*

fears of devolution sparked by Darwinism and the cutthroat competition of industrial capitalism, Dracula/Grayson, as scientist, inventor, and entrepreneur, offers a more egalitarian alternative to Stoker's atavistic vampire king.

While the NBC *Dracula, Penny Dreadful,* and *Castlevania* can stimulate student engagement with Stoker's novel, they likewise illustrate *Dracula's* transition into "transmedia storytelling" through their expansion into graphic novels, streaming video, and fan-produced adaptations. Both the NBC *Dracula* and *Penny Dreadful* courted fans through official fan websites that presented additional narrative materials, links to social media accounts, video documentaries, and series-related merchandise. And each series' extensive fan base survived the television show's cancellation, extending the narrative through online blogs, *Twitter* and *Tumblr* threads, fan fiction forums, and fan-produced *YouTube* videos, most notably those created by the Westenray LGBTQ fan community to celebrate the queer potential of Lucy and Mina's relationship in the NBC series and tribute videos created by the #Dreadfuls to ensure *Penny Dreadful's* "continued circulation within contemporary popular culture" in a manner that mimicked the show's own "mash-up" format (Griggs 54). Directing my students to some of these fan-produced examples, I conclude courses in which I teach *Dracula* with a project that allows students to create their own adaptation of a literary work we have studied in another medium, accompanied by an analytical essay scrutinizing their interpretive approach to the source text and its intertexts. Stimulating more creative, personal engagement with the literature we study than the traditional research project, this has become a favorite project with my students, particularly those who are already participants in fan cultures accustomed to elaborating beloved narratives through fan-created content. Intermedial appropriations of literature like those within the *Dracula* culture-text can thus encourage readers to "rewrite" a literary text for greater relevance by demonstrating its interpretive possibilities, inspiring further creative appropriations that extend the life and power of the original. If, as the educators Ladislaus M. Semali and Ann Watts Pailliotet have claimed, "modern literacy is intermedial" (6), the continual shape-shifting of Stoker's characters and narrative across assorted media makes Stoker's novel an ideal text for literature classrooms in our "convergence culture" (H. Jenkins, *Convergence Culture* 2), which offers new methods for instructors to engage with the literature we love and enhance its significance for our students.

NOTE

1. Steampunk is a subgenre of science fiction, usually set in an alternative history of the Victorian age, that features futuristic technologies driven by steam power.

BOARD GAMES AND STUDY ABROAD

Fury of Dracula:
Board Games as Participatory Pedagogy

David Smith

Bram Stoker's *Dracula* presents a multifaceted and challenging experience to readers and educators. Its transmedia and patchwork structure and its themes of fin-de-siècle anxiety, vampiric contagion, progressivism-atavism conflict, and exploration of nonnormative social and sexual behaviors infuse an electricity that explains its profound impact on subsequent popular media and scholarly attention. The novel's procedural structure as well as its Victorian prose at times erect obstacles for student comprehension and involvement, and the sheer breadth of potential topics can overwhelm students, resulting in the privileging of certain topics over others. Analyzing themes of narrative construction, contagion, and modernity can mean giving short shrift to participatory and creative strategies that resonate with students.[1] The board game *Fury of Dracula* illuminates thematic material in the novel while also inviting imaginative participation and immersion, making it an interactive multimedia pedagogical tool.

Scholarship on games and ludic theory has expanded rapidly in the last generation, primarily in video games (see Michael and Chen), as game design and narrative have become more sophisticated and greater attention to factual detail has allowed for submersion into other times and places.[2] Accordingly, educators are embracing the pedagogical potential of games. John Lean and colleagues highlight games' "immediately accessible shared social space . . . [and] tactile sensory experience" (2). Similarly, Benjamin Hoy asserts that games allow "students to experience historical settings and systems rather than simply reading about them" (116). The capacity for games to provide students immersive experiences and performative activities has validated the use of board games' "statements about leisure, about socialization, and about mediation" (Booth 57). Board games can even serve to illustrate and empower previously marginalized and disenfranchised groups, as Kaitlynn Mendes and Kumarini Silva contend (246). Narrative reimagining occurs as gameplay "opens up gamers' engagement with tabletop games to a myriad of possible 'readings' and uses of any game (perhaps to a greater extent than most other media)" (Brown and

168   BOARD GAMES

Waterhouse-Watson, "Reconfiguring" 8). Among the various media forms popularly included in pedagogical practice, board games offer unique intersections of educational content with imaginative engagement.

Fury of Dracula, a board game in which a team of hunters pursues Dracula across a map of Europe to catch and kill him, was first released in 1987 by the designer Stephen Hand. Four editions have been subsequently released, the latest in 2019 ("*Fury of Dracula*"). This game's distinctive design combines cooperative and competitive play, offering players a range of choices and roles to inhabit. Additionally, the game's adaptation of the original novel rather than cinematic interpretations facilitates its use as a pedagogical tool in teaching Stoker's text. The game's faithfulness to the novel, its participatory aspect, and the incorporation of vampiric contagion offer a unique opportunity to explore thematic and scholarly facets of the novel in a fun and engaging experience for students.

Adapting Dracula *as a Game*

Fury of Dracula, which occurs chronologically after the events of the original novel, embodies several key elements of the novel, most notably the "power of combination" that Abraham Van Helsing cites as the hunters' main advantage over their fiendish opponent (Stoker, *Dracula* 223). Furthermore, *Fury* cleverly intertwines character traits and abilities from the novel with the individual hunters' abilities to dramatize each character's particularities, and the gameplay mirrors the procedural aspects and various dichotomies of the novel.

From the outset the game capitalizes on Stoker's notion of collaboration versus individualistic egotism. The game's five roles divide players into two teams: the team of hunters consists of Arthur Godalming, John Seward, Van Helsing, and Mina Harker, all of whom always take part in the game; the other "team" is Dracula, played by another player. At once this theme of cooperation versus isolation emerges; all five characters must participate in the game, and with a full contingent of players enacting each role, four players will compete against one. This type of game, called "cooperative-competitive" in board name nomenclature, offers a balance between competition and collaboration that disrupts a typical binary between cooperative and competitive formats. *Fury*'s combination of different types of games resembles *Dracula*'s own multifaceted narrative form, which in its composite of textual artifacts exemplifies the theory of transmedia storytelling—that is, a narrative's dispersal "across multiple delivery channels for the purpose of creating a unified and coordinated entertainment experience"—developed by Henry Jenkins ("Transmedia Storytelling" 944). In contrast to cooperative games, which feature all players confronting a common enemy, or competitive games, in which all players vie for supremacy, *Fury of Dracula* combines these two styles for a hybridized experience of cooperative-competitive gameplay that illustrates *Dracula*'s multifaceted narrative and the opposition of individual versus collective in the novel.

Fury also participates in the "hidden movement" genre, in which one player moves around a shared board without openly revealing their actions; the other players' central task is to discover and arrest the enemy's movement. In *Fury*, the Dracula player moves by playing a trail of location cards face down once per round. A round consists of a day phase, when hunters move or perform actions; a night phase, in which hunters cannot move but perform other actions; and the Dracula phase, in which Dracula moves and performs actions. After the day and night turns by all hunters, Dracula moves to an adjacent city by sliding the facedown location card of the city where he currently lurks, along with any encounter cards, to the next space on the track and placing a new location card and encounter card face down on his current location. Encounter cards are cards describing traps or adversaries that hinder hunters and benefit the Dracula player when matured. Thus, a trail of Dracula's current and previous locations emerges, complete with nasty surprises to delay or defeat the hunters. There are six spaces for location cards on the trail; once a seventh location is placed, the card farthest from the current location is removed from the board, which triggers possible "mature effects" on the accompanying encounter card. If a vampire encounter card matures, Dracula will gain influence on the influence track, which is how he wins the game. A hunter who enters a city on the trail instantly reveals that location card, and from there hunters can track and defeat the vampire by inflicting damage equal to the vampire's health. This "hidden movement" mechanic deftly captures the uncertainty and frustration the characters face in the novel as they struggle to discover Dracula's movements and whereabouts and ultimately race to confront and defeat him in the final sequence. The novel's procedural sequence translates into the hunters' need to deduce Dracula's whereabouts from the location cards' placement on the trail. Hunters must coordinate in their search for the trail and use supplies and events that they acquire in cities and towns. Here the game already extends narrative possibilities beyond the original novel; both Dracula and the hunters may begin anywhere across the continent.

Features of the modern age, such as newspapers, chartered carriages and railroads, and telegraphs all assist the game's hunters in their pursuit, reflecting the reading of Dracula as the archaic and atavistic force who is defeated by modern science and innovations. While this reading may serve as an entry point into discussions of the novel, Dracula's own adoption of modern techniques and mindsets becomes a critical motive for his speedy elimination; as Van Helsing warns, Dracula's "child-brain" is learning to exploit technology and bureaucracy, which, combined with his supernatural strength and longevity, will make him unstoppable if he continues to evolve and modernize (Stoker, *Dracula* 278). This nuance appears in event cards that misdirect or delay hunters.

170   BOARD GAMES

Other examples of the game's instantiation of novelistic elements heighten Dracula's atavism. The game board connects cities and towns through roads and railways, but Dracula can move only via roads since he mistrusts rail technology (c.f. Stoker, *Dracula* 321). Similarly, players can move into sea zones, which allow for quicker movement from one end of Europe to the other; however, Dracula takes damage when entering a sea zone from a port and continues taking damage at sea, creating tactical considerations as well as maintaining the novel's depiction of his relative helplessness when crossing bodies of water. This vampire lore appears in the novel at various points; Van Helsing reports Dracula's inability to cross running water except at slack tide (225), and Mina reiterates his powerlessness while surrounded by water (321). *Fury* applies this weakness to penalize Dracula for escaping to sea, where he cannot be defeated in combat.

Beyond the expression of resident themes of collaboration versus individualism and Old World–New World polarities, board games like *Fury* offer students creative engagement and narrative construction. Studies conducted by several scholars on the educational merits of board games found that games with a clear progressive narrative allow players to retell familiar texts according to their own choices and to inhabit, and therefore personalize, set characters in the world of the game (Costikyan 6; Brown and Waterhouse-Watson, "Reconfiguring" 7; Bowman 127–28). *Fury* allows players to reimagine the original narrative in new ways specific to the ludic interaction of the hunters' decisions and Dracula's responses. Each player, including Dracula, selects their character's starting location, which expands the variety of the game's progression almost limitlessly. If Dracula starts in Spain and the hunters are spread across eastern Europe, play proceeds rather differently than it does when Dracula starts in England or Italy. Players also control their characters' actions and can role-play as the character they control. One of the hallmarks of modern board games evolved from the classic role-playing game (RPG) *Dungeons and Dragons*, developed by Gary Gygax, in which players create their characters, writing backstories and selecting traits from the handbook. Although *Fury* offers less opportunity for customizing characters than RPGs, players can enact their own version of the characters in the novel.[3] The player acting out Mina's character may choose to portray her as more agential and decisive than in the novel, sparking conversations about female characterizations in gothic fiction. During a game a student observed the increased agency for Mina that *Fury* provided, leading to a brief discussion of whether her crucial deduction concerning Dracula's movements during the chase constituted female agency in the novel. The Dracula player can perform their own vision of the vampire as villainous or more complex. Though players' ability to reimagine the vampire is limited by the structure of the game, there is space for improvisation and revision in the ways they enact their intentions. The players' opportunity to personalize and reimagine the characters breathes dynamism and imagination into the study of *Dracula*.

As a tangible experience, *Fury* allows players not only to consider facets in the original story but also to alter and extend the narrative beyond the original text; Dracula may never venture to England, for example. Questions of narrative construction, collaboration-individualist dynamics, archaic-modern binaries, and interpretive extension of the story allow for a participatory engagement with the novel that transcends theoretical discussions in the classroom. What is more, the game also presents opportunities to consider a theme relevant to the modern pandemic crisis: vampirism as a disease.

Vampiric Contagion

As a supplement to study of the novel, *Fury* facilitates the consideration of vampirism as a metaphor for infectious disease and contagion studies that has informed both scholarly approaches and mainstream adaptations. Mary Hallab describes how the novel's "Victorian background, when Europe was still plagued by numerous endemic illnesses and epidemics whose nature and cure were yet unknown," particularly resonates with the Ireland into which Stoker was born, which was still recovering from potato famines and cholera outbreaks ("Vampires" 172). The numerous films that directly adapt vampire novels or are based in the vampiric world quite often establish vampires' embodiment of disease and contagion. Hallab observes the 1922 film *Nosferatu*'s proximity to the Spanish influenza pandemic of 1918 (174) and traces implicit and explicit corollaries throughout the twentieth century (175), including AIDS and West Nile virus (177). An invasive infection communicated interpersonally through fluid transfer readily correlates to the vampiric myth. Martin Willis articulates the Victorian etiologies of contagionism: "Contagionists believed that infectious diseases were passed from one person to another through close contact or touch" (305). This theory endorsed quarantine as a means of combating the spread of disease as well as identifying and neutralizing a known spreader, in particular a "Typhoid Mary" or patient zero. Dracula as an exotic carrier of the vampiric contagion, conveyed by ship to England, where he begins to infect healthy women like Lucy and Mina, plays powerfully on xenophobic suspicions that accompanied England's imperialist globalization in the nineteenth century.[4]

Stoker draws upon other etiological and epidemiological theories in late Victorian science, primarily miasmatism. Miasmatism attributed disease and infection to unsanitary atmospheres and environmental factors. Certain types of soil or water were believed to breed microbial agents that in the form of mist or fog became detectable through senses like smell and sight; the vapors and rancorous odors of Dracula's crypt and its soil are indicators of the outdated yet persistent theory of etiological and epidemiological origins of disease. Willis records the various instances of Dracula and the vampire brides' appearing as mist or minuscule particles that suggest miasma to the Victorian mind as well as the mentions of smells of putrefaction and contamination in Lucy's mausoleum and the Carfax mansion (311).

Fury incorporates disease allusions from the novel and centralizes the notions of contagionism and miasmatism in the game. In *Fury*, Dracula's objectives

172 BOARD GAMES

incorporate contagionist and miasmatic elements; the "Object of the Game" section in the instruction manual states that "Dracula's objective is to advance the influence track to space '13' by creating new vampires and defeating the Hunters" ("Learn to Play" 5). The influence track charts Dracula's progress toward victory as Dracula matures vampires on the location trail and defeats hunters in battle. Dracula's miasmatic influence corresponds to the number of Despair tokens on the board when hunters are defeated; "Despair tokens represent Dracula's creeping influence over the unsuspecting citizens" (10); one token is placed after every week. Once all three Despair tokens have been placed, the influence track advances every time Dracula moves on the trail; the game ends very quickly once Dracula has completed spreading despair across Europe. Both contagion and miasma are represented in this mechanic; Dracula gains influence through spreading his contagion to hunters (through bites or winning combats) or by creating and maturing vampires from his encounter cards on the trail. These events trigger miasmatic phenomena wherein Dracula's influence and despair spread across Europe in a kind of atmospheric epidemiology.

The themes of contagion and miasma also occur in other cards and abilities in the game, mostly in Dracula's encounter cards featuring animal carriers of contagion—rats and bats that attack and confound hunters. His bites in combat weaken the hunters; multiple bites result in male hunters' eventual defeat, while Mina, already weakened by Dracula's attack in the novel, succumbs to a single bite. Miasmatic elements also include the encounter cards "Unnatural Fog" and "Desecrated Soil"; the combat card "Escape as Mist," which prematurely ends a combat, makes use of Dracula's miasmatic incorporeality. One final reference to epidemiology lies in the conundrum of contact tracing that players confront once they stumble upon Dracula's trail. Because of the possibility of vampires seeded in the trail's hideouts, players cannot entirely ignore the trail and simply pursue Dracula. Although hunters must defeat Dracula to win, they must balance that necessity with preventing vampire encounter cards from maturing, since this maturation generates the most influence that Dracula needs to win. Hunters may choose to follow and clear the trail of potential instances of contagion, an example of contact tracing to "sanitize" the infectious elements left in the carrier's wake.

Fury of Dracula contains an array of allusions or references to the competing notions of disease and contagion associated with vampirism. Coupled with a grounding in the scientific debate over contagionism and miasmatism that defined etiology and epidemiology in the nineteenth century, the game provides a tactile experience in which players confront a disease's origins and spread, allowing for continued discussions of Victorian ideas of disease.

Pedagogies of Enactment

One of the pedagogical justifications of board games involves socialization. Board games have been used to teach multicultural awareness and sympathy,[5]

David Smith   173

advocate feminist inclusion and expression,[6] and enhance overall learning.[7] Stuart Woods notes that board games by their nature encourage socialization: "The very act of sitting together to engage in competitive play establishes a framework for social interaction that can never be entirely separated from the play of the game itself" (206). *Fury*'s combination of competitive and cooperative game formats creates opportunities for an even wider spectrum of interaction; hunters must coordinate to strategize and search and to defeat Dracula. They must simultaneously consider the mind and personality of their collective opponent to anticipate Dracula's movements and the risk-reward calculations of ignoring the card trail to pursue Dracula. In turn, Dracula must analyze the board's setup and the hunters' positions to predict his opponents' movements and avoid detection, calling upon a high degree of empathy.[8] Players are thus forced to understand one another in competitive and cooperative ways.

Board games allow players' identification with actions and perspectives that may seem strange or even disturbing to them. The "hidden traitor" genre of games involves one or more players secretly working against the interests of the group while attempting to avoid detection, often inhabiting the role of villain or monster in games like *Battlestar Galactica* (Brown and Waterhouse-Watson, "Reconfiguring" 11 and "Playing" 11). This requirement confounds the narrow perspective of traditional power structures and paradigms. Adam Brown and Deborah Waterhouse-Watson endorse the benefits of perspectival reversal, which "can result in the narrative perspective being reversed to position all gamers against those with whom they would conventionally identify via the source text, reversing and marginalizing the narrative's core drivers" ("Reconfiguring" 8). In *Fury*, the Dracula player must operate in direct opposition to the group, laying traps and engaging in combat to defeat them and to spread their vampiric influence. The player must identify with the goals and perspective of an infamous monster—to empathize with nefarious motives as well as experience the isolation and suspicion Dracula must adopt toward literally everyone around him. Playing as Dracula means sympathizing with the extreme other to win the game, and *Fury* creates a powerful effect of role reversal that facilitates this projection. In volunteering to be Dracula, students face an uneasy but also potentially liberating chance to behave in nonnormative ways and embody socially subversive perspectives that few pedagogical strategies afford. Board games give students a chance to deviate from linear narrative trajectories and literally chart a new path, revising and reimagining behaviors and tactics in ways informed by their own thoughts and experience. As Greg Costikyan observes, "A game is nonlinear. Games must provide at least the illusion of free will to the player; players must feel that they have freedom of action—not absolute freedom, but freedom within the structure of the system" (6). Players have this limited freedom to interpret a story and to enact their interpretations within parameters defining contexts and goals; doing so in the guise of a simple entertaining activity, they can transform the potentially disorienting adoption of unfamiliar perspectives into a lighthearted and fun exercise.

174   BOARD GAMES

Fury of Dracula equips educators with a unique transmedia tool for teaching Stoker's novel. The text's thematic complexity appears in the game's continuums of modernity and atavism and individual and collective action, in the cooperative-competitive gameplay, and in various specific rules and roles. Furthermore, *Fury* illustrates the vampiric disease through Dracula's win conditions and gameplay as well as the trail of contact tracing. Finally, players' immersion in and enactment of their characters energizes the performative participation afforded by video games or dramatic adaptations. Board games' textured layers of design and gameplay capture the complexity and fascination that continues to render Stoker's novel relevant to this day.

NOTES

1. As Bowman observes, "Educators are beginning to recognize the value of 'participatory, experiential modes of thinking' as complementary to the standard 'distanced, reflective modes,' such as detached observation and analysis" (82).

2. Natalie Underberg-Goode and Peter Smith address Andean culture, while Rose Namubiru Kirumira explores Ugandan cultural rituals.

3. Bowman contends that "[r]ole-playing provides the opportunity for participants to evaluate and understand the consequences of their actions, both tactically and emotionally" (85).

4. This theory, Willis explains, lends itself both to quarantine and to targeted marginalization of certain lower socioeconomic and ethnic groups (305).

5. Underberg-Goode and Smith discuss how their homemade game "leaves the players with a greater understanding of Andean culture through actual play experience as opposed to being told or compelled to adopt an Andean stance in the game" (163).

6. Mendes and Silva cite the ability of art forms to provide "a powerful form of expression for women, children and other marginalized groups" (246).

7. Underberg-Goode and Smith cite a study that found "that cooperation was the stronger goal structure for learning" (168).

8. Hoy (127) and Bowman (86) note the scholarly attention paid to this empathetic development.

vEmpire 2.0: How to Teach *Dracula*: Where, When, and Why

Dragan Kujundžić

Few novels attract as many curious and enthusiastic student readers as Bram Stoker's *Dracula*. This account therefore examines various pedagogical tools of benefit to those who would like to start teaching a course related to the novel. Drawn from personal experience, it offers practical, hands-on advice on how to prepare a course or start a program abroad in London related to *Dracula* along with some theoretical ideas I have generated while teaching the novel.

The novel and the attending cinematic and theoretical tradition that it spawned give numerous opportunities for investigation of their many implications. The courses I taught, regardless of level (undergraduate or graduate), form and inform venues for and of my research. I started teaching the course at the University of California, Irvine, in the Department of Comparative Literature and English, some twenty years ago, responding to a demand for some larger courses, with an idea of cultivating and drawing in majors to the program and of broadening my own teaching portfolio and interests. At the time, I knew little about vampire narratives, but I had a sense that they presented an opportunity that could justify a course on vampire cinema taught concomitantly with Stoker's *Dracula*. My colleagues in film studies introduced me to a B list of vampire cinema: *Cat People, The Hunger, Daughters of Darkness, Vampyros Lesbos,* and *Irma Vep.* In addition, I started teaching the course at the University of California, Santa Barbara, where at the time Laurence Rickels taught a celebrated undergraduate course, The Vampire Lectures, to some nine hundred students. These lectures became the eponymous book, which encouraged me in thinking that such an enterprise could be relevant and replicable. In addition to the course, I started an annual Halloween vampire lecture and invited Rickels to give the inaugural talk. We all dressed up for the occasion, which started after dark; the food was catered, and a Romanian "Vampire" wine (an utter plonk) was served to carded students and attendees. My class immediately drew 150 students. When I moved five years later to the University of Florida (UF), the course again began with 150 students and increased to over 180. Only the size of the room and the logistics prevented me from offering it to an even larger body of students, all thirsty for knowledge. I teach it now at UF regularly every fall, sometimes as two courses, Vampire Literature and Vampire Cinema, in the fall and spring, to fully enrolled and well-attended classes. Stoker's *Dracula* is obligatory literature in both. But the California campuses where I worked in particular, as Rickels convincingly argues, begged for such a course to be taught. Within the vicinity of Hollywood, they observed or embraced a vampiric

176   WHERE, WHEN, AND WHY TO TEACH *DRACULA*

culture of undead beautiful bodies, including movie stars, the transported "Old World" (specifically, Germany and Austria), psychoanalysis, East Coast culture brought west, and the *Körperkultur* ("body culture") of Botox and mummification to preserve skin and beauty. An Austrian world bodybuilding champion and actor was the state governor who signed my checks. At the very least, Hollywood is the place where all cultures go to die and to be resurrected every time the light in the movie theater goes dark.

Written at the end of the nineteenth century, *Dracula* is a fertile depository, a rich vein, so to speak, of psychoanalytic, biopolitical, historical, and postcolonial discourses that come to the reader in a reverse way, in a mirror that does not give back a reflection. It is a text that begs and refuses to be read, tantalizing the reader with the terror of self-recognition, or with terror *tout court*. The novel condenses discourses of modernity but also constitutes in and of itself a temporal machine out of time, an untimely temporal deferral of its valence and meanings. It is a testimony of Victorian culture with the attending implications regarding the birth of the clinic, including discipline and punishment and treatment of hysteria (Dr. Van Helsing is the student of Jean-Martin Charcot, Sigmund Freud's mentor and inspiration), and the inventions of the apparatuses of phonic and visual reproduction—typewriters, photography and cinema— all incorporated into the narrative. The novel also enacts the drama of dying empires soon to be dissolved after World War I into smaller nation-states. The tele-technological aspects of the novel, to paraphrase slightly the words of J. Hillis Miller and his *The Medium Is the Maker*, where he speaks about telecommunication devices and new telepathic technologies, are "prosthetic replacements for religion, for spiritualism, and for psychoanalysis, all three, in a four stage historical process that of course does not sublate the earlier stages in a definitive *Aufhebung*, but retains each stage throughout, as when Freud compares telepathy to talking on the phone" (14–15).

The vampire narrative operates on delay time, the countertime of mourning and melancholia, of the past that refuses to die, the undead trauma of massification of bodies in cinema and in war, the deferred account of the undead effects of modernity. *Dracula* is an exemplary illustration of temporality that rises in darkness, with artificial light, every time the novel is being read; and technical, prosthetic, mediatic time, the medium as the maker, opens it to the experience of finitude and spectrality, "time created by the performative media, the media as makers, including makers of human time" (J. Miller 25). Dracula rising from the coffin in darkness, with the invocation in the novel of every possible technical apparatus available at the end of the nineteenth century and put to use in the novel, is the emblem of that technomediatic performance at the end of literature. It is the text that in an exemplary way articulates, or puts to use, and is itself used toward the ends and dead ends of modernity. For example, and there could be many, the vampire is hunted and the novel haunted by technologies of mass media and mass death, from cinema to sulfur gases, and the vampire's lair at the Carfax Abbey is purged with fire in order to smoke out the stench of

"Ole Jerusalem" (Stoker, *Dracula*, 214). Thus, the novel anticipates the purges with fire and massification of death in the Holocaust. Jack Halberstam wrote in "Technologies of Monstrosity: Bram Stoker's *Dracula*" that the vampire is "the Jew of anti-Semitic discourse" (92).

At the same time, the novel is skin deep, a "skin show," as Halberstam says, cathecting fantasies of limitless transgression of any corporeal limit (corporeal as in physical body or the body of work). It is an incessant machine of conversion of blood, semen, and milk, of gender role inversions, of interracial and intergenerational sexuality, of the human body becoming animal and of an animal becoming human. Judith Butler and Gilles Deleuze can be your guides into that maze of lines of both escape and escapism. The polymorphously perverse body of the vampire invites erotic and thanatotic hunger, often amplified in the classroom with cinematic images, the pleasure principle serving the technically and prosthetically reproduced death drive. Thus unleashed by the novel are the topics of psychoanalysis, mourning and melancholia, hysteria and female sexuality, exquisite corpses and the jubilation of and in mourning analyzed by Nicolas Abraham and Maria Torok. The subject of mourning and melancholia advertised in a course title would probably appeal to few students, but psychoanalytic theory offered through the lens of Stoker's novel and Francis Ford Coppola's *Bram Stoker's* Dracula, with its many erotic reversals and perversions—copulation with the lycanthropic animal in human form; the sapphic attraction between Mina and Lucy; the polyamorous fantasies, Lucy's polyandric and Harker's polygamic; and female orgasms misdiagnosed as illness and male orgasm projected as castration (the Medusa's head scene of Harker's imprisonment in Coppola's film)—animates even first-year undergraduate students who have never had a single class in "theory" to interiorize and write essays on Abraham and Freud, make short films about their correspondence, and read Jacques Derrida on the crypt and mourning or Halberstam and Rickels on the politics of skin.

The course also provides a space for play. I used to allow creative projects that had to be explained with an academic final paper (four single-spaced pages) until I ran out of space for the creative projects in my office. Students submitted numerous boxes of putrid cursed earth, vampire cookbooks (only one ingredient for the vampire meal but many recipes for the "thirsty" food Harker tastes on the way to Romania), baked goods oozing red jelly, garlands of garlic, paintings, mock transfusion apparatuses, and smaller and larger coffins, and almost everyone in the final class dressed in Victorian fashion and Goth makeup, without my having suggested it. Other final projects included a ritual kung fu slaying of a vampire piñata and a punctured oil painting depicting a neck and vampire kiss that squirted blood-red pigment. Students collaborated to make short feature films or documentaries; tourism majors made flyers, CDs, and brochures for BYOB (Bring Your Own Body) tours. One student documentary featured a group that met in a club in Los Angeles to drain actual blood from one another. The course, in a word, allows tremendous creativity to be unleashed—and opens access to texts in theory, film,

178   WHERE, WHEN, AND WHY TO TEACH *DRACULA*

media, and psychoanalysis, all of which inspire large enrollment or eagerness of appropriation. Some of this bore fruit that I could see almost immediately. Some six months after the class, one of my undergraduate students from the course at UF wrote a review of the first *Twilight* saga film and published it in the *Seattle Times*, the newspaper with the largest circulation in the Pacific Northwest, quoting discussions we had had in class. My undergraduate teaching also bore professional fruit, including invitations to give a plenary lecture at the annual meeting of the American Comparative Literature Association in Austin, Texas (with the obligatory conference riverboat tour of the bat colonies at dusk), which was subsequently published in *The Comparatist* as "vEmpire, Glocalisation, and the Melancholia of the Sovereign," and to give talks in London on the Irish subtext of Stoker's *Dracula*. I gave numerous press interviews on the topic. My undergraduate classes often influenced and directed my research, more so than graduate teaching did. I thus urge my young colleagues to consider their undergraduate teaching as such a conduit to academic success.

The history of cinema is another topic addressed in this course. The course provides an opportunity to review many screenings of the novel, making historical surveys of the birth of cinema, including F. W. Murnau's *Nosferatu*, the Hollywood cinema, and Bela Lugosi, and continuing to the present with recent productions, including *Twilight* and *What We Do in the Shadows*. Stoker's *Dracula* is a protocinematic apparatus, already operating at the end of literature and projecting its demise. Students become aware of how the novel multiplies itself by means of typewriters, Kodak snapshots, phonographs, and stenographs. The novel is in the end filed and archived in triplicate, anticipating computers and modern-day technologies of archivization, the literary text vampirized by the technologies of technical reproducibility that it puts into motion. Friedrich Kittler's "*Dracula's* Legacy" remains to this day an indispensable analysis in this regard.

The novel is a nexus to cinema, an apparatus that mimics, anticipates, and imitates the film. "The Vampire rises from a secret crypt in centuries long anticipation of cinema," says Rickels, and the novel is "the ultimate double of the film medium" (93). The figure of the vampire operates as a cinematic apparatus, its skin burnt by light, just as film is. The pellicle, the skin of the filmic substrate, is written on by light that leaves ashen, burnt traces then stabilized in chemicals, fixed in all senses of the word, including cutting by scissors or the stake and sword, and then projected on the screen, rising when the light goes out. The course thus allows a reflection on the cinematic as vampiric and a larger interrogation of modernism and its aftermath, qua Walter Benjamin on technical reproducibility, André Bazin on the mummification of skin qua the origin of photography, Jean-François Lyotard on "acinema" and the transparency of the cinematic skin, Bernard Stiegler on the history of technics, Samuel Weber on "mass mediauras" and the theatricality and spectrality of the medium (Hamlet's father ghost!), or Derrida on spectrographies and echographies of television and cinema (Derrida and Stiegler) and the fragile testamentary properties of the burnt trace (Derrida, *Cinders*).

The where of *Dracula*, its geopolitics, constitutes another aspect of the novel that provides a fertile territory of exploration. What caught my attention the first time I read the novel with an eye to a possible course was the fact that Dracula fashions himself as the avenger of "the shame of Cassova" (that is, Kosovo; Stoker, *Dracula* 38). Coppola's film prominently stages this conflict in its introduction. At the time, I knew little about Victorian London, but I certainly knew a lot about the Battle of Kosovo (1389), the conflict between the Ottoman (Muslim) and Serbian (Christian) forces, that clash of civilizations if there was ever one, and its cultural implications, especially for the South Slavic literatures and cultures in which I had been raised. We are now crossing the Danube at Budapest, leaving the West and entering the East, "into the traditions of Turkish rule" (Stoker, *Dracula* 11). I was reading the novel in the United States at the time of the war in Yugoslavia provoked by another avenger of Kosovo, Slobodan Milošević, "the butcher of the Balkans," often drawn in caricatures in the United States as a vampire (I show students an example by David Levine in the *New York Review of Books* [Judah]). Milošević was in turn being punished by the "little band of men together" (Stoker, *Dracula* 344)—a.k.a. NATO, led by the United States—bombing Serbia with technical superiority from afar and reenacting the scenario of *Dracula*. That Milošević died in the hands of Dutch doctors, the modern-day Van Helsings, just shows the incredible valence of the novel and its ability to serve as an interpretive tool for subsequent history, actual or literary. James Lyon's novel *Kiss of the Butterfly* tells a story set at the time of the war in Yugoslavia, a mini-empire of the South Slavs come to self-destruction, in which a vampire is awakened from the Petrovaradin fortress built by the Austro-Hungarian Empire (today Novi Sad, my hometown), and goes to wreak genocide in Srebrenica. Geopolitics is the bloodline of *Dracula*, arguably its main artery.

Dracula stages the end of empire through the figure of the vampire, who forms the underbelly, the beneath-the-skin, of imperial decay. The empire may be the Ottoman one invoked by the killing technique borrowed, as myth has it, by the historical Dracula from the Ottomans and applied against his own Christian folk, hence the name Vlad the Impaler;[1] it may be the Austro-Hungarian Holy Roman Empire, which gave the historical Dracula his knighthood title, "of the Dragon," against which then he turned; or indeed it may be the staging of the end of the British Empire, as explicitly narrated in the novel. We could invoke also the 2021 autoimmunitary implosion in the Congress of the US Empire, with its attending vampire narrative (discussed further below).

The novel lends itself to a discussion of history, geopolitics, and empire and may serve as both their lure and their interpretation. Naturally, first and foremost it is a novel about the British Empire at the end of an era when the sun never set on it, in its twilight and life after dark. *Dracula*, as both novel and vampire, has a timeless capacity to operate at the undead ends of empire, an

180   WHERE, WHEN, AND WHY TO TEACH *DRACULA*

effect I call the vEmpire. This dominant aspect of the novel pertaining specifically to the imperial politics of the British Empire motivated me to respond to an invitation from colleagues at the University of Florida International Center to teach the novel on-site in London, incorporating interpretation of the British Empire up to and including its sovereignist self-immolation in Brexit. Thus UF in London was born.

The course consists of two courses, Vampire London and Empire London, taught by myself, and on-location lectures given by myself or by notable invited lecturers. Vampire London, naturally, assesses Stoker's *Dracula*, along the lines familiar to the readers of "The Occidental Tourist," a foundational essay by Stephen D. Arata that is obligatory reading in the course. Empire London discusses the imperial politics of Britain, from the Roman imperial settings in England to the modern-day England of Brexit. I include in the appendix two excerpts from the syllabi that I submitted for the course proposal.

The program turned out to be extremely successful. In addition to courses and film screenings in a classroom setting and regular student presentations, lectures were given at four or more different locations per week. I presented the lecture and discussion on Victorian sexuality in the sex and sexuality portion of the nineteenth-century section of the Victoria and Albert Museum and in the Victorian fashion wing. Marxism, capitalism, and vampirism were discussed at Karl Marx's grave at Highgate; students were asked to read Franco Moretti's "The Capital *Dracula*" (see Marx, *Critique* 342: "Capital is dead labour, which, vampire-like, only lives by sucking living labour"), and Derrida's *Specters of Marx* was invoked as an explanatory background of the spectrality of capital. At the Freud Museum in Hampstead, I taught on Freud's "Mourning and Melancholia," "The Medusa's Head," and "Beyond the Pleasure Principle"; the students went through the guided exhibit and attended the screening of the rare footage of Freud made on the spot in Maresfield Gardens shortly before his death ("Home 1939"). Imperial mean time was discussed at the Royal Observatory and the National Maritime Museum in Greenwich. I lectured on empire and the Jews at the Jewish Museum in Camden (including the history of notable Jews in England, the history of modern Israel, the Balfour Declaration, and the British Mandate for Palestine) and on anti-Semitism, vampirism, and the Shoah in the new permanent Holocaust exhibition in the Imperial War Museum (the two courses I teach are cross-listed between Jewish studies, English, and international studies).

The real treat, for students and for myself, was provided by invited lecturers. A specialist of English landscape and gardens gave a talk at Kew Gardens combining an analysis of Virginia Woolf's story "Kew Gardens" with the history of English landscape; Pamela Gilbert, one of the foremost specialists of the Victorian era, gave a talk called "London: The Blood of the Living City: Urban Planning, Sickness and Death" at the Royal London Hospital Museum; the best-selling author Vesna Goldsworthy, the chair of creative writing at several prestigious universities in the United Kingdom, delivered the lecture

"Ruritania, London, the Empire, and East and Central Europe"; and the highlight of all of these talks was a presentation of the history of English political caricature from Hogarth to Brexit, by the leading political cartoonist, satirist, and commentator Martin Rowsen. Rowsen indulged the students with the history of caricature and then showed his current work, published weekly in *The Guardian*. His drawing of Theresa May as a ghost, his caricatural variations on William Hogarth's celebrated *Gin Lane* in relation to the Tories and Boris Johnson, and his political commentaries on the clowns, ghosts, and ends of the empire coalescing as Brexit allowed us to witness the history of the United Kingdom, an empire in decline, in the making.

This leads me to just a few concluding remarks on why I teach Stoker's *Dracula*. I said that *Dracula* operates as both the lure and interpretation of history. It is a literary machine of incredible semantic valence, displaying its relevance every time some political monster rises from the crypt. It prefigures the rise of fascism and anti-Semitism. By court order Murnau's *Nosferatu* was burned (with only one print saved), and such a holocaustic burning (from the Greek *holos* ["whole"] and *kaustos* ["burnt"]) and attendant anti-Semitism have been used to produce an allegory of German trauma left by Nazism in Werner Herzog's *Nosferatu the Vampyre*. Herzog sets Harker's journey to the castle to Siegfried's funeral march from Richard Wagner's *Götterdämmerung* (*The Twilight of the Gods*—as a phrase the epitome and the most fitting description of the vampire narrative), and images of the Alpine sublime, channeling Leni Riefenstahl, lead Harker to the door of the Vampyre-Führer: "Welcome to my castle!" Herzog is showing what went into the making of the project to "make Germany great again" and sending an urgent warning not to repeat it. Recent war in Yugoslavia and the rising specters of nationalism as well as US militarism have been discussed through the lens of *Dracula* (Tomislav Longinović's *Vampires like Us* and *Vampire Nation* are indispensable in this regard); a more recent global pandemic is said to have started with the vampire bat and, in an uncanny coincidence, has paralleled the autoimmunitary implosion of the United States.[2] Let us not forget that Vlad, the sovereign prince of Wallachia, the defender of the Christian world, turned against his own Christian brethren and started impaling his own people.

Dracula is a story about blood and a vampire that, like a virus carried by a vampire bat, propagates itself as an undead spore affixing itself to a living body. Thus, a certain parallel between COVID-19 and the MAGA movement imposes itself and demands a reading through the prism of *Dracula*—not least because MAGA's favorite trope, that the Democrats are bloodsucking pedophiles and vampires feasting on children, is a blood libel straight from *The Protocols of the Wise Men of Zion*, the anti-Semites' manifesto. The monster that rose out of the coffin on 6 January 2021 in the United States is familiar to anyone who has read Stoker's *Dracula* and understood its undead historical implications and warnings. *Dracula* needs to be read and reread

182 WHERE, WHEN, AND WHY TO TEACH *DRACULA*

today, and taught to American students, more than ever, maybe forever. The stakes are high.

NOTES

This essay is dedicated to J. Hillis Miller, who passed away as I was finishing this essay, on 7 February 2021. Hillis was a colleague at UC Irvine, a mentor, and a friend. His contributions to the study of literature and theory are colossal. Among other things, he was a president of the MLA (1986) and a recipient of the MLA Award for Lifetime Scholarly Achievement (2005).

1. A lengthy scene in the *Bridge on the Drina*, by the Yugoslav Nobel laureate Ivo Andrić, describes the impaling of the "Christian peasant" Radosav by the Ottoman forces in Bosnia led by Mehmed Paša Sokolović in the sixteenth century as punishment for interfering with their construction of the bridge on the Drina at Višegrad.

2. We live a situation of double suicide, both "natural" and political, that Derrida spoke and warned about after the "event of 9-11." This political suicide by implosion affects both capital and Capitol "with extraordinary *economy*" (Derrida, "Autoimmunity" 95). This implosion started with building the wall of hyperdefense to the point where these defensive forces, in the manner of an autoimmunitary cytokine storm, mimicking the viral epidemics, infected and affected the very seat of the US government, the US Congress, and attempted to destroy it. I am grateful to Patricia Pierson for the discussion of these aspects of the novel.

APPENDIX

My proposal for UF in London included the following descriptions of the courses Vampire London and Empire London.

Vampire London

Vampire London will discuss the setting of Bram Stoker's signature novel, located in London. It will follow the novel's rich trajectory in cinema, history, and literature and discuss its multifaceted and enduring cultural impact. Lectures related to the novel and its historical context will take place at sites in London such as Highgate Cemetery, the Tower of London, the Freud Museum, the Jewish Museum, the Science Museum, the British Museum, and St. Paul's Cathedral for on-location instruction and on-site learning. The course will discuss the figure of the vampire in cinema and literature (*Bram Stoker's* Dracula will be read or screened and analyzed, among other films; particular attention will be given to the novel as a protocinematic medium) as well as the rendering of the vampire in cinema (from Murnau's *Nosferatu* to *The Fearless Vampire Slayers, An American Werewolf in London, Buffy the Vampire Slayer, Twilight*, and others).

Student learning objectives: students will learn about the rich tradition of vampires in literature and cinema, both as this tradition relates to the history of London and the British Empire and as it informs the novel *Dracula*.

Empire London

Empire London will discuss the imperial politics of Britain, from the Roman imperial settings in England to the modern-day England of Brexit. Contemporary media representations of the royal family will be discussed in the context of globalization and mediatic imperialism (the royal bloodline and weddings like that of Prince Harry and Meghan Markle as selling the imperial brand, the nonbiodegradable imperial kitsch of "tea with the Queen" in Madame Tussauds). The course will start by defining empire (using the work of Hardt and Negri) and follow the origins of the British Empire in the context of the Roman conquest of Britain. Joseph Conrad's *Heart of Darkness* and Bram Stoker's *Dracula* will serve as the overarching metaphors of British imperial politics. Each week students will read and report on a chapter from *The Oxford History of British Empire* and relate it to the British imperial politics discussed on location at renowned places of imperial learning or culture, such as the Royal Museums Greenwich, the Victoria and Albert Museum, the Royal College of Physicians, the Imperial War Museum, Buckingham Palace Garden, Kew Gardens, and the Natural History Museum.

Student learning objectives: students will learn about the rich tradition of vampires in literature and cinema, both as it relates to the history of London and the British Empire and as it informs Bram Stoker's *Dracula*.

NOTES ON CONTRIBUTORS

Agnes Andeweg is associate professor of modern literature at University College Utrecht. She has published widely on literature as cultural memory in both English and Dutch and edited the volume *Gothic Kinship* with Sue Zlosnik (2013). Her essay "Manifestations of the Flying Dutchman: On Materializing Ghosts and (Not) Remembering the Colonial Past" was awarded the essay prize of the International Society for Cultural History in 2014.

Zan Cammack is a lecturer in the Department of English and Literature at Utah Valley University, specializing in Irish studies, material culture, and digital humanities. Her book *Ireland's Gramophones: Material Culture, Memory, and Trauma in Irish Modernism* (2021) examines the gramophone as an object of cultural significance during the revolutionary era of Ireland in the early twentieth century. She is also the cohost of *The Thing about Austen,* a podcast about Jane Austen and her material world.

Srirupa Chatterjee is associate professor of English, gender, and body image studies at the Indian Institute of Technology, Hyderabad, where she teaches genres, world literature, gender studies, and popular fiction. Her research interests include gender and body image studies, and her recent publications include *Female Body Image and Beauty Politics in Contemporary Indian Literature and Culture* (2024) and *Gendered Violence in Public Spaces: Women's Narratives of Travel in Neoliberal India* (2023). Her forthcoming monograph is titled *Body Image in Contemporary American Young Adult Literature.*

Christopher G. Diller is professor of English, rhetoric, and writing at Berry College. He is the editor of the Broadview edition of *Uncle Tom's Cabin* (2009), and some of his most recent publications have appeared in *African American Review, MLQ: Modern Language Quarterly,* and *Resources for American Literary Study.*

Peter Gölz is associate professor of Germanic and Slavic studies at the University of Victoria. He regularly teaches German language and film courses and Vampires in Literature and Film. He has published on German literature and film, cyberpunk, computer-assisted language learning and new media, humor studies, and cinematic vampires.

Joshua Gooch is professor of English at D'Youville University. He is the author of *Dickensian Affects: Charles Dickens and Feelings of Precarity* (2020) and *The Victorian Novel, Service Work, and the Nineteenth-Century Economy* (2015), and his teaching and research interests include film, literature, and critical theory.

Richard Haslam is associate professor of English at Saint Joseph's University, where he teaches Irish literature and film. Among his many articles he has published "Negotiating the Poetics of Irish Gothic via Casuistry" and "The Hermeneutic Hazards of Hibernicizing Oscar Wilde's *The Picture of Dorian Gray.*"

Jerrold E. Hogle is emeritus professor and university distinguished professor in the Department of English, University of Arizona. He has written and edited a wealth of articles and books on the gothic, including *The Cambridge Companion to Gothic Fiction* (2002) and *The Gothic and Theory: An Edinburgh Companion* (2019).

186 NOTES ON CONTRIBUTORS

Shari Hodges Holt is instructional associate professor of English at the University of Mississippi. She teaches film adaptations of fiction and drama, nineteenth-century British Victorian novelists, sensation fiction, science fiction, and the gothic. Her publications include "The Wonderful Worlds of Dickens and Disney: Animated Adaptations of *Oliver Twist* and *A Christmas Carol*" and the coauthored *Ouida the Phenomenon: Evolving Social, Political, and Gender Concerns in Her Fiction* (2008).

William Hughes is professor of English at the University of Macau, where he has developed medically informed teaching in the fields of Victorian and contemporary gothic, ecocriticism, and imperial fictions. He has published extensively on *Dracula* in works including *Beyond* Dracula: *Bram Stoker's Fiction and Its Cultural Context* (2000), *Bram Stoker's* Dracula: *A Reader's Guide to Essential Criticism* (2009), and, coedited with Andrew Smith, *Bram Stoker: History, Psychoanalysis and the Gothic* (1998). He is an honorary research fellow of the University of East Anglia, Norwich, and a fellow of the Royal Historical Society.

Jerry Rafiki Jenkins is assistant director of the Institute for African American Studies at the University of Georgia. He is the author of *Anti-Blackness and Human Monstrosity in Black American Horror Fiction* (2024) and *The Paradox of Blackness in African American Vampire Fiction* (2019). He also coedited, with Martin Japtok, *Human Contradictions in Octavia E. Butler's Work* (2020) and *Authentic Blackness / Real Blackness: Essays on the Meaning of Blackness in Literature and Culture* (2011).

Dragan Kujundžić is professor of Germanic, Slavic, and Jewish studies at the University of Florida (UF) and serves as the director of UF in London. He is the author of five books and numerous edited volumes in several languages, on the works of Mikhail Bakhtin and Jacques Derrida among others. His film and book *The First Sail* are dedicated to the work of J. Hillis Miller. He is currently completing "Cinetaphs," concerned with the spectrality of cinema.

William Thomas McBride is associate professor of English at Illinois State University, where he teaches film, drama, and the Bible as literature. His most recent publications on film may be found in the MLA's *Approaches to Teaching Baraka's* Dutchman (2018) and the forthcoming *Neglected Scorsese: Overlooked Films, Television Shows, and Commercials* (2025). His most recent publications in biblical hermeneutics appear in *Troubling Topics, Sacred Texts: Readings in Hebrew Bible, New Testament, and Qur'an* (2021) and *Sacred Tropes: Tanakh, New Testament, and Qur'an as Literature and Culture* (2009).

Lisa Nevárez is professor of English at Siena College, where she directs the race and ethnic studies minor. She teaches courses in Latinx literature, early-nineteenth-century British literature, literary theory, and gothic and horror fiction. She is the editor of *The Vampire Goes to College: Essays on Teaching with the Undead* (2014).

Patrick R. O'Malley is professor of English at Georgetown University. He teaches classes in nineteenth-century British, Irish, and Anglo-Irish literature and culture; gender and sexuality; and the gothic novel. He has published *Catholicism, Sexual Deviance, and Victorian Gothic Culture* (2006), *Liffey and Lethe: Paramnesiac History in Nineteenth-Century Anglo-Ireland* (2017), and *The Irish and the Imagination of Race: White Supremacy across the Atlantic in the Nineteenth Century* (2023) as well as essays on the work of Oscar Wilde, James Joyce, and Ann Radcliffe.

NOTES ON CONTRIBUTORS 187

Ess Pokornowski is a trans, queer, and crip researcher, writer, and educator. They have published public-facing research on censorship and academic freedom and on issues of equity and access in higher education in prison. Their teaching and academic research examine how political and medical rhetoric is used to justify violence in popular culture. Pokornowski is also an author of creative nonfiction and a volunteer staff reader at *The Adroit Journal*.

Ana Raquel Rojas is assistant professor of English at the University of San Francisco. Her research and teaching interests include decadent literature, the femme fatale, and the vampire. Her publications include "The Mustachioed Woman; or, The Problem of Androgyny," in *Cahiers Victoriens et Édouardiens*, and "Vampires and Unicorns: Atavism, Futurism, and Disruption in a Twenty-First-Century Reading of *Dracula*," in *Victorians Institute Journal*.

Andrew Smith is professor of English at University of Sheffield. His publications include *Dickens and the Gothic* (2024), *Gothic Fiction and the Writing of Trauma, 1914–1934: The Ghosts of World War One* (2022), *Gothic Death, 1740–1914: A Literary History* (2016), and *The Ghost Story 1840–1920: A Cultural History* (2012). He is a past president of the International Gothic Association.

David Smith is assistant professor of English at the University of Science and Arts of Oklahoma. His research and teaching interests include interdisciplinary studies in Western and non-Western literature, the gothic, Romanticism, and new media. He has published on the Romanticism of William Blake and J. R. R. Tolkien, as well as gothic texts like Charles Brockden Brown's *Wieland* and Samuel Taylor Coleridge's *Christabel*.

Elizabeth Way is assistant professor of English at High Point University. Her most recent publications include "'By Unholy Arts?': The Craft of Protest in Joanna Baillie's *The Phantom* and *Witchcraft*," in *European Romantic Review*, and "'Stuck Through with a Pin, and Beautifully Preserved': Curating the Life of Elizabeth Barrett Browning (1806–1861)," in *Biographical Misrepresentations of British Women Writers: A Hall of Mirrors and the Long Nineteenth Century* (2017). She contributed an essay on Mary Seacole to the MLA volume *Teaching Anglophone Caribbean Literature* (2012). Her monograph entitled *Romantic Compositions: Gender, Genre, and Authority in Women's Writing, 1790–1836* is forthcoming.

Jeffrey Andrew Weinstock is associate professor of English at Central Michigan University, where he teaches a variety of courses in American literature, film, fantasy, and science fiction. The author of *Pop Culture for Beginners* (2022) and editor of *The Monster Theory Reader* (2020), he has published prolifically in media studies and on Monty Python, Edgar Allan Poe, Tim Burton, and Goth music.

Jolene Zigarovich is associate professor of English at the University of Northern Iowa, where she teaches a variety of classes with an emphasis on Victorian fiction. She has been a visiting fellow at the Netherlands Institute for Advanced Study and at the University of Edinburgh's Institute for Advanced Studies in the Humanities. She is the author of *Writing Death and Absence in the Victorian Novel: Engraved Narratives* (2012) and editor of *Sex and Death in Eighteenth-Century Literature* (2013) as well as *TransGothic in Literature and Culture* (2018). Her monograph *Death and the Body in the Eighteenth-Century Novel* (2023) received support from the National Endowment for the Humanities.

SURVEY RESPONDENTS

Agnes Andeweg, *University College Utrecht*
Susan Bernardo, *Wagner College*
Nicole Blair, *University of Washington, Tacoma*
Abigail Burnham Bloom, *Hunter College, City University of New York*
Lauren Byler, *California State University, Northridge*
Zan Cammack, *Utah Valley University*
Peter Chapin, *New York University*
Srirupa Chatterjee, *Indian Institute of Technology, Hyderabad*
Lisa Di Bartolomeo, *West Virginia University*
Christopher G. Diller, *Berry College*
James Doan, *Nova Southeastern University*
Sharon M. Gallagher, *Penn State University*
Andrea Gazzaniga, *Northern Kentucky University*
Caroline Gelmi, *University of Massachusetts, Dartmouth*
Peter Gölz, *University of Victoria*
Joshua Gooch, *D'Youville College*
Lesley Goodman, *Albright College*
Lynda A. Hall, *Chapman University*
David Hansen, *Illinois State University*
Donald M. Hassler, *Kent State University*
Mark M. Hennelly, Jr., *California State University, Sacramento*
Shari Hodges Holt, *University of Mississippi*
Jerry Rafiki Jenkins, *University of Georgia*
Dragan Kujundžić, *University of Florida*
Jonathan Malcolm Lampley, *Austin Peay State University*
Sara L. Maurer, *University of Notre Dame*
Holly J. McBee, *Dickinson State University*
John McBratney, *John Carroll University*
Renata Kobetts Miller, *City College, City University of New York*
Patrick R. O'Malley, *Georgetown University*
Patricia O'Neill, *Hamilton College*
Sylvia A. Pamboukia, *Robert Morris University*
Elizabeth L. Rambo, *Campbell University*
Susanna Rich, *Kean University*
Kelsey Ridge, *University of Birmingham*
John Paul Riquelme, *Boston University*
Ana Raquel Rojas, *University of San Francisco*
Elizabeth Sheckler, *University of New Hampshire*
Beth Sherman, *Queens College, City University of New York*
Eric Sterling, *Auburn University, Montgomery*
Michael Torregrossa, *Bristol Community College*
Tom Ue, *Dalhousie University*

190 SURVEY RESPONDENTS

Elizabeth Way, *High Point University*
Jeffrey Andrew Weinstock, *Central Michigan University*
Karen Winstead, *Ohio State University*
Livia Arndal Woods, *University of Illinois, Springfield*
Jolene Zigarovich, *University of Northern Iowa*

WORKS CITED

Abbott, Stacey. "Dracula on Film and TV from 1960 to the Present." Luckhurst, *Cambridge Companion*, pp. 192–206.

Abel, Jessica, et al. *Life Sucks.* First Second, 2008.

Abraham, Nicolas, and Maria Torok. *The Shell and the Kernel.* Edited and translated by Nicholas T. Rand. U of Chicago P, 1994. Vol. 1 of *Renewals of Psychoanalysis.*

"The Age of Union." *The Story of Ireland*, episode 4, BBC/RTÉ, 2011, www.bbc.co.uk/iplayer/episode/b00zj0rx/story-of-ireland-4-the-age-of-union.

Ahmad, Aalya, and Sean Moreland, editors. *Fear and Learning: Essays on the Pedagogy of Horror.* McFarland, 2013.

———. "Horror in the Classroom." Ahmad and Moreland, *Fear,* pp. 5–18.

Ahuja, Neel. *Bioinsecurities: Disease Interventions, Empire, and the Government of Species.* Duke UP, 2016.

Alberge, Dalya. "Christopher Marlowe Credited as One of Shakespeare's Co-writers." *The Guardian*, 23 Oct. 2016, www.theguardian.com/culture/2016/oct/23/christopher-marlowe-credited-as-one-of-shakespeares-co-writers.

An American Werewolf in London. Written and directed by John Landis, Universal Pictures, 1981.

Anderson, Gregory. *Victorian Clerks.* U of Manchester P, 1976.

Anyiwo, U. Melissa, editor. *Race in the Vampire Narrative.* Sense Publishers, 2015.

Arata, Stephen D. "The Occidental Tourist: *Dracula* and the Anxiety of Reverse Colonization." *Victorian Studies*, vol. 33, no. 4, 1990, pp. 621–45.

Archer, Jodie, and Matthew L. Jockers. *The Bestseller Code: Anatomy of the Blockbuster Novel.* St. Martin's Press, 2016.

Armstrong, Nancy. "Feminism, Fiction, and the Utopian Promise of Dracula." *Differences: A Journal of Feminist Cultural Studies*, vol. 16, no. 1, spring 2005, https://doi.org/10.1215/10407391-16-1-1.

Artenie, Cristina. Dracula *Invades England: The Text, the Context, and the Readers.* Universitas Press, 2015.

Aubrey, James, editor. *Vampire Films around the World: Essays on the Cinematic Undead of Sixteen Cultures.* McFarland, 2020.

Auerbach, Nina. *Our Vampires, Ourselves.* U of Chicago P, 1995.

Azzarello, Robert. "Unnatural Predators: Queer Theory Meets Environmental Studies in Bram Stoker's *Dracula.*" *Queering the Non/Human*, edited by Noreen Giffney and Myra J. Hird, Taylor and Francis, 2016, pp. 140–48.

Bak, John S. "Bad Blood; or, Victorian Vampires in the Postmodern Age of AIDS." *Post/modern Dracula: From Victorian Themes to Postmodern Praxis*, edited by Bak, Cambridge Scholars Publishing, 2007, pp. xi–xxiv.

Barber, Paul. *Vampires, Burial, and Death: Folklore and Reality.* Yale UP, 1988.

Barker-Benfield, Ben. "The Spermatic Economy: A Nineteenth-Century View of Sexuality." *Feminist Studies*, vol. 1, no. 1, summer 1972, pp. 45–74.

192 WORKS CITED

Barsam, Richard, and Dave Monahan. *Looking at Movies: An Introduction to Film.* W. W. Norton, 2013.

Bauman, Kurt. "School Enrollment of the Hispanic Population: Two Decades of Growth." United States Census Bureau, 28 Aug. 2017.

Bazin, André. "The Ontology of the Photographic Image." Translated by Hugh Gray. *Film Quarterly*, vol. 13, no. 4, summer 1960, pp. 4–9.

Belford, Barbara. *Bram Stoker: A Biography of the Author of* Dracula. Alfred A. Knopf, 1996.

———. *Bram Stoker and the Man Who Was Dracula.* Hachette Books, 2002.

Benjamin, Walter. "The Work of Art in the Age of Mechanical Reproduction." *Illuminations*, edited by Hannah Arendt, translated by Harry Zohn, Schocken Books, 1969, pp. 217–53.

Benshoff, Harry. "Blaxploitation Horror Films: Generic Reappropriation or Reinscription?" *Cinema Journal*, vol. 39, no. 2, 2000, pp. 31–50.

Bentley, C. F. "The Monster in the Bedroom: Sexual Symbolism in Bram Stoker's *Dracula*." Carter, *Dracula*, pp. 25–35.

Beresford, Matthew. *From Demons to Dracula: The Creation of the Modern Vampire Myth.* Reaktion, 2008.

Berni, Simone. Dracula, *by Bram Stoker: The Mystery of the Early Editions.* Translated by Stefano Bigliardi, Bibliohaus, 2016.

Bierman, Joseph S. "Dracula: Prolonged Childhood Illness, and the Oral Triad." *American Imago*, vol. 29, no. 2, summer 1972, pp. 186–98.

Blacula. Directed by William Crane. American International Pictures, 1972.

"Blood for Sale: Gothic Goes Global." *The Art of Gothic: Britain's Midnight Hour*, episode 3, *BBC*, 2014.

"The Blood Is the Life." Written by Cole Haddon. *Dracula*, created by Haddon and Daniel Knauff, season 1, episode 1, NBC, 2013. *Amazon Prime*, www.amazon.com.

Blundell, James. "Observations on Transfusion of Blood, with a Description of His Gravitator." *The Lancet*, vol. 2, 1828–29, pp. 321–24.

———. "A Successful Case of Transfusion." *The Lancet*, vol. 1, 1828–29, pp. 431–32.

Boltanski, Luc, and Eve Chiapello. *The New Spirit of Capitalism.* Translated by Gregory Elliot, Verso Books, 2018.

Booth, Paul. "Missing a Piece: (The Lack of) Board Game Scholarship in Media Studies." *The Velvet Light Trap*, no. 81, 2018, pp. 57–60.

Bowen, John. "The Gothic." *British Library*, www.britishlibrary.cn/en/articles/video-the-gothic/.

———. "Gothic Motifs." *British Library*, 15 May 2014, www.britishlibrary.cn/en/articles/gothic-motifs/.

Bowman, Sarah Lynne. *The Functions of Role-Playing Games: How Participants Create Community, Solve Problems and Explore Identity.* McFarland, 2010.

Braddon, Mary Elizabeth. *Lady Audley's Secret.* Edited by Jenny Bourne Taylor, Penguin Books, 1998.

WORKS CITED   193

Bram Stoker's Dracula. Directed by Francis Ford Coppola, performance by Gary Oldman, Columbia Pictures, 1992.

Brantlinger, Patrick. "Imperial Gothic: Atavism and the Occult in the British Adventure Novel, 1880–1914." *English Literature in Transition, 1880–1920*, vol. 28, no. 3, 1985, pp. 243–52.

Braverman, Harry. *Labor and Monopoly Capital: The Degradation of Work in the Twentieth Century*. Monthly Review Press, 1998.

Briggs, Laura. "The Race of Hysteria: 'Overcivilization' and the 'Savage' Woman in Late Nineteenth-Century Obstetrics and Gynecology." *American Quarterly*, vol. 52, no. 2, June 2000, pp. 246–73.

Bristow, Joseph. *Oscar Wilde on Trial: The Criminal Proceedings, from Arrest to Imprisonment*. Yale UP, 2022.

Brontë, Emily. *Wuthering Heights*. Edited by Pauline Nestor, Penguin Books, 2003.

Brown, Adam, and Deborah Waterhouse-Watson. "Playing with the History of Middle Earth: Board Games, Transmedia Storytelling, and *The Lord of the Rings*." *Journal of Tolkien Research*, vol. 3, no. 3, Oct. 2016, scholar.valpo.edu/journaloftolkienresearch/vol3/iss3/4/. PDF download.

———. "Reconfiguring Narrative in Contemporary Board Games: Story-Making across the Competitive-Cooperative Spectrum." *Intensities: The Journal of Cult Media*, no. 5, summer 2014, pp. 5–19.

Brown, Henry Box. *Narrative of Henry Box Brown, Who Escaped from Slavery Enclosed in a Box Three Feet Long and Two Wide*. Edited by Charles Stearns, Boston, 1849.

Brown, Sarah Annes. *Devoted Sisters: Representations of the Sister Relationship in Nineteenth-Century British and American Literature*. Ashgate, 2003.

Browning, John Edgar. *Bram Stoker's* Dracula: *The Critical Feast: An Annotated Reference of Early Reviews and Reactions, 1897–1913*. Apocryphile Press, 2012.

Browning, John Edgar, and Caroline Joan Picart. *Dracula in Visual Media*. McFarland, 2011.

Browning, Robert. "Tray." *Browning's Shorter Poems*, edited by Franklin T. Baker, 4th ed., Macmillan, 1919, pp. 15–17.

Buffy the Vampire Slayer. Written by Joss Whedon, directed by Fran Rubel Kuzui, 20th Century Fox, 1992.

"Buffy vs. Dracula." *Buffy the Vampire Slayer*, created by Joss Whedon, season 5, episode 1, 2000. *Dailymotion*, dailymotion.com.

Butler, Judith. *Gender Trouble: Feminism and the Subversion of Identity*. Routledge, 2006.

Butler, Octavia. *Fledgling*. Seven Stories, 2005.

Byron, Glennis, editor. Dracula: *Contemporary Critical Essays*. Macmillan, 1999.

Cain, Jimmie E., Jr. *Bram Stoker and Russophobia: Evidence of the British Fear of Russia in* Dracula *and* The Lady of the Shroud. McFarland, 2006.

Cantú, Francisco. *The Line Becomes a River*. Riverhead, 2018.

Carpenter, Edward. *The Intermediate Sex: A Study of Some Transitional Types of Men and Women*. George Allen and Unwin, 1908.

194   WORKS CITED

Carpenter, William. *Principles of Mental Physiology*. 4th ed., London, 1876.

Carroll, Noël. *The Philosophy of Horror; or, Paradoxes of the Heart*. Routledge, 1990.

Carter, Margaret L. *Dracula: The Vampire and the Critics*. U of Michigan Research P, 1988. Studies in Speculative Fiction 19.

———. "The Vampire as Alien in Contemporary Fiction." *Blood Read: The Vampire as Metaphor in Contemporary Culture*, edited by Joan Gordon and Veronica Hollinger, U of Pennsylvania P, 1997, pp. 27–44.

Carter, Robert Brudenell. *On the Pathology and Treatment of Hysteria*. London, 1853.

Castle, Gregory. "Ambivalence and Ascendancy in Bram Stoker's *Dracula*." Stoker, *Dracula* [Riquelme 2002], pp. 518–37.

Castlevania: Lords of Shadow. Konami, 2010. PlayStation 3 and Xbox 360 game.

Castlevania: Lords of Shadow—Mirror of Fate. Konami, 2013. Nintendo 3DS game.

Castlevania: Lords of Shadow 2. Konami, 2014. PlayStation 3 and Xbox 360 game.

Catalogue of Valuable Books, Autograph Letters, and Illuminated and Other Manuscripts: First Day's Sale: The Property of Bram Stoker, Esq. (Deceased). Stoker, *Forgotten Writings*, pp. 222–41.

Cat People. Directed by Jacques Tourneur, RKO, 1942.

Cave, Stephen. *Immortality: The Quest to Live Forever and How It Drives Civilization*. Crown, 2012.

Cerveza Cristal [@xoDrVenture]. "I'm reading Dracula for the first time. . . .'" *X*, 26 Oct. 2019, x.com/xoDrVenture/status/1188222250513850373.

Chaykin, Howard, et al. *Bite Club*. DC Comics, 2004, 2007.

Chen, Mel Y. *Animacies: Biopolitics, Racial Mattering, and Queer Affect*. Duke UP, 2012.

Chitty, Christopher. *Sexual Hegemony*. Duke UP, 2020.

Chwala, Gregory Luke. "Subdue Our Fears: Displacing Homophobia in Bram Stoker's *Dracula*." *Fascination of Queer*, edited by Stefano Ramello, Inter-Disciplinary Press, 2011, pp. 49–58.

Ciemniewski, Marcin. "Indian Spooks." *Politeja*, vol. 16, no. 2, 2019, pp. 161–76.

Clemens, Ruthner. "Bloodsuckers with Teutonic Tongues: The German Speaking World and the Origins of Dracula." Miller, Dracula, pp. 54–67.

Clery, E. J. *The Rise of Supernatural Fiction, 1762–1800*. Cambridge UP, 1995.

———. *Women's Gothic: From Clara Reeve to Mary Shelley*. Northcote, 2000.

"Closer Than Sisters." *Penny Dreadful*, written by John Logan, season 1, episode 5, Showtime, 2014.

Cohen, Jeffrey Jerome, editor. *Monster Theory: Reading Culture*. U of Minnesota P, 1996.

Coker, Cait, et al., editors. *The Global Vampire: Essays on the Undead in Popular Cultures around the World*. McFarland, 2020.

Collins, Wilkie. *Heart and Science: A Story of the Present Time*. Edited by Steve Farmer, Broadview, 1996.

———. *The Woman in White*. Edited by John Sutherland, Oxford World's Classics, 2008.

WORKS CITED   195

Conrad, Joseph. *Heart of Darkness*. Edited by Robert Hampson, Penguin Books, 1995.

Constable, Liz. *"Fin-de-Siècle* Yellow Fevers: Women Writers, Decadence, and Discourses of Degeneracy." *L'Esprit Créateur,* vol. 37, no. 3, 1997, pp. 25–37.

Copeland, Rita, and Peter Struck. Introduction. *The Cambridge Companion to Allegory,* edited by Copeland and Struck, Cambridge UP, 2010, pp. 1–12.

Costikyan, Greg. "Games, Storytelling, and Breaking the String." *EBR: The Electronic Book Review,* 28 Dec. 2007, electronicbookreview.com/essay/games-storytelling-and-breaking-the-string/.

Crabapple, Molly, et al. "Restrict AI Illustration from Publishing: An Open Letter." *Center for Artistic Inquiry and Reporting,* 2 May 2023, artisticinquiry.org/AI-Open-Letter.

Craft, Christopher. Excerpt from "'Kiss Me with Those Red Lips': Gender and Inversion in Bram Stoker's *Dracula."* Stoker, *Dracula* [Auerbach and Skal], pp. 444–59.

———. "'Kiss Me with Those Red Lips': Gender and Inversion in Bram Stoker's *Dracula." Representations,* no. 8, fall 1984, pp. 107–33.

Cribb, Susan M. "'If I Had to Write with a Pen': Readership and Bram Stoker's Diary Narrative." Holte, *Century,* pp. 133–41.

"Crimson Peak—Official Theatrical Trailer [HD]." *YouTube,* uploaded by Legendary, 13 May 2015, www.youtube.com/watch?v=oquZifON8Eg.

Crişan, Marius-Mircea, editor. *Dracula: An International Perspective.* Palgrave Macmillan, 2017.

Crofts, Matthew. "Untold Draculas: Textual Estrangements, Cinematic Reincarnations, and the Popular *Dracula* Legend." *Gothic Afterlives: Reincarnations of Horror in Film and Popular Media,* edited by Lorna Piatti-Farnell, Rowman and Littlefield, pp. 61–78.

Culler, Jonathan. *Literary Theory: A Very Short Introduction.* 2nd ed., Oxford UP, 2011.

Curran, Bob. "Was Dracula an Irishman?" *History Ireland,* vol. 8, no. 2, summer 2000, pp. 12–15.

Dalby, Richard. *Bram Stoker: A Bibliography of First Editions.* Dracula Press, 1983.

Daly, Nicholas. "Incorporated Bodies: Dracula and the Rise of Professionalism." *Texas Studies in Literature and Language,* vol. 39, no. 2, summer 1997, pp. 181–203.

———. *Modernism, Romance and the* Fin-de-Siècle: *Popular Fiction and British Culture, 1880–1914.* Cambridge UP, 1999.

Dan, Peter. "How Vampires Became Jewish." *Studia Hebraica,* vols. 9–10, 2009, pp. 419–30.

Darwin, Charles. *The Descent of Man.* London, 1871.

Daugherty, Anne, and Jerri L. Miller. "Luring Online Students with the Power of the Vampire." Nevárez, pp. 192–203.

Daughters of Darkness. Ciné Vog Films et al., 1971.

Davis, Leonard J. "Constructing Normalcy: The Bell Curve, the Novel, and the Invention of the Disabled Body in the Nineteenth Century." *Beyond Bioethics:*

196 WORKS CITED

Toward a New Biopolitics, edited by Osagie K. Obasogie and Marcy Darnovsky, U of California P, 2019, pp 63–72.

Davis, Paul. *The Lives and Times of Ebenezer Scrooge*. Yale UP, 1990.

Davison, Carol Margaret. *Anti-Semitism and British Gothic Literature*. Palgrave Macmillan, 2004.

———. *Bram Stoker's* Dracula: *Sucking through the Century, 1897–1997*. With Paul Simpson-Housley, Dundurn Press, 1997.

Deane, Hamilton, and John L. Balderston. Dracula: *The Ultimate, Illustrated Edition of the World-Famous Vampire Play*. Edited by David J. Skal, St. Martin's Press, 1993.

Deane, Seamus. *Reading in the Dark*. Vintage, 1996.

———. *A Short History of Irish Literature*. Hutchinson, 1986.

———. *Strange Country: Modernity and Nationhood in Irish Writing since 1790*. Oxford UP, 1997.

De Block, Andreas, and Pieter R. Adriaens. "Pathologizing Sexual Deviance: A History." *Journal of Sexual Research*, vol. 50, nos. 3–4, 2013, pp. 276–98.

Deleuze, Gilles. *A Thousand Plateaus: Capitalism and Schizophrenia*. U of Minnesota P, 1987.

Del Toro, Guillermo. "Guillermo del Toro's Guide to Gothic Romance." *Rookie*, no. 50, 29 Oct. 2015.

Demetrakopoulos, Stephanie. "Feminism, Sex Role Exchanges, and Other Subliminal Fantasies in Bram Stoker's *Dracula*." *Frontiers: A Journal of Women Studies*, vol. 2, no. 3, autumn 1977, pp. 104–13.

Derrida, Jacques. "Autoimmunity: Real and Symbolic Suicides." *Philosophy in a Time of Terror: Dialogues with Jürgen Habermas and Jacques Derrida*, edited by Giovanna Borradori, U of Chicago P, 2003.

———. *Cinders*. Translated by Ned Lukacher. Minnesota UP, 2014.

———. *Specters of Marx: The State of the Debt, The Work of Mourning, and the New International*. Translated by Peggy Kamuf, Routledge, 2006.

———. *Writing and Difference*. Translated by Alan Bass, U of Chicago P, 1978.

Derrida, Jacques, and Bernard Stiegler. *Echographies of Television*. Polity Press, 2002.

Dijkstra, Bram. *Idols of Perversity: Fantasies of Feminine Evil in Fin-de-siècle Culture*. Oxford UP, 1986.

Doan, James E. "The Vampire in Native American and Mesoamerican Lore." *The Universal Vampire: Origins and Evolution of a Legend*, edited by Barbara Brodman and Doan, Fairleigh Dickinson UP, 2013.

Dracula. Directed by John Badham, Universal Pictures, 1979.

Dracula. Directed by Tod Browning, performances by Bela Lugosi and Edward Van Sloan, Universal Pictures, 1931.

Dracula. Directed by Dan Curtis, Dan Curtis Productions, 1973.

Dracula. Directed by George Melford, Spanish adaptation by Baltasar Fernández Cué, Universal Pictures, 1973.

"*Dracula*: Summary and Analysis: Bram Stoker." *YouTube*, uploaded by Course Hero, 20 May 2018, www.youtube.com/watch?v=_UYAI2Vswus.

WORKS CITED 197

Dracula Untold. Directed by Gary Shore, Universal Pictures, 2014.

Drakula halála. Directed by Károly Lajthay, Lapa Film Studio, 1921.

Drakula İstanbul'da. Directed by Mehmet Muhtar, And Film, 1953.

Eagleton, Terry. *Heathcliff and the Great Hunger: Studies in Irish Culture.* Verso Books, 1995.

Eighteen-Bisang, Robert. "Hutchinson's Colonial Library Edition of *Dracula*." Melton, *All Things* Dracula, www.cesnur.org/2003/dracula/.

Eighteen-Bisang, Robert, and Elizabeth Miller, editors. *Bram Stoker's Notes for* Dracula: *A Facsimile Edition.* McFarland, 2008.

———. Dracula: *A Century of Editions, Adaptations and Translations: Part One: English Language Editions.* Transylvanian Society of Dracula, 1998.

———, editors. *Drafts of* Dracula. Tellwell Talent, 2019.

Eliot, T. S. *Collected Poems, 1909–1962.* Harcourt, Brace and World, 1963.

Ellis, Havelock, and John Addington Symonds. *Sexual Inversion.* 1897. Ayer, 1994.

Ellmann, Maud. Introduction. *Dracula,* by Bram Stoker, Oxford UP, 1998, pp. vii–xxviii.

Eltis, Sos. "Corruption of the Blood and Degeneration of the Race: Dracula and Policing the Borders of Gender." Stoker, *Dracula* [Riquelme 2002], pp. 450–65.

Ewence, Hannah. "Blurring the Boundaries of Difference: *Dracula,* the Empire, and 'the Jew.'" *Jewish Culture and History,* vol. 12, nos. 1–2, 2012, pp. 213–22.

Farson, Daniel. *The Man Who Wrote* Dracula: *A Biography of Bram Stoker.* Michael Joseph, 1975.

The Fearless Vampire Slayers. Directed by Roman Polanski, Metro-Goldwyn-Mayer, 1967.

Field, Kelly. "More Hispanics Are Going to College." *The Hechinger Report,* 14 May 2018, hechingerreport.org/rising-college-rates-spur-hispanic-progress-in-higher-education/.

Fincher, Max. *Queering Gothic in the Romantic Age: The Penetrating Eye.* Palgrave Macmillan, 2007.

Flood, David Hume. "Blood and Transfusion in Bram Stoker's Dracula," *Studies in English, New Series,* vol. 7, 1989, pp. 180–92, egrove.olemiss.edu/studies_eng_new/vol7/iss1/21/.

Florescu, Radu, and Raymond T. McNally. *Dracula: A Biography of Vlad the Impaler.* Hawthorn Books, 1973.

Fontana, Ernest. "Lombroso's Criminal Man and Stoker's *Dracula*." *Victorian Newsletter,* no. 66, 1984, pp. 25–27.

Foster, Dennis. "'The Little Children Can Be Bitten': A Hunger for Dracula." Stoker, *Dracula* [Riquelme 2002], pp. 483–99.

Foucault, Michel. *The History of Sexuality: An Introduction.* Translated by Robert Hurley, Penguin, 1984.

Fox, Renée. "Building Castles in the Air: Female Intimacy and Generative Queerness in *Dracula*." Stoker, *Dracula* [Riquelme 2016], pp. 590–607.

Frank, Frederick. *The First Gothics: A Critical Guide to the English Gothic Novel.* Garland, 1987.

198   WORKS CITED

Frayling, Christopher. "Bram Stoker's Working Papers for *Dracula*." Stoker, *Dracula* [Auerbach and Skal], pp. 339–50.

———. "Mr. Stoker's Holiday." *Bram Stoker: Centenary Essays*, edited by Jarlath Killeen, Four Courts Press, 2014, pp. 179–200.

———. *Vampyres: Lord Byron to Count Dracula*. Faber and Faber, 1991.

Frazel, Midge. *Digital Storytelling: Guide for Educators*. International Society for Technology in Education, 2010.

Freud, Sigmund. "Beyond the Pleasure Principle." *The Standard Edition of the Complete Psychological Works of Sigmund Freud*, translated by James Strachey et al., vol. 18, Hogarth Press, 1955, pp. 7–64.

———. "Heredity and the Aetiology of the Neuroses." *The Standard Edition of the Complete Works of Sigmund Freud*, translated by James Strachey et al., vol. 3, Hogarth Press, 1953, pp. 151–56.

———. *Introductory Lectures on Psychoanalysis*. Translated and edited by James Strachey, W. W. Norton, 1966.

———. "The Medusa's Head." *The Standard Edition of the Complete Psychological Works of Sigmund Freud*, translated by James Strachey et al., vol. 18, Hogarth Press, 1964, p. 57.

———. "Mourning and Melancholia." *The Standard Edition of the Complete Psychological Works of Sigmund Freud*, translated by James Strachey et al., vol. 14, Hogarth Press, 1964, pp. 243–58.

———. *Three Essays on the Theory of Sexuality*. *On Sexuality:* Three Essays on the Theory of Sexuality *and Other Works*, translated by James Strachey, Penguin, 1991. Vol. 7 of Penguin Freud Library.

———. "The 'Uncanny.'" *The Norton Anthology of Theory and Criticism*, edited by Vincent B. Leitch, W. W. Norton, 2001, pp. 929–52.

From Dusk till Dawn. Directed by Robert Rodríguez, Miramax, 1996.

Fry, Carrol L. *Primal Roots of Horror Cinema: Evolutionary Psychology and Narratives of Fear*. McFarland, 2019.

Frye, Northrop. *An Anatomy of Criticism: Four Essays*. Princeton UP, 1957.

Fuentes, Carlos. *Vlad*. 2004. Translated by E. Shaskan Burmas and Alejandro Branger, Dalkey Archive Press, 2012.

"The Fury of Dracula." *Wikipedia: The Free Encyclopedia*, Wikimedia Foundation, 4 Aug. 2020, en.wikipedia.org/wiki/The_Fury_of_Dracula.

Galvan, Jill. "Occult Networks and the Legacy of the Indian Rebellion in Bram Stoker's *Dracula*." *History of Religions*, vol. 54, no. 4, May 2015, pp. 434–58.

Ganja and Hess. Written and directed by Bill Gunn, Kelly-Jordan Enterprises, 1973.

Gerard, Emily. "Transylvanian Superstitions." *The Nineteenth Century*, vol. 18, July–Dec. 1885, pp. 130–50.

"German Expressionism: Crash Course Film History #7." *YouTube*, uploaded by Crash Course, 25 May 2017, www.youtube.com/watch?v=K6XDyth0qxc.

"*Get Out* Official Trailer 1—Daniel Kaluuya Movie." *YouTube*, uploaded by Rotten Tomatoes Trailers, 4 Oct. 2016, www.youtube.com/watch?v=DzfpyUB60YY.

Ghost Dance. Directed by Ken McMullen, Channel Four Films, 1983.

WORKS CITED   199

Gibson, Matthew. *Dracula and the Eastern Question: British and French Vampire Narratives of the Nineteenth-Century Near East.* Palgrave, 2006.

Gilman, Charlotte Perkins. "The Yellow Wall-Paper." *The New England Magazine,* vol. 11, no. 5, 1982, pp. 647–56. *National Library of Medicine,* www.nlm.nih .gov/exhibition/theliteratureofprescription/exhibitionAssets/digitalDocs/The -Yellow-Wall-Paper.pdf.

Glover, David. "*Dracula* in the Age of Mass Migration." Luckhurst, *Cambridge Companion,* pp. 85–94.

———. "'Our Enemy Is Not Merely Spiritual': Degeneration and Modernity in Bram Stoker's *Dracula.*" *Victorian Literature and Culture,* vol. 22, 1994, pp. 249–65.

———. "Travels in Romania: Myths of Origins, Myths of Blood." *Discourse: Journal for Theoretical Studies in Media and Culture,* vol. 16, no. 1, 1994, pp. 126–44.

———. *Vampires, Mummies and Liberals: Bram Stoker and the Politics of Popular Fiction.* Duke UP, 1996.

Glut, Donald F. *The Dracula Book.* Scarecrow Press, 1975.

Golub, Adam, and Heather Richardson Hayton, editors. *Monsters in the Classroom: Essays on Teaching What Scares Us.* McFarland, 2017.

Gomez, Jewelle. *The Gilda Stories.* Firebrand Books, 1991.

Gooch, Joshua. *The Victorian Novel, Service Work, and the Nineteenth-Century Economy.* Palgrave Macmillan, 2015.

Goss, Sarah. "Dracula and the Spectre of Famine." *Hungry Words: Images of Famine in the Irish Canon,* edited by George Cusack and Goss, Irish Academic Press, 2006, pp. 77–107.

Graeber, David. *Bullshit Jobs: A Theory.* Simon and Schuster, 2018.

Grand, Sarah. "The New Aspect of the Woman Question." *A New Woman Reader: Fiction, Articles, and Drama of the 1890s,* edited by Carolyn Christensen Nelson, Broadview Press, 2001, pp. 140–46. Originally published in *North American Review,* 1894.

Griggs, Yvonne. *Adaptable TV: Rewiring the Text.* Palgrave Macmillan, 2018.

Grondin, Jean. *Introduction to Philosophical Hermeneutics.* Translated by Joel Weinsheimer, Yale UP, 1994.

"Guide to Bram Stoker Holdings in the Rosenbach Museum and Library." *Rosenbach Museum,* 2020, rosenbach.org/wp-content/uploads/2020/08/Bram-Stoker-holdings-20200819.pdf.

Haefele-Thomas, Ardel. *Queer Others in Victorian Gothic: Transgressing Monstrosity.* U of Wales P, 2009.

Haggerty, George E. *Queer Gothic.* U of Illinois P, 2006.

Halberstam, Jack. *Skin Shows: Gothic Horror and the Technology of Monsters.* Duke UP, 1995.

———. "Technologies of Monstrosity: Bram Stoker's *Dracula.*" *Victorian Studies,* vol. 36, no. 3, spring 1993, pp. 333–52.

Hallab, Mary Y. *Vampire God: The Allure of the Undead in Western Culture.* State U of New York P, 2009.

. "Vampires and Medical Science." *Journal of Popular Culture*, vol. 48, no. 1, Feb. 2015, pp. 168–83. *EBSCOhost*, doi:10.1111/jpcu.12241.

Hamilton, Susan. "Reading and the Popular Critique of Science in the Victorian Anti-Vivisection Press: Frances Power Cobbe's Writing for the Victoria Street Society." *Victorian Review*, vol. 36, no. 2, fall 2010, pp. 66–79.

Hand, Stephen, et al. *Fury of Dracula*. 3rd ed., Fantasy Flight Games, 2015.

Hanlon, Aaron. "The Trigger Warning Myth." *The New Republic*, 14 Aug. 2015, newrepublic.com/article/122543/trigger-warning-myth.

Hanson, Ellis. "Queer Gothic." Spooner and McEvoy, pp. 174–182.

Hardt, Michael, and Antonio Negri. *Empire*. Harvard UP, 2001.

Harris, G. W. "Bio-Politics." *The New Age*, vol. 10, no. 9, 1911, p. 197.

Harse, Katie. "High Duty and Savage Delight: The Ambiguous Nature of Violence in 'Dracula.'" Holte, *Century*, pp. 115–23.

Harvard Law Review Association. "Cooperation or Resistance? The Role of Tech Companies in Government Surveillance." *Harvard Law Review*, vol. 131, no. 6, 2018, pp. 1722–41.

Haslam, Richard. "The Hermeneutic Hazards of Hibernicizing Oscar Wilde's *The Picture of Dorian Gray*." *English Literature in Transition, 1880–1920*, vol. 57, no. 1, Jan. 2014, pp. 37–58.

. "Investigating Irish Gothic: The Case of *Sophia Berkley*." *Gothic Studies*, vol. 19, no. 1, May 2017, pp. 34–56.

. "Irish Gothic." Spooner and McEvoy, pp. 83–94.

. "Irish Gothic: A Rhetorical Hermeneutics Approach." *The Irish Journal of Gothic and Horror Studies*, no. 2, Mar. 2007.

. "Negotiating the Poetics of Irish Gothic via Casuistry." *"The Common Darkness Where the Dreams Abide": Perspectives on Irish Gothic*, edited by Annalisa Volpone and Ilaria Natali, Aguaplano, 2018, pp. 29–53.

. "Revisiting the 'Irish Dimension' in Oscar Wilde's *The Picture of Dorian Gray*." *Victorian Literature and Culture*, vol. 42, no. 2, June 2014, pp. 267–79.

. "Seeking the 'Irish Dimension' in Oscar Wilde's *The Picture of Dorian Gray*: 'What Does This Mean?'" *English Literature in Transition, 1880–1920*, vol. 63, no. 4, Apr. 2020, pp. 533–58.

Heiss, Lokke. "Madame Dracula: The Life of Emily Gerard." Holte, *Century*, pp. 174–86.

Herbert, Christopher. "Vampire Religion." *Representations*, vol. 79, no. 1, 2002, pp. 100–21.

Hindle, Maurice. Introduction. Stoker, *Dracula* [Hindle], pp. xvii–xxxix.

"Hispanics: College Majors and Earnings." *Georgetown University Center on Education and the Workforce*, 14 Oct. 2015, cew.georgetown.edu/cew-reports/hispanicmajors/.

Hobson, Amanda, and U. Melissa Anyiwo, editors. *Gender in the Vampire Narrative*. Sense Publishers, 2016.

Hochschild, Arlie Russell. *The Managed Heart: Commercialization of Human Feeling*. U of California P, 2003.

WORKS CITED

Hoeveler, Diane Long. *Gothic Feminism: The Professionalization of Gender from Charlotte Smith to the Brontës.* Pennsylvania State UP, 1988.

Hoffmann, E. T. A. "The Sandman." 1816. Translated by John Oxenford. *German Stories,* edited by Robert Godwin-Jones, 1994–99, archive.vcu.edu/germanstories/hoffmann/sand_e.html.

Hogle, Jerrold E. "Abjection as Gothic and the Gothic as Abjection." *The Gothic and Theory: An Edinburgh Companion,* edited by Hogle and Robert Miles, Edinburgh UP, 2019, pp. 108–25.

———. "The Gothic Image at the Villa Diodati." *The Wordsworth Circle,* vol. 47, no. 1, 2017, pp. 16–26.

———. "The Mutations of the Vampire in Nineteenth-Century Gothic." *Gothic in the Nineteenth Century,* edited by Dale Townshend and Angela Wright, Cambridge UP, 2020, pp. 65–84. Vol. 2 of *The Cambridge History of the Gothic.*

———. "Stoker's Counterfeit Gothic: *Dracula* and Theatricality at the Dawn of Simulation." Hughes and Smith, pp. 205–24.

Holte, James Craig. "A Century of Draculas." Holte, *Century,* pp. 109–14.

———, editor. *A Century of Draculas.* Special issue of *Journal of the Fantastic in the Arts,* vol. 10, no. 2 (38), 1999.

"Home 1939." Sigmund Freud Archives Collection, Library of Congress, control no. 2018601155.

Hope, Andrew. "Biopower and School Surveillance Technologies 2.0." *British Journal of Sociology of Education,* vol. 37, no. 7, 2016, pp. 885–904.

Hopkins, Lisa. *Bram Stoker: A Literary Life.* Palgrave Macmillan, 2007.

Horner, Avril, and Sue Zlosnik. "Female Gothic." *Teaching the Gothic,* edited by Anna Powell and Andrew Smith, Palgrave Macmillan, 2006, pp. 107–20.

Horror of Dracula. Directed by Terence Fisher, performances by Christopher Lee and Peter Cushing, Hammer Film Productions, 1958.

"How Did Dracula Become the World's Most Famous Vampire?—Stanley Stepanic." *YouTube,* uploaded by TED-Ed, 20 Apr. 2017, www.youtube.com/watch?v=7uiyz3139tE.

Hoy, Benjamin. "Teaching History with Custom-Built Board Games." *Simulation and Gaming,* vol. 49, no. 2, Apr. 2018, pp. 115–33. *EBSCOhost,* https://doi.org/10.1177/1046878118763624.

Hughes, Eamonn. "Dracula's Irish Blood." *BBC News,* 18 Oct. 2012, www.bbc.com/news/uk-northern-ireland-19960728.

Hughes, William. *Beyond* Dracula: *Bram Stoker's Fiction and Its Cultural Context.* Macmillan, 2000.

———. *Bram Stoker:* Dracula. Red Globe Press, 2008. Reader's Guides to Essential Criticism 69.

———. *Bram Stoker:* Victorian Secrets. 1996, victorianfictionresearchguides.org/bram-stoker/. Victorian Fiction Research Guides 25.

———. "A Singular Invasion: Revisiting the Postcoloniality of Bram Stoker's Dracula." *Empire and the Gothic: The Politics of Genre,* edited by Andrew Smith and Hughes, Palgrave Macmillan, 2003, pp. 88–103.

———. "'So unlike the Normal Lunatic': Abnormal Psychology in Bram Stoker's *Dracula*." *Studies in English*, new series, vol. 11, article 5, 1993. *University of Mississippi*, egrove.olemiss.edu/studies_eng_new/vol11/iss1/5/.

———. *That Devil's Trick: Hypnotism and the Victorian Popular Imagination*. Manchester UP, 2015.

Hughes, William, and Andrew Smith, editors. *Bram Stoker: History, Psychoanalysis and the Gothic*. Palgrave Macmillan, 1998.

———. Introduction. *Queering the Gothic*, edited by Hughes and Smith, Manchester UP, 2011, pp. 1–10.

The Hunger. Directed by Tony Scott, Metro-Goldwyn-Mayer, 1983.

Hutcheon, Linda, and Siobhan O'Flynn. *A Theory of Adaptation*. 2nd ed., Routledge, 2013.

Huyssen, Andreas. *After the Great Divide: Modernism, Mass Culture, Postmodernism*. Indiana UP, 1986.

Ingelbien, Raphaël. "Gothic Genealogies: Dracula, Bowen's Court, and Anglo-Irish Psychology." *ELH*, vol. 70, no. 4, 2003, pp. 1089–105.

Interview with the Vampire. Directed by Neil Jordan, Warner Bros., 1994.

Irma Vep. Written and directed by Olivier Assayas, Dacia Films, 1996.

James, Henry. *The Tragic Muse*. 1890. Penguin, 1995.

Jenkins, Henry. *Convergence Culture: Where Old and New Media Collide*. New York UP, 2006.

———. "Transmedia Storytelling and Entertainment: An Annotated Syllabus." *Continuum: Journal of Media and Cultural Studies*, vol. 24, no. 6, 2010, pp. 943–58.

Jenkins, Jerry Rafiki. "*Blacula* and the Question of Blackness." *Screening Noir*, vol. 1, no. 1, 2005, pp. 49–79.

———. *The Paradox of Blackness in African American Vampire Fiction*. Ohio State UP, 2019.

Jentsch, Ernst. "On the Psychology of the Uncanny." 1906. Translated by Roy Sellars, *Angelaki*, vol. 2, no. 1, 1997, pp. 7–16.

Johnson, Alan. "Bent and Broken Necks: Signs of Design in Stoker's *Dracula*." *Victorian Newsletter*, no. 72, 1987, pp. 17–24.

Johnson, Roy. *Dracula: A Study Guide*. *Mantex*, 2011, mantex.co.uk/dracula/.

Jones, Jennifer A. "Scaffolding Self-Regulated Learning through Student-Generated Quizzes." *Active Learning in Higher Education*, vol. 20, no. 2, Oct. 2017, https://doi.org/10.1177/1469787417735610.

Jordan, Neil. *Mistaken*. Soft Skull Press, 2011.

Joslin, Lyndon W. *Count Dracula Goes to the Movies: Stoker's Novel Adapted*. 3rd ed., McFarland, 2017.

Joyce, James. *Finnegans Wake*. Faber and Faber, 1939.

———. *Ulysses*. Shakespeare and Company, 1922.

Judah, Tim. "The Star of the Hague." *The New York Review of Books*, 25 Apr. 2002, www.nybooks.com/articles/2002/04/25/the-star-of-the-hague/.

Kaes, Anton, and Eric Rentschler. Reading a Film Sequence. Sixth German Film Institute, 18–24 June 1995, University of Chicago.

Kaplan, Sidney. "The Miscegenation Issue in the Election of 1864." *The Journal of Negro History*, vol. 34, no. 3, 1949, pp. 274–343.

Kavanaugh, Lydia, et al. "Design Considerations." Reidsema et al., pp. 15–35.

Keatley, Avery. "Try as She Might, Bram Stoker's Widow Couldn't Kill 'Nosferatu.'" *National Public Radio*, 15 Mar. 2022, www.npr.org/2022/03/15/1086605684/try-as-she-might-bram-stokers-widow-couldnt-kill-nosferatu.

Kelly, Jane. "Dissecting 'Dracula': A Chat with Vampire Expert Stanley Stepanic." *UVA Today*, 29 Oct. 2018, news.virginia.edu/content/dissecting-dracula-chat-vampire-expert-stanley-stepanic.

Kennedy, Randall. *Interracial Intimacies: Sex, Marriage, Identity, and Adoption*. Vintage, 2004.

Keogh, Calvin W. "The Critics' Count: Revisions of *Dracula* and the Postcolonial Irish Gothic." *Cambridge Journal of Postcolonial Literary Inquiry*, vol. 1, no. 2, Sept. 2014, pp. 189–206.

Kevles, Daniel J. *In the Name of Eugenics: Genetics and the Uses of Human Heredity*. Harvard UP, 1998.

Kiberd, Declan. *Irish Classics*. Harvard UP, 2001.

Kiberd, Declan, and P. J. Matthews. *Handbook of the Irish Revival: An Anthology of Irish Cultural and Political Writings 1891–1922*. U of Notre Dame P, 2016.

Killeen, Jarlath, editor. *Bram Stoker: Centenary Essays*. Four Courts Press, 2014.

———. "Bram Stoker, *Dracula*, and the Irish Dimension." *Irish Gothic: An Edinburgh Companion*, edited by Jarlath Killeen and Christina Morin, Edinburgh UP, 2023, pp. 174–93.

———. *The Emergence of Irish Gothic Fiction: History, Origins, Theories*. Edinburgh UP, 2014.

———. "The Greening of Oscar Wilde: Situating Ireland in the Wilde Wars," *Irish Studies Review*, vol. 23, no. 4, 2015, pp. 424–50.

———. "Irish Gothic: A Theoretical Introduction." *The Irish Journal of Gothic and Horror Studies*, no. 1, Oct. 2006, pp. 12–26.

———. "Irish Gothic Revisited." *The Irish Journal of Gothic and Horror Studies*, no. 4, June 2008, pp. 30–51.

———. "Remembering Bram Stoker." *Bram Stoker: Centenary Essays*, edited by Jarlath Killeen, Four Courts Press, 2014, pp. 15–36.

Kirtley, Bacil F. "Dracula, the Monastic Chronicles and Slavic Folklore." Carter, *Dracula*, pp. 11–18.

Kirumira, Rose Namubiru. "Reconfiguring the Omweso Board Game: Performing Narratives of Buganda Material Culture." *African Arts*, vol. 52, no. 2, 2019, pp. 52–65. *EBSCOhost*, search.ebscohost.com.

Kittler, Friedrich A. *Discourse Networks, 1800/1900*. Translated by Michael Metteer, with Chris Cullens, Stanford UP, 1985.

———. "Dracula's Legacy." *Literature, Media, Information Systems*, by Kittler, edited and translated by John Johnston, GB Arts International, 1997, pp. 50–84.

204 WORKS CITED

Klein, Naomi. "AI Machines Aren't 'Hallucinating.' But Their Makers Are." *The Guardian*, 8 May 2023, www.theguardian.com/commentisfree/2023/may/08/ai-machines-hallucinating-naomi-klein.

Klinger, Leslie S. *In the Shadow of Dracula*. IDW Publishing, 2011.

Koch-Rein, Anson. "Monster." *TSQ: Transgender Studies Quarterly*, vol. 1, nos. 1–2, 2014, pp. 134–35.

Koerber, Amy. *From Hysteria to Hormones: A Rhetorical History*. Penn State UP, 2018.

Kohlke, Marie-Luise. "The Lures of Neo-Victorian Presentism (with a Feminist Case Study of *Penny Dreadful*)." *Literature Compass*, vol. 15, no. 7, 2018.

Kooyman, Ben. "The Pedagogical Value of Mary Shelley's *Frankenstein* in Teaching Adaptation Studies." Ahmad and Moreland, *Fear*, pp. 245–63.

Krafft-Ebing, Richard von. *Psychopathia Sexualis with Special Reference to Contrary Sexual Instinct: A Medico-Legal Study*. Translated by Franklin S. Klaf, Stein and Day, 1965.

Kreider, Jodie A., and Meghan K. Winchell, editors. *Buffy in the Classroom: Essays on Teaching with the Vampire Slayer*. McFarland, 2010.

Kristeva, Julia. *Powers of Horror: An Essay on Abjection*. Translated by Leon S. Roudiez, Columbia UP, 1982.

———. *Strangers to Ourselves*. Translated by Leon S. Roudiez, Columbia UP, 1991.

Kuzmanovic, Dejan. "Vampiric Seduction and Vicissitudes of Masculine Identity in Bram Stoker's *Dracula*." *Victorian Literature and Culture*, vol. 37, no. 2, Sept. 2009, pp. 411–25.

Lampert-Weissig, Lisa. "Taking Dracula's Pulse: Historicizing the Vampire." Nevárez, pp. 32–43.

Lankester, Edwin. *Degeneration: A Chapter in Darwinism*. London, 1880.

"Latino Students in Higher Education." *Postsecondary National Policy Institute*, 19 June 2020, pnpi.org/factsheets/latino-students/.

LaVey, Anton Szandor. *The Satanic Bible*. William Morrow, 1969.

Laycock, Thomas. *Mind and Brain; or, The Correlations of Consciousness and Organisation*. Andesite Press, 2017.

Lean, John, et al. "Unhappy Families: Using Tabletop Games as a Technology to Understand Play in Education." *Research in Learning Technology*, vol. 26, 2018, pp. 1–13.

"Learn to Play *Fury of Dracula*." Games Workshop, 2018. Instruction booklet.

Leatherdale, Clive. *Dracula: The Novel and the Legend: A Study of Bram Stoker's Gothic Masterpiece*. Aquarian Press, 1985.

Le Bon, Gustave. *The Crowd: A Study of the Popular Mind*. T. F. Unwin, 1903.

Leeder, Murray. "A Tale of Three Draculas: Teaching Evolution and Genre Conventions." Nevárez, pp. 146–53.

Le Fanu, Joseph Sheridan. *Carmilla*. *Project Gutenberg*, 6 Aug. 2021, www.gutenberg.org/files/10007/10007-h/10007-h.htm.

WORKS CITED 205

———. "The Fortunes of Sir Robert Ardagh; Being a Second Extract from the Papers of the Late Father Purcell." *The Dublin University Magazine*, vol. 11, no. 63, Mar. 1838, pp. 313–24.

———. *In a Glass Darkly*. Edited by Robert Tracy, Oxford UP, 1993.

———. "Ultor de Lacy: A Legend of Cappercullen." *The Dublin University Magazine*, vol. 58, no. 348, Dec. 1861, pp. 694–707.

Let the Right One In. Directed by Thomas Alfredson, Mongrel, 2008.

Levine-Clark, Marjorie. "'I Always Prefer the Scissors': Isaac Baker Brown and Feminist Histories of Medicine." *The Health Humanities Reader*, edited by Therese Jones et al., Rutgers UP, 2014, pp. 215–25.

Linebaugh, Peter. *The London Hanged: Crime and Civil Society in the Eighteenth Century*. Verso Books, 2006.

Littlefield, Henry. "*The Wizard of Oz*: Parable on Populism." *American Quarterly*, vol. 16, no. 1, 1964, pp. 47–58.

Livingston, Paisley. *Art and Intention: A Philosophical Study*. Clarendon Press, 2005.

Lloyd, David. *Anomalous States: Irish Writing and the Post-colonial Moment*. The Lilliput Press, 1993.

Lombroso, Cesare. *Criminal Man*. 1880. Duke UP, 2006.

Lombroso, Cesare, and William Ferrero. *The Female Offender*. New York, 1895. The Criminology Series.

Lombroso-Ferrero, Gina. *Criminal Man, according to the Classification of Cesare Lombroso*. G. P. Putnam's Sons, 1911.

Longinović, Tomislav. *Vampire Nation: Violence as Cultural Imaginary*. Duke UP, 2011.

———. *Vampires like Us: Writing down "the serbs."* Belgrade Circle, 2005.

Lordon, Frédéric. *Willing Slaves of Capital: Spinoza and Marx on Desire*. Verso Books, 2014.

The Lost Boys. Directed by Joel Schumacher, Warner Bros., 1987.

Love at First Bite. Directed by Stan Dragoti, American International Picture, 1979.

Lovecraft, H. P. "Supernatural Horror in Literature." 1927. Dover Publications, 1973, pp. 12–106.

Luckhurst, Roger, editor. *The Cambridge Companion to* Dracula. Cambridge UP, 2017.

———. Introduction. Luckhurst, *Cambridge Companion* pp. 1–8.

———. Introduction. Stoker, *Dracula* [Luckhurst], pp. vii–xxxii.

Ludlam, Harry. *A Biography of Dracula: The Life Story of Bram Stoker*. Fireside Press / W. Foulsham, 1962.

Luiselli, Valeria. *Tell Me How It Ends: An Essay in Forty Questions*. Coffee House Press, 2017.

Lynch, Jack, editor. *Critical Insights*: Dracula, *by Bram Stoker*. Salem Press, 2009.

Lyon, James. *Kiss of the Butterfly*. 2013.

Lyotard, Jean-François. *Acinema*. Edited by Graham Jones and Ashley Woodward, Edinburgh UP, 2017.

206   WORKS CITED

Mackenzie, W. J. *Home Medicine and Surgery.* London, 1890.

Malchow, H. L. *Gothic Images of Race in Nineteenth-Century Britain.* Stanford UP, 1996.

Marcus, Sharon. *Between Women: Friendship, Desire, and Marriage in Victorian England.* Princeton UP, 2017.

Marshall, P. J., and Alaine Low, editors. *The Oxford History of the British Empire.* Oxford UP, 1998.

Marx, Karl. *A Critique of Political Economy.* Translated by Ben Fowkes, Penguin, 1976. Vol. 1 of *Capital.*

Masco, Joseph. "Preempting Biosecurity: Threats, Fantasies, Futures." *Bioinsecurity and Vulnerability,* edited by Nancy N. Chen, S.A.R. Press, 2014, pp. 5–24.

Mason, Diane. *The Secret Vice: Masturbation in Victorian Fiction and Medical Culture.* Manchester UP, 2008.

Matsuoka, Mitsuharu. *A Hyper-concordance to the Works of Bram Stoker. The Victorian Literary Studies Archive,* Nagoya U, 2003, victorian-studies.net/concordance/stoker/.

Maturin, Charles. "Leixlip Castle." 1825. *Project Gutenberg,* 2006, gutenberg.net.au/ebooks06/0605961h.html.

———. *Melmoth the Wanderer.* Oxford UP, 1989.

Maunder, Andrew. *Bram Stoker.* Northcote House Publishers, 2006.

May, Leila Silvana. *Disorderly Sisters: Sibling Relations and Sororal Resistance in Nineteenth-Century British Literature.* Bucknell UP, 2005.

Mbembe, Achille. *On the Postcolony.* U of California P, 2001.

McBride, William Thomas. "Dracula and Mephistopheles: Shyster Vampires." *Literature/Film Quarterly,* vol. 18, no. 2, 1990, pp. 116–21.

McCabe, Patrick. "Was Dracula Irish?" *BBC Radio 4,* 8 Oct. 2012, www.bbc.co.uk/programmes/b01n61sr.

McCormack, W. J. "Irish Gothic and After, 1820–1945." *The Field Day Anthology of Irish Writing,* edited by Seamus Deane, vol. 2, Field Day, 1991, pp. 831–949.

McCrea, Barry. "Heterosexual Horror: Dracula, the Closet, and the Marriage-Plot." *Novel: A Forum on Fiction,* vol. 43, no. 2, July 2010, pp. 251–70.

McIntyre, Dennis. *Bram Stoker and the Irishness of* Dracula. Shara Press, 2013.

McKee, Patricia. "Racialization, Capitalism, and Aesthetics in Stoker's *Dracula.*" *Novel: A Forum on Fiction,* vol. 36, no. 1, 2002, pp. 42–60.

McLean, Thomas. "Dracula's Blood of Many Brave Races." *Fear, Loathing, and Victorian Xenophobia,* edited by Marlene Troup et al., Ohio State UP, 2013, pp. 331–46.

McLoughlin, George. "The British Contribution to Blood Transfusion in the Nineteenth Century." *British Journal of Anaesthesia,* vol. 31, no. 11, 1959, pp. 503–16.

McLuhan, Marshall. *Understanding Media: The Extensions of Man.* MIT Press, 1994.

McNally, Raymond T., and Radu Florescu. *In Search of Dracula: A True History of Dracula and Vampire Legends.* New York Graphic Society, 1972.

A Medical Man. *Cassell's Family Doctor.* London, 1897.

Melton, J. Gordon, editor. *All Things* Dracula: *A Bibliography of Editions, Reprints, Adaptations, and Translations of* Dracula. CESNUR: Center for Studies on New Religions, 2003, www.cesnur.org/2003/dracula/. Joint project of the Transylvanian Society of Dracula, US and Italian chapters.

———. *The Vampire Book: The Encyclopedia of the Undead.* Visible Ink Press, 2010.

Melton, J. Gordon, and Alysa Hornick, editors. *The Vampire in Folklore, History, Literature, Film and Television: A Comprehensive Bibliography.* McFarland, 2015.

Mendes, Kaitlynn, and Kumarini Silva. "Feminist Games, Play, and Expression." *Feminist Media Studies*, vol. 11, no. 2, June 2011, pp. 245–57. *EBSCOhost*, search.ebscohost.com.

Meyer, Stephenie. *Twilight.* Little, Brown, 2005.

Michael, David, and Sande Chen. *Serious Games: Games That Educate, Train and Inform.* Thomson Course Technology, 2006.

Mighall, Robert. *A Geography of Victorian Gothic Fiction: Mapping History's Nightmares.* Oxford UP, 1999.

Milbank, Alison. "'Powers Old and New': Stoker's Alliances with Anglo-Irish Gothic." Hughes and Smith, pp. 12–28.

Miller, Elizabeth. "Back to the Basics: Re-Examining Stoker's Sources for 'Dracula.'" Holte, *Century*, pp. 187–96.

———. *A Dracula Handbook.* Xlibris, 2005.

———, editor. Dracula: *The Shade and the Shadow.* Desert Island Books, 1998.

———. "Filing for Divorce: Count Dracula vs. Vlad the Impaler." 1998. *Bram Stoker's* Dracula: *A Documentary Journey into Vampire Country and the* Dracula *Phenomenon*, edited by Elizabeth Miller, Pegasus Books, 2009, pp. 212–17.

Miller, J. Hillis. *The Medium Is the Maker: Browning, Freud, Derrida, and the New Telepathic Ecotechnologies.* Brighton: Sussex Academic Press, 2009.

Mittman, Asa Simon, and Marcus Hensel. *Classic Readings on Monster Theory.* Arc Humanities Press, 2020.

Moers, Ellen. *Literary Women.* Doubleday, 1976.

Monk, Leland. "Undead Images, Images of the Undead: Dracula on Film." Stoker, *Dracula* [Riquelme 2016], pp. 490–506.

Mooney, Graham. "Infectious Diseases and Epidemiologic Transition in Victorian Britain? Definitely." *Social History of Medicine*, vol. 20, 2007, pp. 595–606.

Moretti, Franco. "A Capital *Dracula*." 1988. Stoker, *Dracula* [Browning and Skal], pp. 508–21.

———. *Graphs, Maps, Trees: Abstract Models for Literary Study.* Verso, 2007.

———. *Signs Taken for Wonders: Essays in the Sociology of Literary Form.* Verso Books, 2006.

Morin, Christina. "*The Adventures of Miss Sophia Berkley*: Piracy, Print Culture, and Irish Gothic Fiction." *Irish University Review*, vol. 49, no. 2, 2019, pp. 229–44.

———. *Charles Robert Maturin and the Haunting of Irish Romantic Fiction.* Manchester UP, 2011.

———. *The Gothic Novel in Ireland, c. 1760–1829.* Manchester UP, 2018.

208 WORKS CITED

Morrisette, Jason J. "Marxferatu: The Vampire Metaphor as a Tool for Teaching Marx's Critique of Capitalism." *PS: Political Science and Politics*, vol. 4, no. 3, July 2013, pp. 637–42, https://doi.org/10.1017/S1049096513000607.

Moses, Michael Valdez. "The Irish Vampire: *Dracula*, Parnell, and the Troubled Dreams of Nationhood." *Journal X*, vol. 2, no. 1, autumn 1997, pp. 67–111.

Moss, Stephanie. "Bram Stoker and the London Stage." Holte, *Century*, pp. 124–32.

Mulvey-Roberts, Marie. *Dangerous Bodies: Historicising the Gothic Corporeal.* E-book ed., Manchester UP, 2016.

———. "*Dracula* and the Doctors: Bad Blood, Menstrual Taboo and the New Woman." Hughes and Smith, pp. 78–95.

Murray, Paul. *From the Shadow of* Dracula*: A Life of Bram Stoker.* Jonathan Cape, 2004.

Nazario, Sonia. *Enrique's Journey.* Random House, 2006.

Nevárez, Lisa A., editor. *The Vampire Goes to College: Essays on Teaching with the Undead.* McFarland, 2014.

Nordau, Max. *Degeneration.* U of Nebraska P, 1985.

Nosferatu: A Symphony of Horror. Directed by F. W. Murnau, performance by Max Schreck, Prana Film, 1922.

Nosferatu: The First Vampire. Directed by F. W. Murnau, Front Row Entertainment, 2000.

Nosferatu the Vampyre. Directed by Werner Herzog, performance by Klaus Kinski, Twentieth Century Fox, 1979.

"Obituary: Mr. Bram Stoker." *The Times*, April 22, 1912, p. 15.

O'Brien, Flann. *The Third Policeman.* Dalkey Archive Press, 1999.

O'Connor, M., and N. Dunbar. "Bayesian Analysis of Blood Transfusion in *Dracula*." *Irish Medical Journal*, vol. 109, 2016, p. 362.

O'Flinn, Paul. "Production and Reproduction: The Case of *Frankenstein*." *Literature and History*, vol. 9, no. 3, 1983, pp. 194–213.

Ormandy, Leslie. "Blood, Lust and Transformation: Vampires in the Community College Classroom." Nevárez, pp. 204–17.

Ostherr, Kirsten. *Cinematic Prophylaxis: Globalization and Contagion in the Discourse of World Health.* Duke UP, 2005.

Otterberg, Henrik. "Dark Darwin: (D)evolutionary Theory and the Logic of Vampirism." *Contesting Environmental Imaginaries: Nature and Counternature in a Time of Global Change*, edited by Steven Hartman, Brill/Rodopi, 2017, pp. 181–93.

Ouida. "The New Woman." *The North American Review*, vol. 158, no. 450, May 1894, pp. 610–19.

Page, Leanne. "Phonograph, Shorthand, Typewriter: High Performance Technologies in Bram Stoker's *Dracula*." *Victorian Network*, vol. 3, no. 2, 2011, pp. 95–113.

Palmer, Paulina. *The Queer Uncanny.* U of Wales P, 2012.

Parker, Kendra R. *Black Female Vampires in African American Women's Novels, 1977–2011: She Bites Back.* Lexington, 2019.

Parker, Robert Dale. *How to Interpret Literature: Critical Theory for Literary and Cultural Studies.* 4th ed., Oxford UP, 2020.

WORKS CITED 209

Passel, Jeffrey S., and D'Vera Cohn. "Mexicans Decline to Less than Half the U.S. Unauthorized Immigrant Population for the First Time." *Pew Research Center*, 12 June 2019, www.pewresearch.org/short-reads/2019/06/12/us-unauthorized-immigrant-population-2017/.

Patterson, Kathy Davis. "Echoes of *Dracula*: Racial Politics and the Failure of Segregated Spaces in Richard Matheson's *I Am Legend*." *Journal of Dracula Studies*, vol. 7, 2005, pp. 19–27.

Peele, Jordan. "Jordan Peele on *Get Out*, His Fears and Cultural Hope." Interview by Eddie S. Glaude. *Time*, 15 Feb. 2018.

Perfume: The Story of a Murderer. Directed by Tom Tykwer, DreamWorks, 2006.

Perlman, Mike. "Dracula: Our Cultural Demon." *Psychological Perspectives: A Quarterly Journal of Jungian Thought*, vol. 12, no. 1, 1981, pp. 89–105.

Phillips, Robert. "Abjection." *TSQ: Transgender Studies Quarterly*, vol. 1, nos. 1–2, 2014, pp. 19–21.

Pick, Daniel. "'Terrors of the Night': *Dracula* and 'Degeneration' in the Late Nineteenth Century." *Critical Quarterly*, vol. 30, 1988, pp. 71–87.

Polidori, John William. *The Vampyre*. 1819. Woodstock Books, 1990.

Poole, W. Scott. Foreword. Golub and Hayton, pp. 1–7.

Pope, Rebecca A., "Writing and Biting in *Dracula*." *LIT: Literature Interpretation Theory*, vol. 1, 1990, pp. 199–216.

"Postsecondary Faculty and Staff." *American Council on Education*, www.equityinhighered.org/indicators/postsecondary-faculty-and-staff/diversity-of-full-time-and-part-time-faculty/. Accessed 2 Jan. 2023.

Prescott, Charles E., and Grace A. Giorgio. "Vampiric Affinities: Mina Harker and the Paradox of Femininity in Bram Stoker's *Dracula*." *Victorian Literature and Culture*, vol. 33, no. 2, Sept. 2005, pp. 487–515.

Primorac, Antonija. *Neo-Victorianism on Screen: Postfeminism and Contemporary Adaptations of Victorian Women*. Palgrave Macmillan, 2017.

The Protocols of the Wise Men of Zion. The Beckwith Company, 1920.

Punter, David. "Dracula and Taboo." Dracula: *The New Casebook*, edited by Glennis Byron, Macmillan, 1999, pp. 22–29.

Radick, Caryn. "'Complete and in Order': Bram Stoker's 'Dracula' and the Archival Profession." *The American Archivist*, vol. 76, no. 2, fall-winter 2013, pp. 502–20.

Ray, Julie. "Half of Hispanic Students Considered Leaving College Last Year." *Gallup*, 27 Sept. 2023, news.gallup.com/opinion/gallup/509603/half-hispanic-students-considered-leaving-college-last-year.aspx.

Regan, Margaret. *The Death of Josseline: Immigration Stories from the Arizona Borderlands*. Beacon Press, 2010.

Reidsema, Carl, et al., editors. *The Flipped Classroom: Practice and Practices in Higher Education*. Springer Singapore, 2017. *Crossref*, https://doi.org/10.1007/978-981-10-3413-8.

Reidsema, Carl, et al. Introduction. Reidsema et al., pp. 3–14.

Renfield. Directed by Chris McKay, Universal Pictures, 2023.

210 WORKS CITED

Review of *Dracula*. *The Athenaeum*, 26 June 1897, p. 835.

Review of *Dracula*. *The Spectator*, 31 July 1897. Stoker, *Dracula* [Auerbach and Skal], p. 365.

Reyes, Xavier Aldana. "Dracula Queered." Luckhurst, *Cambridge Companion*, pp. 125–35.

Richards, Leah. "Mass Production and the Spread of Information in *Dracula*: 'Proofs of So Wild a Story.'" *English Literature in Translation, 1880–1920*, vol. 52, no. 4, 2009, pp. 440–57.

Richardson, Maurice. "The Psychoanalysis of Ghost Stories." *Twentieth Century*, vol. 166, no. 994, 1959, pp. 419–31.

Rickels, Laurence A. *The Vampire Lectures*. U of Minnesota P, 1999.

Rider, John M. "The Victorian Aura of the Recorded Voice." *New Literary History*, vol. 32, no. 3, summer 2001, pp. 769–86.

Riquelme, John Paul. "A Critical History of *Dracula*." Stoker, *Dracula* [Riquelme 2016], pp. 441–67.

———. "Doubling and Repetition/Realism and Closure in *Dracula*." Stoker, *Dracula* [Riquelme 2002], pp. 559–72.

———. "Toward a History of Gothic and Modernism: Dark Modernity from Bram Stoker to Samuel Beckett." *Modern Fiction Studies*, vol. 46, no. 3, fall 2000, pp. 585–605.

Roos, Hans Corneel de. "Castle Dracula: Its Exact Location Reconstructed from Stoker's Novel, His Research Notes and Contemporary Maps." Linköping U Electronic P, 2012, www.diva-portal.org/smash/get/diva2:1385303/FULLTEXT01.pdf.

Rose, Brian A. *Jekyll and Hyde Adapted: Dramatizations of Cultural Anxiety*. Greenwood Press, 1996.

Rossetti, Christina G. "Goblin Market." *Poems*, by Rossetti, *Project Gutenberg*, 11 Sept. 2006, www.gutenberg.org/files/19188/19188-h/19188-h.htm.

Roth, Phyllis A. *Bram Stoker*. Twayne Publishers, 1982.

———. "Suddenly Sexual Women in Bram Stoker's *Dracula*." Stoker, *Dracula* [Browning and Skal], pp. 542–53. Originally published in *Literature and Psychology*, 1977.

Ruskin, John. *Sesame and Lilies*. 1865. Edited by Deborah Epstein, Yale UP, 2002.

Rymer, James Malcolm. *The Illustrated* Varney the Vampire; or, The Feast of Blood: A Romance of Exciting Interest. With Thomas Preskett Prest, edited by Finn J. D. John, Pulp Lit, 2020. 2 vols.

———. *Varney the Vampire; or, The Feast of Blood*. Edited by Curt Herr, Zittaw Press, 2008.

Sage, Victor. *Horror Fiction in the Protestant Tradition*. St. Martin's Press, 1988.

Said, Edward W. *Orientalism*. Vintage Books, 1979.

Salem's Lot. Directed by Tobe Hooper, performance by Reggie Halder, Warner Bros. Television, 1979.

Schaffer, Talia. Excerpt from "'A Wilde Desire Took Me': The Homoerotic History of *Dracula*." Stoker, *Dracula* [Browning and Skal], pp. 557–70.

———. "'A Wilde Desire Took Me': The Homoerotic History of *Dracula*." *ELH*, vol. 61, no. 2, 1994, pp. 381–425.

WORKS CITED 211

Schatz, Thomas. *Hollywood Genres: Formulas, Filmmaking, and the Studio System.* McGraw-Hill, 1981.

Schmitt, Cannon. *Alien Nation: Nineteenth-Century Gothic Fictions and English Nationality.* U of Pennsylvania P, 1997.

Schopf, Sue Weaver. "'Legitimizing' Vampire Fiction as an Area of Literary Study." Nevárez, pp. 9–20.

Sedgwick, Eve Kosofsky. *Between Men: English Literature and Male Homosocial Desire.* Columbia UP, 1985.

———. *The Coherence of Gothic Conventions.* Methuen, 1986.

———. *Touching Feeling: Affect, Pedagogy, Performativity.* Duke UP, 2003.

Seed, David. "The Narrative Method of *Dracula*." *Nineteenth-Century Fiction*, vol. 40, 1985, pp. 61–75.

Selzer, Mark. *Serial Killers: Death and Life in America's Wound Culture.* Routledge, 1998.

Semali, Ladislaus M., and Ann Watts Pailliotet. "What Is Intermediality and Why Study It in U.S. Classrooms?" *Intermediality: The Teacher's Handbook of Critical Media Literacy*, edited by Semali and Pailliotet, Kindle ed., Routledge, 2018.

Sen, Aditi, and Alok Sharma. "Meet Dracula's Indian Ancestor Vetala." *The Hindu*, 20 Jan. 2018, www.thehindu.com/society/meet-draculas-indian-ancestor-vetala/article22479854.ece.

Senf, Carol. *The Critical Response to Bram Stoker.* Bloomsbury, 1993.

———. *Dracula: Between Tradition and Modernism.* Twayne Publishers, 1998.

———. "*Dracula*: The Unseen Face in the Mirror." Stoker, *Dracula* [Browning and Skal], pp. 474–84. Originally published in *The Journal of Narrative Technique*, 1979.

———. *The Vampire in Nineteenth Century English Literature.* U of Wisconsin P, 1988.

"Series: Dracula." *Internet Speculative Fiction Database*, www.isfdb.org/cgi-bin/pe.cgi?25425.

Sha, Raj. "Counterfeit Castles: The Age of Mechanical Reproduction in Bram Stoker's *Dracula* and Jules Verne's *Le Château des Carpathes*." *Texas Studies in Literature and Language*, vol. 56, no. 4, 2014, pp. 428–71.

Shapsay, Sandra. "At Once Tiny and Huge: What Is This Feeling We Call 'Sublime'?" *Aeon*, 4 Dec. 2018, aeon.co/ideas/at-once-tiny-and-huge-what-is-this-feeling-we-call-sublime.

Shelley, Mary. *Frankenstein.* Edited by J. Paul Hunter, Norton Critical Edition, 2nd ed., W. W. Norton, 2012.

Shuster, Seymour. "*Dracula* and Surgically Induced Trauma in Children." *British Journal of Medical Psychology*, vol. 76, 1973, pp. 259–70.

Skal, David J. "*Dracula* Unearthed: The Seldom-Seen Turkish Adventure Emerges from the Vaults." *Cinefantastique*, vol. 30, nos. 7–8, Oct. 1998, pp. 93, 125.

———. "'His Hour upon the Stage': Theatrical Adaptations of Dracula." Stoker, *Dracula* [Browning and Skal], pp. 371–80.

———. *The Hollywood Gothic: The Tangled Web of Dracula from Novel to Stage to Screen.* Faber and Faber, 2004.

———. "Ninetieth Spanish *Drácula* Anniversary Interview with David J. Skal." Interview by Justina Bonilla. *Latin Horror*, 28 June 2021, latinhorror.com/90th-spanish-dracula-anniversary-interview-with-david-j-skal/#.

———. Preface. Stoker, *Dracula* [Browning and Skal], pp. vii–xi.

———. *Something in the Blood: The Untold Story of Bram Stoker, the Man Who Wrote* Dracula. Liveright, 2017.

———. "The Spanish *Dracula*." *American Film*, vol. 15, no. 12, Sept. 1990, pp. 38–41.

Smallwood, Christine. "Infiltrating Literature." Interview by Daniel Drake. *The New York Review of Books*, 22 Apr. 2023, www.nybooks.com/online/2023/04/22/infiltrating-literature-christine-smallwood/.

Smart, Robert A. "Postcolonial Dread and the Gothic: Refashioning Identity in Sheridan Le Fanu's *Carmilla* and Bram Stoker's *Dracula*." *Transnational and Postcolonial Vampires: Dark Blood*, edited by Tabish Khair and Johan A. Hoglund, Palgrave Macmillan, 2013, pp. 10–45.

Smart, Robert A., and Michael Hutcheson. "'Negative History' and Irish Gothic Literature: Persistence and Politics." *Anglophonia/Caliban*, no. 15, 2004, pp. 105–18.

Smith, Andrew. *Gothic Literature*. Edinburgh UP, 2013.

———. *Victorian Demons: Medicine, Masculinity, and the Gothic at the Fin-de-Siècle*. Manchester UP, 2017.

Smith, Andrew, and Diana Wallace. "The Female Gothic: Then and Now." *Gothic Studies*, no. 6, 2004, pp. 1–7.

Smith, David Livingstone. "A Theory of Creepiness." *Aeon*, 19 Sept. 2016, aeon.co/essays/what-makes-clowns-vampires-and-severed-hands-creepy.

Smith, Neil. *Uneven Development: Nature, Capital and the Production of Space*. Blackwell, 1984.

Spence, Joseph. "'The Great Angelic Sin': The Faust Legend in Irish Literature, 1820–1900." *Bullán: An Irish Studies Journal*, vol. 1, no. 2, autumn 1994, pp. 47–58.

Spooner, Catherine, and Emma McEvoy. *The Routledge Companion to Gothic*. Routledge, 2007.

The State of Higher Education 2023. Gallup / Lumina Foundation, 2023.

Steinmetz, Lilith. *Bram Stoker's* Dracula: *A Critical Study Guide*. CreateSpace, 2016.

Stepanic, Stanley. "How Did Dracula Become the World's Most Famous Vampire?" *TED-Ed*, ed.ted.com/lessons/how-did-dracula-become-the-world-s-most-famous-vampire-stanley-stepanic.

"The Sterner Sex!" *Punch*, 26 Sept. 1891, p. 147. *The Racketeer*, www.the-racketeer.co.uk/the-sterner-sex-punch-1891-sep-26th-4321-p.asp.

Stevenson, John Allen. "A Vampire in the Mirror: The Sexuality of Dracula." *PMLA*, vol. 103, no. 2, 1988, pp. 139–49.

Stewart, Bruce. "Bram Stoker's *Dracula*: Possessed by the Spirit of the Nation." *Irish University Review*, vol. 29, no. 2, autumn-winter 1999, pp. 238–55.

Stiegler, Bernard. *Technics and Time, 3: Cinematic Time and the Question of Malaise*. Translated by Steven Baker, Stanford UP, 2011.

WORKS CITED   213

Stiles, Ann. "The Rest Cure, 1873–1925." *BRANCH: Britain, Representation and Nineteenth-Century History*, Oct. 2012, branchcollective.org/?ps_articles=anne-stiles-the-rest-cure-1873-1925.

Stoker, Bram. "The American 'Tramp' Question and the Old English Vagrancy Laws." *North American Review*, no. 648, Nov. 1909, pp. 605–14.

———. *The Annotated* Dracula. Edited by Leonard Wolf, Crown Publishers, 1975.

———. *Bram Stoker and the Stage: Reviews, Reminiscences, Essays and Fiction.* Edited by Catherine Wynne, Pickering and Chatto, 2012. 2 vols.

———. *The Bram Stoker Bedside Companion.* Edited by Charles Osborne, Gollancz, 1973.

———. *The Bram Stoker Omnibus.* Orion, 1992.

———. "The Censorship of Fiction." *The Nineteenth Century and After: A Monthly Review*, no. 379, Sept. 1908, pp. 479–87.

———. *The Chain of Destiny. The Shamrock*, 1–22 May 1875.

———. *The Complete Short Stories of Bram Stoker*. CreateSpace, 2015.

———. *Dracula.* Edited by Nina Auerbach and David J. Skal, Norton Critical Edition, W. W. Norton, 1997.

———. *Dracula.* Edited by John Edgar Browning and David J. Skal, Norton Critical Edition, 2nd ed., W. W. Norton, 2022.

———. *Dracula.* Edited by Maurice Hindle, Penguin Books, 2003.

———. *Dracula.* Edited by William Hughes and Diane Mason, Artswork Books, 2007.

———. *Dracula.* Edited by Roger Luckhurst, Oxford UP, 2011.

———. *Dracula.* Edited by John Paul Riquelme, Bedford / St Martin's, 2002. Case Studies in Contemporary Criticism.

———. *Dracula.* Edited by John Paul Riquelme, 2nd ed., Bedford / St Martin's, 2016. Case Studies in Contemporary Criticism.

———. "*Dracula's Guest*" *and Other Weird Stories.* George Routledge and Sons, 1914.

———. Dracula: *The Definitive Edition.* Edited by Marvin Kaye, illustrated by Edward Gorey, Barnes and Noble, 1996.

———. Dracula: *The Postcolonial Edition.* Edited by Cristina Artenie and Dragos Moraru, Universitas Press, 2016.

———. Dracula *Unearthed.* Edited by Clive Leatherdale, Desert Island Books, 1998.

———. *Drakula: Angol regény: Harker Jonathan naplója.* Edited by Jenő Rákosi, Budapest, 1898.

———. *The Essential* Dracula: *A Completely Illustrated and Annotated Edition of Bram Stoker's Classic Novel.* Edited by Raymond McNally and Radu Florescu, Mayflower Books, 1979.

———. *Famous Impostors.* Sidgwick and Jackson, 1910.

———. *The Forgotten Writings of Bram Stoker.* Edited by John Edward Browning, Palgrave Macmillan, 2012.

———. *Gibbet Hill.* 1890. Rotunda Foundation, 2024.

———. *A Glimpse of America: A Lecture Given at the London Institution.* London, 1886.

214 WORKS CITED

———. "The Great White Fair in Dublin." *The World's Work: An Illustrated Magazine of National Efficiency and Social Progress*, May 1907, pp. 570–76.

———. *The Jewel of the Seven Stars*. Heinemann, 1903.

———. *Lady Athylene*. Heinemann, 1908.

———. *The Lady of the Shroud*. Heinemann, 1909.

———. *The Lair of the White Worm*. William Rider and Son, 1911.

———. "Lecture on Abraham Lincoln." *Irish Studies Review*, vol. 10, no. 1, 2002, pp. 10–27.

———. *The Lost Journal of Bram Stoker: The Dublin Years*. Edited by Elizabeth Miller and Dacre Stoker, Robson Press, 2012.

———. *Makt Myrkranna*. Translated by Valdimar Ásmundsson, Reykjavik, 1901.

———. *The Man*. Heinemann, 1905.

———. *Miss Betty*. London, 1891.

———. *Mörkrets makter*. Dagen, 10 June 1899–7 Feb. 1900.

———. *The Mystery of the Sea*. 1902. Sutton, 1997.

———. *The New Annotated* Dracula. Edited by Leslie S. Klinger, W. W. Norton, 2008.

———. *The Primrose Path*. The Shamrock, 6 Feb.–6 Mar. 1875.

———. *The Shoulder of Shasta*. London, 1895.

———. *The Snake's Pass*. London, 1890.

———. *Snowbound: The Record of a Theatrical Touring Party*. Collier, 1908.

———. "The Squaw." Stoker, *Dracula's Guest*, Arrow, 1974, pp. 50–66.

———. *Under the Sunset*. London, 1882.

———. *The Watter's Mou'*. London, 1895.

———. "The World's Greatest Ship-building Yard: Impressions of a Visit to Messrs. Harland and Wolff's Ship-building Yards at Belfast." *The World's Work: An Illustrated Magazine of National Efficiency and Social Progress*, May 1907, pp. 647–50.

Stoker, Bram, and Valdimar Ásmundsson. *Powers of Darkness: The Lost Version of* Dracula. Translated and annotated by Hans Corneel de Roos, Abrams Books, 2017.

Stryker, Susan. "My Words to Victor Frankenstein above the Village of Chamounix: Performing Transgender Rage." *GLQ: A Journal of Lesbian and Gay Studies*, vol. 1, no. 3, 1994, pp. 237–54.

Stryker, Susan, and Stephen Whittle, editors. *The Transgender Studies Reader*. Vol. 1, Routledge, 2006.

Stuart, Regina. *Stage Blood: Vampires of the Nineteenth-Century Stage*. Bowling Green State U Popular Press, 1994.

Stuart, Thomas M. "Out of Time: Queer Temporality and Eugenic Monstrosity." *Victorian Studies*, vol. 60, no. 2, 2018, pp. 218–27.

Study Guide for Bram Stoker's Dracula. Gale, Cengage Learning, 2015.

Süskind, Patrick. *Perfume: The Story of a Murderer*. Vintage, 2001.

WORKS CITED   215

Taylor, Drew Hayden. *The Night Wanderer*. Annick Press, 2007.

"Teaching Large Classes." *Centre for Teaching and Learning*, Western University, teaching.uwo.ca/teaching/engaging/large-class-teaching.html.

Thompson, Tyechia Lynn. "Mapping Narratives of Reversal in 'Baldwin's Paris.'" *CLA Journal*, vol. 59, no. 3, March 2016, pp. 279–94.

Thomson, Spencer. *A Dictionary of Domestic Medicine and Household Surgery*. Philadelphia, 1856.

Tieken, Herman. "On the Use of *Rasa* in Studies of Sanskrit Drama." *Indo-Iranian Journal*, vol. 43, no. 2, 2000, pp. 115–38.

Titley, Alan. *Nailing Theses: Selected Essays*. Lagan Press, 2011.

Todorov, Tzvetan. *The Fantastic: A Structural Approach to a Literary Genre*. Translated by Richard Howard, P of Case Western Reserve U, 1973.

Todorova, Maria. *Imagining the Balkans*. Oxford UP, 1997.

Tomaszewska, Monika. "Vampirism and the Degeneration of the Imperial Race— Stoker's *Dracula* as the Invasive Degenerate Other." *Journal of Dracula Studies*, vol. 6, 2004, pp. 1–8.

Torabi, Katayoun. "If (Not 'Quantize, Click, and Conclude') {Digital Methods in Medieval Studies}." *Meeting the Medieval in a Digital World*, edited by Matthew Evan Davis et al., Arc Humanities Press, 2018.

Townshend, Dale. "Vampire Fiction." *Oxford Bibliographies*, 20 Sept. 2012, https:// doi.org/10.1093/OBO/9780199846719-0059.

Traubel, Horace. *With Walt Whitman in Camden, January 21–April 7, 1889*. Edited by Bradley Sculley, U of Pennsylvania P / Oxford UP, 1953. Vol. 4 of *With Walt Whitman in Camden*.

"Treehouse of Horror IV." *The Simpsons*, season 5, episode 5, Fox, 28 Oct. 1993.

Tronti, Mario. *Workers and Capital*. Translated by David Broder, Verso Books, 2019.

Twilight. Directed by Catherine Hardwicke. Summit Entertainment, 2008.

Twitchell, James. "The Vampire Myth." M. Carter, *Dracula*, pp. 109–16.

"Undead, Adj." *Oxford English Dictionary*, Oxford UP, 2023, www.oed.com/ dictionary/undead_adj?tab=meaning_and_use.

Underberg-Goode, Natalie, and Peter Smith. "Proceso de Lana: Playing Andean Culture through Board Games." *Catalan Journal of Communication and Cultural Studies*, vol. 10, no. 2, 2018, pp. 161–76. *EBSCOhost*, https://doi.org/10.1386/ cjcs.10.2.161_1.

Urrea, Luis Alberto. *The Devil's Highway*. Little, Brown, 2004.

"US Immigration Trends." *Migration Policy Institute*, www.migrationpolicy.org/ programs/data-hub/us-immigration-trends#source. Accessed 2 January 2023.

Valente, Joseph. *Dracula's Crypt: Bram Stoker, Irishness, and the Question of Blood*. U of Illinois P, 2002.

———. "Stoker's Vampire and the Vicissitudes of Biopower." Stoker, *Dracula* [Riquelme 2016], pp. 649–66.

"Vampire, N. (2a)." *Oxford English Dictionary*, Jan. 2024, www.oed.com/dictionary/ vampire_n?tab=meaning_and_use.

WORKS CITED

"Vampires: Folklore, Fantasy, and Fact—Michael Molina." *YouTube*, uploaded by TED-Ed, 29 Oct. 2013, www.youtube.com/watch?v=_0ThKRmySoU&feature=emb_logo.

Vampires vs. the Bronx. Directed by Oz Rodriguez, Broadway Video / Caviar, 2020.

Vampyr: Der Traum des Allan Gray. Directed by Carl Dreyer, Vereinigte Star-Film GmbH, 1932.

Vampyros Lesbos. Fénix Films / CCC Telecine Film, 1971.

Villareal, Raymond. *A People's History of the Vampire Uprising*. Mulholland Books, 2018.

Vint, Sherryl. *Science Fiction: A Guide for the Perplexed*. Bloomsbury, 2014.

Virno, Paolo. *A Grammar of the Multitude*. Translated by Isabella Bertoletti et al., Semiotext(e), 2004.

Waal, Ariane de. "Letting Dracula out of the Closet." *Dracula and Philosophy: Dying to Know*, edited by Nicolas Michaud and Janelle Pötzsch, Open Court Publishing, 2015, pp. 175–85.

Wailoo, Keith, et al., eds. *Genetics and the Unsettled Past: The Collision of DNA, Race, and History*. Rutgers UP, 2012.

Wald, Priscilla. *Contagious: Cultures, Carriers, and the Outbreak Narrative*. Duke UP, 2008.

Walkowitz, Judith. *City of Dreadful Delight: Narratives of Sexual Danger in Late-Victorian London*. U of Chicago P, 1992.

Wallace, Diana, and Andrew Smith, editors. *The Female Gothic: New Directions*, Palgrave Macmillan, 2009.

Walpole, Horace. *The Castle of Otranto: A Gothic Story*. Edited by W. S. Lewis and E. J. Clery, Oxford UP, 1996.

Warburton, Nigel, and Andrew Park. "Edmund Burke on the Sublime." *Aeon*, 19 Feb. 2015, aeon.co/videos/what-separates-the-beautiful-from-the-sublime.

Wark, Mackenzie. *Capital Is Dead: Is This Something Worse?* Verso Books, 2019.

Warwick, Alexandra. "Vampires and the Empire: Fears and Fictions of the 1890s." *Cultural Politics at the Fin de Siècle*, edited by Sally Ledger and Scott McCracken, Cambridge UP, 1995, pp. 202–20.

Watters, Audrey. "The Ed-Tech Imaginary." *Hack Education*, 21 June 2020, hackeducation.com/2020/06/21/imaginary.

We Are the Night. Directed by Dennis Gansel, IFC, 2011.

Weber, Samuel. *Mass Mediauras*. Stanford UP, 1996.

Welles, Orson, and Peter Bogdanovich. *This Is Orson Welles*. HarperCollins Publishers, 1992.

Wells, H. G. "The Stolen Bacillus." 1895. *The Stolen Bacillus and Other Incidents, Project Gutenberg*, 31 Oct. 2018, www.gutenberg.org/files/12750/12750-h/12750-h.htm.

———. "Zoological Retrogression." *Gentleman's Magazine*, vol. 271, 1891, pp. 246–53.

What We Do in the Shadows. Written and directed by Jemaine Clement and Taika Waititi, The Orchard, 2014.

White, Dennis L. "The Poetics of Horror: More than Meets the Eye." *Cinema Journal*, vol. 10, no. 2, spring 1971, pp. 1–18.

Wicke, Jennifer. "Vampiric Typewriting: *Dracula* and Its Media." Stoker, *Dracula* [Riquelme 2002], pp. 577–99.

Wilde, Oscar. *The Picture of Dorian Gray*. Oxford UP, 2006.

Wilkens, Matthew. "Canons, Close Reading, and the Evolution of Method." *Debates in the Digital Humanities*, edited by Matthew K. Gold, U of Minnesota P, 2012.

Williams, Anne. *Art of Darkness: A Poetics of Gothic*. U of Chicago P, 1995.

———. "Dracula: Si(g)ns of the Fathers." *Texas Studies in Literature and Language*, vol. 33, no. 4, Dec. 1991, pp. 445–63.

Williams, Mai'a. "Radical Mothering as a Pathway to Liberation." *Millennium: Journal of International Studies*, vol. 47, no. 3, 2019, pp. 497–512.

Williams, Raymond. "Dominant, Residual, and Emergent." *Critical Theory: A Reader for Literary and Cultural Studies*, edited by Robert Dale Parker, Oxford UP, 2012, pp. 461–66.

Willis, Martin. "'The Invisible Giant,' *Dracula*, and Disease." *Studies in the Novel*, vol. 39, no. 3, 2007, pp. 301–25.

Wilsman, Adam. "Teaching Large Classes." *Vanderbilt University*, 2013, cft.vanderbilt.edu/guides-sub-pages/teaching-large-classes/.

Wilson, A. N. Introduction. *Dracula*, by Bram Stoker, Oxford UP, 1983, pp. vii–xix.

Wimsatt, W. K., and Monroe Beardsley. "The Intentional Fallacy." *The Verbal Icon: Studies in the Meaning of Poetry*, by Wimsatt, U of Kentucky P, 1954, pp. 3–18.

Wolf, Leonard. *A Dream of Dracula: In Search of the Living Dead*. Little, Brown, 1972.

Woods, Stuart. *Eurogames: The Design, Culture and Play of Modern European Board Games*. McFarland, 2012.

Yu, Eric Kwan-Wai. "Productive Fear: Labor, Sexuality, and Mimicry in Bram Stoker's *Dracula*." *Texas Studies in Literature and Language*, vol. 48, no. 2, summer 2006, pp. 145–70.

Zamora, Javier. *Solito*. Hogarth, 2023.

———. *Unaccompanied*. Copper Canyon, 2017.

Zanger, Jules. "Metaphor into Metonymy: The Vampire Next Door." *Blood Read: The Vampire as Metaphor in Contemporary Culture*, edited by Joan Gordon and Veronica Hollinger, U of Pennsylvania P, 1997, pp. 17–26.

Zigarovich, Jolene, editor. "Transing the Gothic." *TransGothic in Literature and Culture*, edited by Zigarovich, Routledge, 2017, pp. 1–22.

Žižek, Slavoj. *For They Know Not What They Do: Enjoyment as a Political Factor*. Verso Books, 1991.

———. "Žižek! (Transcript/Subtitles)." 1990. *Žižek.UK*, 3 Dec. 2016, zizek.uk/2016/12/03/zizek-transcriptsubtitles/.